Setting the Stage for Creative Writing

Plot Scaffolds for Beginning and Intermediate Writers

SHANNON O'DAY

INTERNATIONAL
Reading Association
800 BARKSDALE ROAD, PO BOX 8139
NEWARK, DE 19714-8139, USA
www.reading.org

The International Reading Association attempts, through its publications, to provide a forum for a wide spectrum of opinions on reading. This policy permits divergent viewpoints without implying the endorsement of the Association.

Director of Publications Dan Mangan
Editorial Director, Books and Special Projects Teresa Curto
Managing Editor, Books Shannon T. Fortner
Acquisitions and Developmental Editor Corinne M. Mooney
Associate Editor Charlene M. Nichols
Associate Editor Elizabeth C. Hunt
Production Editor Amy Messick
Books and Inventory Assistant Rebecca A. Fetterolf
Permissions Editor Janet S. Parrack
Assistant Permissions Editor Tyanna L. Collins
Production Department Manager Iona Muscella
Supervisor, Electronic Publishing Anette Schütz
Senior Electronic Publishing Specialist R. Lynn Harrison
Electronic Publishing Specialist Lisa M. Kochel
Proofreader Stacey Lynn Sharp

Project Editor Charlene M. Nichols

Art Cover: Design, Linda Steere; Curtain Photo, © Comstock Images/Jupiterimages Corporation; Student Photos, Shannon O'Day. Interior Photos (pp. 1, 27, 60, 87), Shannon O'Day.

Web addresses in this book were correct as of the publication date but may have become inactive or otherwise modified since that time. If you notice a deactivated or changed Web address, please e-mail books@reading.org with the words "Website Update" in the subject line. In your message, specify the Web link, the book title, and the page number on which the link appears.

Library of Congress Cataloging-in-Publication Data
O'Day, Shannon, 1953-
  Setting the stage for creative writing : plot scaffolds for beginning and intermediate writers / Shannon O'Day.
       p. cm.
  Includes bibliographical references and index.
  ISBN-13: 978-0-87207-595-5
  1. English language--Composition and exercises--Study and teaching (Elementary) 2. English language--Composition and exercises--Study and teaching (Middle school) 3. Language arts (Elementary) 4. Language arts (Middle school) 5. Creative writing (Elementary education) 6. Creative writing (Middle school) I. Title.
   LB1576.O33 2006
   372.62'3--dc22
                                                                          2006006665

CONTENTS

Wearing the remains of last year's inflatable Brussels sprout costume, a student dressed as Grendel waddles across the cafeteria and flops down at an overturned plastic children's pool.

"Mom, what was all that noise next door last night? I couldn't get my beauty sleep and now I am ugly!" he whines, throwing the plastic food off the pool top.

While facilitating this student production of a plot scaffold based on the classic epic poem *Beowulf* (Heaney, 2000), the teacher is able to witness students' problem-solving skills in action. Students use the plastic pool as a swamp but realize that if they turn it over in Act One, it can be used as a table in Grendel's home. Students also recall last year's Brussels sprout costume, which was used in a science fiction interpretation of *The Wizard of Oz* (Fleming, 1939); its unique bulky shape and color are ideal for Grendel's costume. The problem-solving strategies that students learn through drama, such as these, can be used later when students turn the play into a written story. Thus, drama acts as a bridge, linking dialogue and imagery to written text. As actors, these students will actually sit with other actors in a play, and, as writers, they will later have mental conversations with these same actors who have become the characters in their stories. Good writers often have "conversations" with the characters they create and let their characters dictate how the story will evolve (Scarborough, McCaffery, McCullugh, Crispin, & Weis, 2003). Thus, performing plot scaffolds teaches students this writing technique.

Origins of This Book

This book is a result of my 20 years of writing and facilitating children's creative drama while watching students transfer creative drama techniques to writing. It all began when I could not find a suitable play for a group of first graders to perform. Writing a play myself, in scaffold form, and letting my students complete it made me aware of how children naturally and constructively use story to express their own ideas, voices, and experiences when solving problems.

Watching this active literacy process led to the creation of more plot scaffolds and eventually to questions about how other teachers might use them. These same questions later surfaced in my own research:

1. How do teachers who have limited drama experience use an open-ended script as a plot scaffold?

2. How do teachers' concepts of literacy change when using creative drama?

3. What literacy processes are used as teachers and students develop a drama from an open-ended script?

I designed the plot scaffolds as part of a doctoral dissertation to answer these questions. The intent of this research was to see what would happen if teachers, who had never used plot scaffolds like the ones in this book, used them in their classrooms. Eight teachers, ranging in teaching experience from 2 to 18 years, were chosen for this qualitative study.

The results of my qualitative research (2000) were that the use of plot scaffolds made the following differences in teaching styles:

1. Participants, both teachers and students, began to explore literacy concepts in a playful, nonthreatening manner. In a sense, the "plays" provided meaningful context for play. For example, the plot scaffold "Tyrant?" with its emphasis on rehearsal, actual movement of characters, and rewrite, allowed students to use pretend play. According to current literature on play, children often use pretend play in order to understand and control emotions, and seek, enact, and rehearse solutions to resolve real conflicts (Annarella, 1992; Barnett, 1998; Pelligrini, 1997; Wagner, 1998). Because "Tyrant?" focuses on the issues of a political leader perhaps becoming dishonest about his true intentions, students were able to use pretend play to understand and resolve real dilemmas such as the scandal between former U.S. President Bill Clinton and his intern Monica Lewinsky. Thus, teachers can use plot scaffolds as a bridge between history lessons of the past and present political situations and to explore issues concerning the rights of citizens and the protection of personal freedom.

With the current governmental pressure to increase student-testing performance in U.S. schools, play may appear a frivolous use of instructional time. However, Barnett (1998) argues that

> the psychologically healthy child is able to use play to articulate, and master those important aspects of his life that would otherwise cause strain, and that play is the medium through which a child's inner world can be seen and better understood. (p. 102)

Using a plot scaffold in the manner of play allows "play" to come to paper. The energy can be transferred and captured by writing.

2. Teachers began to act more as facilitators rather than gatekeepers. Teachers and students worked collaboratively to produce stories using open-ended scaffolds. Using the plot scaffold strategy allowed for a sharing of knowledge between teacher and student such that teachers did not find themselves having to play autocrats. Bruner (1996) states,

> Knowledge is what is shared within discourse, within a "textual" community. Truths are the product of evidence, argument, and constructing rather than of authority, textual or pedagogic. This model of education is mutualistic and dialectical, more concerned with interpretation and understanding than with the achievement of factual knowledge or skilled performance. (p. 57)

It is important to note that students' creativity can be suppressed if prior knowledge is used as the ending point rather than as a starting point for addressing a problem. This scenario, otherwise known as "gate keeping" (Eichenberger & King, 1995), occurs when teachers limit students' participation within the event frame. Scaffolding, on the other hand, occurs when teachers help students participate and have voice (Eichenberger & King).

3. Literacy concepts expanded because of the emphasis on elaboration and fluency. Students could elaborate on plots, and through repeated readings and rewriting of scripts, meaning making became more fluent. Reading and writing were seen as an interactive process rather than as two separate daily instructional units.

Participant teachers reported that the plot scaffold strategy encourages originality, elaboration, fluency, and flexibility of students' ideas. By using the plot scaffolds provided in this book, teachers' stances regarding literacy broadened from viewing literacy as a decoding skill to viewing literacy as an awareness of empathy, imagination, voice, prediction, and reflection. Participants reported that empathy, resulting from the creation of active characters that "got up and walked around" as students acted them out, encouraged communication at greater, elaborative depths, as students worked collaboratively to convey meaning. Even in noisy or cramped spaces, such as hallways and small modular classrooms, students' imagination provided focus for attention. Students' voice inflection helped to identify their level of understanding of the characters. Students were able to use prediction and reflection skills to explore different solutions to dilemmas. Thus, students became active creators rather than passive recipients of literacy.

Teachers who have used plot scaffolds found that they work on several levels. One teacher stated,

> It works better on teaching some of the higher level things...predicting, open-endedness, logical reasoning, making sure that things make sense, which drama gives kids a chance to do. It also gives them the chance to realize that what is written can be said and that it needs to make sense. That it is not just on paper and that's it. One can interpret things differently, which would give them a chance to realize that one interpretation is not the only interpretation.

Becoming Part of the Literacy Process

I define *literacy* as communication, not just "reading" print, because the etymology of the word *read* itself conveys communication on many levels. In its original form, *reading* means "giving counsel, taking charge, explaining the obscure" (Levison, 1983, p. 49). Only in the last two centuries, and then only in English, has reading come to be identified almost exclusively with the interpretation of written material (Levison). For the purposes of this book, literacy is seeking to explain the obscure, to inquire; and along the lines of constructivist viewpoints, literacy is a building of meaning because of the emphasis on the process of inquiry rather than finding the right answer or product of an end result. Literacy as communication is such an active mental process that when a transaction between the reader and text occurs, the reader is, in fact, in a state of empathy with the writer's message (Rosenblatt, 1985). As a dancer becomes an extension of a composer's music, so does a reader become a part of the process and the material that is read; thus, literacy comes to have a far broader meaning than a simple decoding of text. In a sense, new texts, like new dances, are created when reader and text enmesh.

Zukav (1979), in his overview of new physics, describes these transactions:

> The subatomic world is a continual dance of recreation and annihilation, of mass changing to energy and energy changing to mass. Transient forms sparkle in and out of existence creating a never-ending, forever-newly-created reality. (p. 197)

Zukav hypothesizes that there is no longer a clear distinction between what is and what happens, between the actor and the action, but rather that the dance and the dancer are one. Transactions between entities are defined through the act of relating to one another and become events, transactions between observer and observed (Zukav). I have observed that when students and teachers use creative drama techniques in literacy scaffolding, then meaning making takes on the same transactions because writer and text become enmeshed, creating a new and vibrant story. Acting out the story allows for empathetic dialogue and vibrant images.

As an educational strategy, plot scaffolds has its origin in constructivist theory (Wagner, 1998). The constructivist process has commonalities with the creative process in that both encourage originality, elaboration, and flexibility. Teachers who have used the plot scaffolds I created, including me, observed similar findings as our own students constructed meaning from plot scaffolds like those in this book. Open-ended writing scaffolds are Socratic in nature—that is, ideas are constantly questioned, and learning is always under construction (Courtney, 1989; Dwyer, 1990; Wolf, Edmiston, & Enisco, 2005). Constructivism in literacy classrooms can provide frameworks for thinking about teaching and learning through emphasis on process-oriented instruction in the language arts curriculum. Process-oriented instruction is a large part of current U.S. national and state language arts standards because evaluation must have a performance-based component. Students must show mastery of a language arts standard by not only passing a standardized written test but also actively using language in a "hands-on" performance. Comprehension instruction based on constructivist principles acknowledges the student's role as a meaning maker in the act of reading. The plot scaffolds presented in this book are based on constructivist principles that acknowledge the student's role in "showing" what they know. Empowering students lent strength to my own awareness of how creativity could help raise standardized test scores because students could develop personal writing style.

Using plot scaffolds for writing dialogue and images adds style and content to students' narratives—elements that are evaluated in mandated standardized writing assessments (e.g., Georgia Writing Tests, 2005 Scholastic Aptitude Test [SAT]). Writing a story is like creating a mental "stage" for the reader. The plot scaffolds in this book are small stages in which students can rehearse or rewrite their stories. Being collaborative in nature, just like actors improvising on stage, students can create these stories as a group project with each student adding his or her own personal voice or gesture to the performance or final written story. Likewise, students also can play the director as they determine the plot, action, costumes, voice tone, stage movement, and dialogue of their players. To quote a master on the subject, "All the world's a stage and all the men and women merely players" (Shakespeare, 1994b, act 2, scene 7, lines 140–141). A writer's world lies in imagination, and the printed page becomes the stage watched by an audience of readers. This book contains strategies for making this dramatic transaction between the writer, text, and reader—a transaction that we call literacy.

Organization of This Book

Setting the Stage for Creative Writing: Plot Scaffolds for Beginning and Intermediate Writers is divided into four chapters. Chapter 1 provides the foundation for using plot scaffolds with beginning and intermediate writers in grades K–8 by presenting research that explains why plot scaffolds are practical, active, and effective. Chapter 2 provides plot scaffold lessons for beginning writers, and chapter 3 provides plot scaffold lessons for intermediate writers. However, because plot scaffolds are based on the "appropriateness" of a writer's ability rather than his or her grade level, teachers should choose the plot scaffolds that best meet their students' needs. Chapter 4 elaborates on the uses of plot scaffolds, such as for larger, cross-curricular theme units or for use in standardized writing test preparation. Chapter 4 differs from the other three chapters because it looks at schoolwide literacy strategies that can be used by teachers who do not normally teach writing. I believe that all teachers, whether they teach math, social studies, art, or science, are teachers of literacy. However, I also have found that those who are not specifically language arts teachers sometimes need to be provided with the strategies necessary to become skilled writing teachers. Personally, I can relate to this dilemma because I would not feel comfortable teaching an algebra class without knowing the appropriate teaching strategies because I do not have a natural inclination for math. Chapter 4 highlights strategies designed for those teachers who are uncomfortable or unsure about teaching writing.

Appendix A contains learning objectives and rubrics for evaluation purposes. Appendix B contains the reproducible plot scaffolds, which can be used as they are or as models to create your own plot scaffolds. I have provided instructions throughout the book so teachers can create their own plot scaffolds to help teach their own individual curriculum. Appendix C contains a research paper model that incorporates the scaffold strategy, which intermediate writers can use to learn how to research and write research papers. Appendix D contains reproducible evaluation forms for writing portfolios. In light of requirements to meet national writing standards as well as move to performance-based assessment, I included these forms in rubric format to cover multiple assessment levels. Finally, I have provided a glossary for quick reference in understanding how literacy and writing terms are defined in this book. These terms may be useful for teachers and students as they use the plot scaffolds.

It is my hope that this book will be helpful not only in raising standardized writing scores but also in raising an awareness of how creativity can be used by teachers and students to give writing originality, elaboration, fluency, and flexibility. With its emphasis on the use of informal, constructed, and performance components, this book will be helpful in acknowledging both product and process as a means of determining whether a literacy standard has been achieved. In education, as in real life, the journey is as important as the end goal.

Acknowledgments

I would like to thank the following people for their inspiration:

- Dr. Jinny Farmer, for her leadership in making the writing mentor program such a success.
- Maureen Clouse and Macy Defnall, for their administrative support and dedication.
- Michael Meade, for being a marvelous storyteller who makes myth dance.
- My fellow teachers of the gifted, for their participation in my doctoral study that "scaffolded" this literacy project.
- The teaching staff, parents, and students of South Paulding Middle School, Dallas, Georgia, for their support and acceptance of my "out of the box" approach and love of play as well as the staff and students of New Georgia Elementary School, Villa Rica, Georgia.
- Charlene Nichols, of the International Reading Association, for her excellent editing help.

ABOUT THE AUTHOR

Shannon O'Day enjoys working hands-on in public school classrooms and is a School Improvement Specialist for Paulding County Schools in Georgia. Her position involves modeling for teachers, developing new curriculums, and presenting state performance standards. Her current focus is on creating literacy strategies for diverse learners. She also teaches educational research courses for the University of Phoenix Online, which allows her to facilitate classes for teachers throughout the world.

Originally from the San Francisco Bay Area, Shannon received her bachelor's degree in humanities with a specialization in medieval literature from the University of California at Berkeley, and her master's in reading education from California State Fullerton, where she was named outstanding graduate student. Her doctorate in language and literacy is from Georgia State University, where her work centered on using creative drama as a literacy strategy.

Shannon's first book, *Setting the Stage for Creative Writing: Plot Scaffolds for Beginning and Intermediate Writers*, is a combination of her love of myth, plays, and writing. Shannon has taught in elementary and middle school, including gifted education and adult literacy. She holds National Board Certification in English language arts/early adolescence. Shannon has published articles on literacy scaffolds for *Gifted Child Today* and *Primary Voices*.

When not teaching or writing, Shannon enjoys travel, including taking her students on Educational Foundations tours of Costa Rica and Italy. Her hobbies include belly dancing, tango, and rapier. She has two children, Alexis and Jeremiah, and also numerous animals including Attila the Pug.

CHAPTER 1

How Plot Scaffolds Work

At exactly twelve o'clock midnight, a squirrel crept silently out of its white-flowered tree that looks as if it was covered in snow, yet the tree smells like a box of dead fish left out in the sun for three days. This tree makes up the squirrel's empire. A few moments later, across the road, a ferret slowly emerged out of trailer fourteen, which makes up the ferret's rebel base.

Back at the squirrel's base, Darth Squader was reporting in to Lord Squithus.

"All was quiet at Ferret Central," Darth Squader reported in a voice like that of someone who gives you nightmares about turning into a robot.

Waving her hands in frustration, a language arts teacher complains, "One of my students is writing fiction stories about ferrets, but the plot I just read sounds like the movie *Star Wars* [Lucas, 1977]. How do you keep students from copying movies and television when they write stories?"

"The ferrets may be carrying lightsabers and invoking the 'Dark Side,' but think of *Star Wars* as a plot scaffold. What is wrong learning from a style you admire?" I offer.

"But it is copying!" the teacher indignantly responds.

"And I suppose *Star Wars* didn't 'copy' heroic plots from classical mythology? Perhaps because the director, George Lucas, changed the setting from ancient times to a futuristic empire, you no longer see the scaffold unless you are looking for it," I suggest.

"OK, I see what you mean, but how do you teach beginning writers to use the stories they hear or see without simply copying them?"

"I propose that you let students use creativity and voice to make the old stories into their own new stories. Ask questions such as, 'Since ferrets have claws, not hands, what kind of weapons might they use? Can they hold a lightsaber? How might the new weapon change the story?' It is all about problem solving. Plot scaffolds based on mythology or older stories provide the base for the story, but as the settings change, each story will have a different set of problems to solve," I explain.

"How do plot scaffolds work?" the teacher inquires.

What Is a Plot Scaffold?

A plot scaffold is a temporary linguistic tool or strategy that teachers can use to assist students in moving to levels of language comprehension performance that they would be unable to obtain at that time without the scaffolding. *Linguistic* refers to the structures languages take in order to convey meaning. For example, a simple sentence conveys meaning, but a complex-compound sentence may be able to show more depth in terms of its meaning because the structure allows for more elaboration and focus. Based on the research on instructional scaffolding, there are five criteria for effective use:

1. **Ownership** allows for students to make their own contributions to ongoing tasks. It makes the learning theirs.

2. **Appropriateness** refers to building on literacy and thinking skills that students already have and helping them accomplish tasks they may not have thought possible on their own. Teachers facilitate students' work when they guide them by using appropriate materials and plot scaffolds.

3. **Support** for the task ensures that a natural sequence of thought and language exists, providing effective routines for students to internalize. Again, teachers act as facilitators by providing this time and routine.

4. **Collaboration** refers to the teacher's role as facilitator rather than evaluator so students feel comfortable exploring different solutions rather than giving a recitation and display of previous learning. The teacher collaboratively works with students in that constructed items or tasks, which are guided by teacher and student feedback, are used to assess process or procedural knowledge. The instructional goal is for constructed learning rather than selected responses (i.e., when students choose responses or answers that are presented to them in objective formats such as true or false, matching, and multiple choice).

5. **Internalization** allows for students to take ownership and control of their newly acquired skills and strategies because they have time for self-assessment and reflection (Applebee, 1991; Bruner, 1996).

Thus, the plot scaffolds in this book emphasize ownership, appropriateness, support, collaboration, and internalization.

What Are the Guidelines for Using Plot Scaffolds?

Although the plot scaffolds in this book may look like play scripts, they represent a creative literacy strategy for classroom use and are not intended for teaching theater. From my own experience, and as Neelands (1998) states, forms of drama found in schools often look and feel very different from professional theater experiences. One major difference is that professional drama is rehearsed and performed for monetary profit. Acting and producing theater is often seen as something only a few can achieve. I have often heard teachers say how uncomfortable they are with the acting that is involved in performing plays because, personally, they have never felt comfortable acting. However, these plot scaffolds are not intended to be used as acting lessons; they are meant to inspire stories that are produced on the basis of constructed response. The stories' meanings belong to the group who produces them and represent their viewpoint about solving a specific problem. Neelands (1998) refers to this as an oral and communal tradition that stresses the processes of production and the quality for participants of the immediate shared experience. That is, stories change and evolve depending on the culture of those using them. A school is a community, and building creative plots is a living practice formed from the literacy within its walls. It is based on students' concerns, needs, and aspirations shared within the school community or a particular classroom. Therefore, these plots used as a literacy strategy in classrooms are not synonymous with theater drama. The closest they come to it is a form of creative drama because the plots are evolving, not set in stone like a prewritten play script. Plot scaffolds look like play scripts so students can make the connection to how dialogue and imagery used in theater or drama may apply to narrative writing. The "script" format is meant to provide a visual aid for spacing dialogue in narrative (something students often have difficulty understanding) because in narrative writing, the writer indents lines when different characters speak to avoid confusion as to who is talking. The basic guideline for using plot scaffolds is to remember they are performed to teach narrative writing, not theater skills. However, the dramatic quality of acting out the story certainly teaches presentation skills such as speaking clearly, body language, and improvisation.

Although many teachers may be accustomed to quiet during the writing process, it is not necessarily effective with plot scaffolding. I feel that literacy floats upon a "sea of talk," a phrase coined by Ruth Hough, a professor in the College of Education, Georgia State University. This metaphor explains the "good noise" that occurs when students are on task but very talkative as they work together in class. This type of plot scaffolding calls for movement and dialogue among the participants, who also have a tendency to take control over their own learning. According to one teacher who used this strategy to build plots,

> They ran the show; they really did. I sat back and let them go unless they were getting off task or they were trying to bite off more than they could chew. Then I would step in and try to size it down so that is was definitely feasible. When the one class was modernizing it, the sixth grade, I did sit down and try to help them write. On the rewriting with each group I just would come up, some of them tried to write it so big that they just didn't know how to condense. So teaching them how to condense and to write for the number of characters they had to do was just one process we did.

What Is the Impact of Plot Scaffolds on Students' Language Learning?

In my work with plot scaffolds, I have found several important implications for language arts teachers. First, creative writing through using plot scaffolds allows for a sharing of knowledge between teacher and student. Teachers find that they do not have to be autocratic. Rather, students become active participants in their own learning because constructive principles are at work. Teachers strive to help students focus the story, provide meaningful support in terms of factual knowledge, and maintain a safe environment where students are free to voice ideas without fear of ridicule by peers.

Second, based on my own classroom observations and my qualitative research observing teacher and student interaction, as teachers and students develop plots using this active, dramatic approach, students' literacy growth evolves in terms of originality, elaboration, fluency, and flexibility. Students take an existing story and create original endings, elaborate on the original story, begin to develop the dialogue and story much more easily, and understand flexibility in terms of rethinking and rewriting stories.

Booth (1985) refers to abstraction that exists in drama as "imaginary gardens with real toads" (p. 197). This is an appropriate definition of what happens when students act out the scaffolds because they "become"—through pretend or play—the characters in their stories. They must use their imaginations to become the characters, and the concepts of imagery, mental imagining, and imagination may be the keys to the deeper processing that occurs when students exhibit higher comprehension in reading (DuPont, 1992; Sadoski & Paivio, 1994). Professional writers often will admit to having conversations with the characters in their stories in order to determine the plot. There are also several researchers who agree that acting out characters improves response to text: "The essential nature of the dramatic medium is a liberating act of imagination...a dual consciousness in which the real and fictional words are held together in the mind" (O'Neill, 1995, p. 159). Sadoski and Paivio (1994) argue that imagery and emotional response are the "sine qua non of esthetic response to text. The sensuous realization of characteristics, objects, and the fundamental basis for living through literature, although the same experiences can occur when reading other types of text as well" (p. 594). Think of all the times as a child, while playing with friends, when you may have pretended to be a character you read about or saw in film. I believe much of this pretend play currently occurs in video games as children create characters and act out plot simulations on computers. This type of play is reflected in the stories students write at school.

However, computer-generated games can be turned off, and the characters cannot provide emotional response or physical touch; therefore, play is limited as far as actually "living through" it. The process of "living through" is an essential aspect of creative drama, though. Wolf, Edmiston, and Enisco (2005) classify process drama as reliant on the teacher's knowledge of aesthetic structuring through improvisation and the use of theatrical and film processes and conventions in order to create multiple and carefully sequenced ways of creating dramatic art with students. (I always interpret this to mean that the teacher gets to "play," too.) The teacher can enter into the fictional world of a text, and the text can provide students and teachers with an initial dilemma or situation. Assessment becomes both informal and performance based. Informal assessment includes oral questioning, observation, interviews, conferences, process description, student self-assessment, and peer review, to name a few. Performance-based evaluation consists of the teacher assessing movement, dramatization, and presentation. *Assess* comes from the Latin word *assessio*, which means "a sitting near" (Handford & Herber, 1966, p. 47). Thus, when the teacher sits near students, the teacher can help students construct stories from plot scaffolds. The original scaffold text is supplemented by the texts that arise among students and teacher as they interact. "It is not that a text is absent from this approach to dramatizing, instead it is 'under construction'" (Wolf et al., 2005, p. 495). Given enough rehearsal or rough draft changes, the student version of the scene from *Star Wars* at the beginning of this chapter will change as the student adds his or her own experiences and voice to the text. Many of these changes occur during rehearsal and in the writer's mind before they are written down.

There are several studies that document the power creative drama has on imagination in literacy (DuPont, 1992; Gourney, Bosseau, & Delgado, 1985; Ignoffo, 1993). One example of reliance on the process of imagination was demonstrated by Ignoffo (1993), who used mental imaging strategies in his "theater of the mind" technique, a kind of creative drama exercise used with low-achieving high school readers. His findings easily translate to younger, beginning and intermediate writers because these students are in the process of learning to read and write, too. Ignoffo had his students create mental pictures to help them "run around old blockages and learn new ways to achieve control over their own mental processes during reading" (p. 310). Ignoffo felt that when he told his students to focus on mental images, he was helping them make use of a mental picture that would empower them as readers to focus on all of their resources, including prior knowledge, sense of structure, problem-solving techniques, and spur-of-the-moment ingenuity. The exercise allowed students to turn concentration into a concrete reality and also helped them filter out distractions. I find the same results when students are allowed to act out plot scaffolds before putting them into written story form. Assessment becomes performance based because students are more actively engaged as they apply knowledge and skills to problem solving.

Ignoffo believes this method reacquaints students with childlike sensory awareness and thus allows for the use of more theater-of-the-mind "special effects" in reading and learning. Students can transform a seemingly dull or bland piece of information into a dramatic experience that has depth in space and extension in time. Acting out the plot scaffolds provides the dimensionality that many kinesthetic, visual, or auditory learners require before putting the story in the more abstract form of print. When the story is acted out, it occurs in the now when questions may arise, and after answering questions and reflecting on what might be the best answers, the story is written down. The transformation process builds self-reliance in the students when they realize how much power they have to bring words and ideas to life. I have seen this occur in the classroom when students who previously had not completed written assignments suddenly became motivated to perform plot scaffolds and then turn those scaffolds into complete stories. This newfound confidence often leads to students mastering other subjects as well.

In his study, Ignoffo found that students who used the theater-of-the-mind technique felt less stress about reading, felt they had discovered a new memory aid, and began to transfer the skills to other academic subjects and even athletic activities. As part of his technique, Ignoffo had students write allegorical scripts that depicted how they saw themselves as readers. These scripts were dramatized, and students came to realize that just as they could create a mental picture, they were also capable of changing it. Ignoffo found that his technique was a powerful antidote for the confused helplessness often experienced by remedial readers. As a result, about 20% of his remedial reading students advanced into the standard language arts program during the course of one semester. More than half of the class improved their verbal SAT scores sufficiently to enter the college of their choice, and the overall improvement on reading tests scores was 1.5 to 2 grade levels during a 4-month semester. Ignoffo states,

> My remedial readers gain[ed] a new sense of being able to dramatize ideas as living characters in a theater of the students' own creation. Learning is thus transferred from the flatness of two-dimensional ink and paper into the three-dimensional world of imagination in which abstract words and ideas can be brought to life as physical experiences in concrete reality. (p. 321)

Ignoffo's students gained control over their reading—a kind of a metacognition—when they used mental imaging. When students use plot scaffolds and act them out, I have noted similar results. In their study of imagery as a neglected correlate of reading instruction, Fillmer and Parkway (1990) indicate that imagery is used infrequently in the classroom. They state that failure to recognize the powerful potential of imagery in the reading program denies students the use of a major correlate in reading instruction. Drama provides a learning situation in which students may share imaginary situations in real life. "Private and shared journeys in imaginary gardens, with real toads" can occur (Booth, 1985, p. 197). Research on mental imagery has proven that it is possible to increase and improve skills of perceiving, imaging, and imagining drama (Wright, 1985). For example, a sixth-grade history class may choose to act out a situation that they have all read in a history text. By sharing and acting out their mental images, an abstract mental process such as reading about past events can become more concrete. Writers use images to set the mood and tone, create the setting, and describe characters. Thus, imagery is a major correlate to reading because the reader must imagine the world created by the writer. Using the plot scaffolding strategy in this book allows students to use imagery as they read and write.

Using plot scaffolds aids in students' language learning because it is a constructive strategy that lends itself to constructed response, informal assessment, and performance-based assessment. Students become more active learners because the plot scaffolds encourage originality, elaboration, fluency, and flexibility of student ideas as students learn the importance of dialogue, images, and conflict in story plots.

How Does the Plot Scaffolding Strategy Affect How I Teach?

Using plot scaffolds allows teachers to reflect on their own practices. My colleagues who participated in using plot scaffolds reported that they more clearly understood how students learn to use language and grow in their independence as learners. Before using plot scaffolds, some of these teachers noted that they were unaware of how much control they had over student meaning in the classroom. After having completed two plot scaffolds, one scripted by me and another constructed by students, one elementary-grade teacher commented,

I was really impressed with the kids. In comparing the two different plots, one of the kids said, "The first one, *Julius Caesar*, was just really hard and so serious. The second one was silly and we could have more fun. You didn't try to control us quite so much." This was really good feedback for me to hear because I wasn't aware that I was controlling them. I have really been giving this comment a lot of thought since I heard that. What exactly was I doing to make [students] feel that I was controlling them?

When teachers use plot scaffolds, they are using a sociocognitive interactive model of literacy. Ruddell and Unrau (1994) describe a sociocognitive interactive model of literacy as a process where the reader, the text, and the teacher work together to construct meaning: It is a "meaning-construction process that enables us to create carefully reasoned as well as imaginary worlds filled with new concepts, creatures, and characters" (p. 996). Following a similar emphasis, plot scaffolding also is a process of creating imaginary worlds filled with new characters and varied solutions to plot. In both cases, the emphasis is on creating or constructing. The sociocognitive interactive model involves an interaction between reader, text, and teacher, with both reader and teacher bringing prior beliefs and knowledge to the task of constructing knowledge. Ruddell and Unrau describe the teacher's role as facilitator within a sociocognitive interactive model:

> Opening the way and not conducting to the end makes (the learner) thoughtful. Socrates emphasized that a teacher does not "teach" in the sense of transferring knowledge to the pupil; rather the teacher serves as a mediator to assist the student in becoming consciously aware of knowledge already possessed. (p. 1022)

Based on my own experience using plot scaffolds, I have found that I become the "director" of learning rather than having to provide all the answers or make all the decisions. As facilitators, teachers encourage students to create their own lines and allow them a voice in the creation of meaning. The main task as manager is to provide a safe, risk-taking environment where students will not be ridiculed for their suggestions or be allowed to make remarks or lines inappropriate for school use.

What About Diverse Learners?

Eichenberger and King (1995) describe the important role that plot scaffolds have in students' language learning because scaffold building occurs when teachers help students to participate and have voice in how and what they create. In addition, English as a second language (ESL) students benefit greatly when given the opportunity to use plot scaffolds that provide meaningful engagements with print (Fitzgerald & Noblit, 1999). In *Culture Bound* (Valdes, 1990), Morain argues that second-language learners need practice in nonverbal as well as verbal channels of expression because "more than 65% of the social meaning of a typical two-person exchange is carried by nonverbal cues" (p. 65).

Plot scaffolds can be a useful strategy for providing ESL students and English-speaking students with exposure to stories and language. When students do not understand the language of a text, frustration and loss of interest may result. Think of an ESL student sitting in an English immersion classroom. He or she might understand only about half of the English vocabulary being used in that classroom and spend more time trying to translate individual words rather than combining them for contextual meaning. The same applies for English speakers if the language of the text is beyond their comprehension. Understanding is difficult unless it is meaningful in terms of prior knowledge and "consequently, new words and information should be drawn from reading or other experiences immediately pertinent to the student and defined in terms and examples that fall within the boundaries of the student's prior knowledge" (Readence, Bean, & Baldwin, 1981, p. 110).

To help ESL students build literacy in English, students can create characters with limited English dialogue, write lines in their native language, and take nonspeaking roles. For example, one of my students who was born in Taiwan played a leading role in the creation of a story in which her lines were spoken and written in English and her native language. ESL students learn language more easily because they, like my English-speaking first-grade students, see a need to use and a purpose for language as a way of communicating with others (Celce-Murcia, Brinton, & Goodwin, 1996). They receive repeated practice in the lines and are supported by the class when they need help. Previewing vocabulary for ESL students is important for their acquisition of English, and the rehearsal aspect of plot scaffolding gives ample time for teachers to define words, make analogies, or provide help with pronunciation. Students also can mime the dialogue without words. As a rationale for this activity, Celce-Murcia and colleagues (1996) argue that the jump from listening to language to speaking may be overwhelming for ESL students at first. By including music, art, and dance in the plots that are acted out later as plays, students can participate more comfortably using these other symbol systems that do not require the user to speak. Students no longer feel silenced; their lives, language, and culture are an integral part of the production of the play. Plot scaffolds allow for the flexibility necessary for second-language learners who may be in different stages of language development. English-speaking students also benefit from observing firsthand the multidimensionality of the world in terms of culture and language.

When working with a group of ESL students, I have students create plot scaffolds that draw on their native languages, as well as English. For example, when I taught a second- and third-grade ESL class, Vietnamese and Hispanic children retold the story of Maximilian and Carlotta to celebrate Cinco de Mayo. Collaboratively, they wrote the following lines, which were spoken in English, French, and Spanish:

Scene:	The court of Maximilian and Carlotta in Mexico.
Mexican citizen:	(speaks in Spanish) We do not like you here. Go back to France where you belong.
Maximilian:	(speaks in French to his interpreter) What did he say?
Interpreter:	(speaks in French) Your Majesty, he says the Mexican people love you.
Maximilian:	(speaks in French) Charlotte, I told you the people wanted us to stay here.

In this story, we later discover that because Maximilian doesn't speak Spanish well, people use this opportunity to lie to him. Ultimately, this weakness costs Maximilian his life. Through this plot scaffold, my second and third graders were discovering and learning this lesson about the dangers of not understanding the language or culture of a native people.

Acting out characters in plot scaffolds is an excellent way for ESL students not only to practice verbal dialogue but also role-play, another form of communication practice. In their work *Teaching Pronunciation: A Reference for Teachers of English to Speakers of Other Languages*, Celce-Murcia and colleagues (1996) suggest simple role-plays as a strategy for ESL students. For example, in one performance my middle school students developed from an intermediate plot, the role of an aggressive chef on a cruise ship was specifically given to a shy Vietnamese student so she could practice being more assertive. This 13-year-old student spoke almost no English and because she was the only Vietnamese student at the school, she spent the first part of the year trying to blend into the back of large classes so she wouldn't be noticed. By getting her involved in the play, she came out of her shell. First, she helped by making some of the backdrops. Next, other students were impressed by her artistic talents and asked her for help with their artwork. Then, they encouraged her to take a part in the actual play. Because a performance can involve art, music, or dance, ESL students have an opportunity to share ideas in sign systems that do not involve speaking English.

Using plot scaffolds allows teachers to include students with varying ability levels, too. Lower ability level students can complete the plot scaffolds at their own pace and participate as the class creates the story. Because the plot scaffolds are rehearsed and acted out, students are allowed repeated practice with oral skills as well as repeated opportunities to offer ideas either orally or through kinesthetic means.

Gardner's (1990) theory on multiple intelligences states that students work best when they are allowed to learn through their own personal, cognitive strengths. For example, a student with verbal/linguistic intelligence has the ability to think in words and to use language to express and appreciate complex meanings. Poets, journalists, authors, speakers, and newscasters exhibit high degrees of linguistic intelligence and use both the auditory and visual mode of perception. A student with logical/mathematical intelligence has the ability to work out complex mathematical operations. According to Gardner, scientists, mathematicians, accountants, engineers, and computer programmers all demonstrate strong logical/mathematical intelligence. Allowing students to use their personal cognitive strengths (e.g., visual/spatial, bodily/kinesthetic, or any of the other identified intelligences; see Gardner, 2000, for more information) enables them to work to their potential because the medium is natural to them.

In addition, most lessons include the option of performing the plot scaffold as a play. Performing the plot scaffold as a play allows all students, regardless of language ability, to work together toward a common goal as they "play." Play, a very powerful learning tool, allows for dimensions of cognitive spontaneity, social spontaneity, physical spontaneity, manifest joy, and a sense of humor (Barnett, 1998). Play encourages risk taking because the players do not "die" when they make mistakes.

Instead, they get to play the game again. Rehearsing a play is very similar to "playing" a game, and each time the players practice, they become more skilled. According to current literature on play, children often use pretend play in order to understand and control emotions, and to seek, enact, and rehearse solutions to resolve conflicts (Annarella, 1992; Barnett, 1998; Pelligrini, 1997; Wagner, 1998). Performing the plot scaffold for an audience gives students a chance to practice oral language and listening skills as well as practice in participating in constructed response and group collaboration. This allows for kinesthetic learners to participate in the language experience because they can move and use body language to tell the story. More than 65% of communication is nonverbal, so body language is an important communication tool (as cited in Morain, 1990). Multiple sign systems can be addressed by giving visual learners the option to create the artwork or backdrop to the story. Multiple sign systems (Harste, 1999) imply that literacy is more than the ability to read and write; it extends to the use of other sign systems such as music and art in order to make sense of the world and communicate with others (Harste, 1999). Finally, remember that when students perform the plot scaffold as a play, they do not necessarily need to read aloud the image sections. In a dramatic presentation, students' actions on stage, their voice inflections, and the scenery help to convey the images.

How Will I Know When My Students Are Good Writers?

Good writing is regarded by many as an art. Michael Meade (2002), noted mythologist and storyteller, states that art is supposed to have a touch or taste of the divine. Art is supposed to spark that touch of the divine in the viewer, listener, and mutually, in the creator as well. Meade believes this spark needs to be an emotional engagement between the parties. (His definition of art as an interactive spark is not unlike the sociocognitive interactive model of literacy.) Artists practice their art. Practice can be defined as finding the way, and, according to Meade, we are always finding our way. "Practice makes perfect" is the good description of creating art. The way must be flexible because, each time, we are a different person and the circumstances have changed. The practice may not change, but we do each time (Meade, 2002).

This definition of art and practice may explain why, for many of us, recognizing a well-written story is easy because through that particular writer's talent and style, we are sparked emotionally and mutually connected. However, the practices or paths that led to that writer's success need to be addressed if we are to teach beginning writers to write well. Frequently, as a K–8 language arts teacher, I find students write countless pages, for example, containing a series of battle scenes, but no interesting, relevant plot twists. Or students write stories consisting of lengthy, wordy dialogue between characters that has no distinctive style or purpose. Ultimately, students receive low writing scores for style and content (and maybe end up boring readers or the standardized test evaluator). Plot scaffolds that are based on good writing techniques provide paths to follow for writers to practice and improve their writing skills.

Plot scaffolds provide a means for teaching beginning and intermediate writers in kindergarten through eighth grade to produce more interesting, cohesive stories. Although there are relatively few plots that are basic to all books and stories (Shah, 1979), how one tells the tale makes for the interesting and distinctive oration that "grabs" the reader's attention. With current high-stakes literacy testing being mandated in many states, student writers need to learn, like Scheherazade in Arabian Nights, that one must hold the listener's attention if one is to keeps one's head. Therefore, dialogue should keep the reader's interest. A character's dialogue can make the reader "see" the character and respond emotionally. The addition of images allows the setting to become a character as well. The inclusion of image writing strategies teaches the beginning writer to "show" not "tell" readers how the character responds emotionally, how the setting appears, and how the plot develops. Good writers in turn can become more critical readers of text. Writing and reading go hand in hand in the production of literacy and communication of thought. Because understanding terminology makes for more effective communication, it is important that teachers clarify terms such as *plot*, *image*, *character*, *scaffold*, and *dialogue* for beginning writers.

What Do Students Need to Know About Plot?

All complete story plots have a beginning, middle, and an end, but what happens to the characters in each section makes for an interesting plot that sells itself. An inquiry approach, like that developed by The Great Books Foundation in their Junior Great Books series, emphasizes the teacher or discussion leader asking questions, not providing answers, so students can explore the many possibilities that may exist as a solution or reason behind a story situation. Often the questions are open-ended (e.g., interpretive or evaluative) in order for students to reach a deeper level of understanding. Students must justify their positions using facts and inference from the text, which helps them learn critical thinking skills. Reading becomes an active, participatory exercise as students learn to share different points of view, which can lead to a better understanding of the story. When teachers take an inquiry approach to teaching story plot, instead of categorizing the three sections of a story as beginning, middle, and end, they ask and have students answer three basic questions:

- What if?
- What is the catch?
- What then?

For example, the inquiry approach might include the following:

- What if a wizard came to tea?
- What is the catch? The wizard wants to take you with him on a wild adventure, but you are very comfortable staying home.
- What happens then? Thirteen dwarves drop in unexpectedly and you find yourself, without your pocket handkerchief, running off after them the next morning.

Many readers may recognize this as the beginning plot to *The Hobbit* (Tolkien, 1966). Another example using the inquiry approach could involve the plot used for many horror stories:

- What if you build your beautiful house next to a dank, creepy swamp?
- Of course, the catch is the creepy swamp has a monster living in it, and he has been there for many years. It was his quiet swamp and your building efforts are very noisy.
- What happens then? Obviously, because he is a monster, he begins to invade your house (although one might argue that you invaded his swamp first). We then need a hero to solve the problem.

Again, readers may recognize this as the beginning plot to the classic Old English tale *Beowulf* (Heaney, 2000), in which a monster, Grendel, lives in a swamp where King Hrothgar decides to build Hall Heorot.

Finally, another example of the inquiry approach focuses on the plot for the movie *Jaws* (Brown, Zanuck, & Spielberg, 1975), based on the novel by Peter Benchley. (As a movie, the story is acted out and one can see the characters just as students using plot scaffolds act out a story before they write it. Acting out a story and then writing it, rather than writing a story and then acting it out, is a process I have found that students today easily accept because they are exposed so much to television and cinema.) In *Jaws*, the shark is the monster in the ocean and people are vacationing at a resort on the shark's beachfront.

- What if you build your expensive, fancy, beachfront resort next to a shark's habitat?
- What is the catch? The shark sees your resort guests as nice "snacks."
- What happens then? The shark begins to eat the guests.

Although *Beowulf* and *Jaws* have similar plots, their different settings led to different story lines. Basically, any good plot involves a problem or dilemma that must be solved, such as Hrothgar building Hall Heorot on Grendel's territory or a rich businessman building a resort next to shark-infested waters. Teachers can explain how conflict is central to plot by showing students how a problem occurs, how it gets worse, and then how it is solved. First, the writer creates a problem. Hrothgar builds Hall Heorot on Grendel's territory and Grendel starts eating Hrothgar's guests. Next, the plot develops as the writer attempts to solve the problem. Numerous men try to kill Grendel, but they can't because he is so strong. Beowulf kills Grendel, but Grendel's mother retaliates. Then, the writer creates a resolution or ending to the story. Beowulf kills Grendel's mother.

Plot structure involving conflict dates back to Greek drama when the first actor, a protagonist, stepped out of the chorus and talked to the audience about his or her problems. These problems generally got worse before they were solved. Therefore, students usually find the following plot structure, which is based on Greek drama, helpful.

- Man gets stuck in tree (state the problem)

- Throw rocks at the man (make the problem worse)

- Man gets out of tree (solve the problem)

Once beginning writers understand the three basic plot questions, teachers can introduce elaboration in terms of the seven elements of plot: hook, problem, backfill, complication, action–reaction, dark moment, and resolution. All complete plots have these seven elements, and they usually follow this order (Scarborough, McCaffery, McCullugh, Crispin, & Weis, 2003).

The first element of plot, **hook**, is used to capture readers' attention and grab their interest so they will become emotionally engaged with the writer's work and read the story. I tell my students to think of the hook as a sale's pitch because you want to get the reader interested in reading the rest of the story. Often the best hooks are made by "twisting" a normal situation into something abnormal or noteworthy (Scarborough et al., 2003). For example, in *Beowulf* a group of people are having a good time at a party celebrating Hall Heorot's construction. The hook occurs when something monstrous and rank suddenly breaks in the door and begins eating the guests. Or, in *Jaws*, the hook occurs when a young woman is swimming happily on a calm night at the beach. Suddenly, she is grabbed by something under water and eaten.

Thus, the writer has presented the reader with a **problem**, the second element of plot, which the main character must solve: Who or what came in the door of Hall Heorot? Who or what ate the young woman who was swimming?

To make a story more credible, the problem needs the third element of plot, **backfill**, or more information about the problem. Who is the hero or heroine of the story, and how will his or her background enable the person to face the problem? Often in more interesting stories, the main character's flaw is mentioned in the backfill, and the internal dilemma that the main character must overcome occurs while he or she solves the problem (Knight et al., 2004). Flaws are character traits that cause further dilemmas for characters during their struggles to solve the plot's main problem. Flaws make more interesting characters because they add an emotional tie or human quality; overcoming flaws is an issue that most people can relate to. For example, in *Jaws*, the main character's problem is that he has to deal with a great white shark, but in the backfill to his character we learn that he is not comfortable in the ocean. Another example of backfill is from *Beowulf* (Nye, 1968), in which we learn that the hero, Beowulf, because of poor eyesight, has cultivated "habits of quickness and concentration that enabled him to be truly *seeing* where others were only looking" (p. 23). Backfill allows readers to discover character flaws, which add good twists to the plot lines. As a reflection of the plot's theme, the main character's fatal flaw deals with ego issues. In most Western literature (from Western in terms of Greek civilization to the American West), heroes and heroines have one tragic flaw or inner dilemma to give them pathos in order to elicit sympathy (with feeling) from the audience. Human failings also give the story an angle when characters need to solve the plot problem while dealing with a personal problem. For example, Achilles had an inflated ego as well as a weak heel. And the main character in the classic Western *Shane* (Schaefer, 1949/

1975) could not escape his past and his love of violence. Both heroes are energized by violence. In addition, instructing students to give their characters flaws helps them to build characterization and purpose for backfill rather than having students create unnecessary details for their stories. However, I instruct students to include backfill only if it serves a purpose. For example, if a character has poor eyesight or a fear of the ocean, these details must add something to the story and help move the action.

The fourth element of plot, **complication**, is a further twist to the plot in which the character attempts to solve a problem but it gets worse instead. A complication is a challenge to a plot solution, and conflict makes for good stories. For example, in *Jaws*, the complication is that the resort town does not want to lose tourist revenue, so they do not want anyone to know that a killer shark is in the water. More "rocks" are thrown at the main character when everyone, including his own family, both expect him to and make it difficult for him to solve the shark problem. Meanwhile, Beowulf's problem is complicated by the fact that Grendel cannot be killed using conventional means—a sword—and that many men have tried and were unsuccessful because of Grendel's thick skin.

The fifth element of plot, **action–reaction**, occurs when the main character makes the first serious attempt to solve the problem, but the problem only gets worse. Although action–reaction may seem similar to complication, the reaction is what differentiates the two. The first reaction puts the plot in motion. Often the problem gets worse because of the main character's attempt to solve it. In addition, complications are often intrinsic (e.g., within a character) but action–reaction is often extrinsic (e.g., physical actions). In *Jaws* the main character attempts to hunt the shark in the ocean, but the shark attacks the boat. In *Beowulf*, Beowulf grabs Grendel by the arm and rips it off. Grendel manages to crawl back to the swamp and his mother, who is justifiably upset and more terrifying than Grendel, and consequently she attacks Hall Heorot. To make matters worse, her attack comes after everyone has just celebrated Beowulf's heroic success over Grendel. Through action–reaction, the writer is throwing more rocks at the man in the tree, similar to using a hook, of which examples abound in most television soap operas to keep viewers tuning in each day.

The sixth element of plot, the **dark moment**, or climax, occurs when the main character must face his or her fears (found in the backfill) and conquer them. A good image for this situation is the "moment of one candle" (Van Doorn, 2004) or when all events lead to this one moment in time. The dark moment in *Jaws* occurs when the main character overcomes his fears and the shark is killed. The dark moment in *Beowulf* occurs when Beowulf swims to Grendel's mother's lair and strangles her.

Finally, the seventh element of plot, **resolution**, occurs when the main character realizes that he or she has won or overcome the dilemma, or able to "get out of the tree," when the problem is solved, and the hero is acknowledged as the "winner" by those around him.

Having students recognize the seven elements of plot as they read helps them to become more critical readers. However, as students critically read works by well-known authors, they may notice that although these authors incorporate the seven plot elements, they often break grammar rules. For example, some authors such as Charles Dickens write using incomplete sentences or run-on sentences. However, as I tell my students, when your style can hold the reader's interest and keep meaning, you may break the rules, too. For now, however, students must follow the basic rules of grammar and be evaluated accordingly. To reinforce these basic rules, I use minilessons in grammar while using the plot scaffolding strategy. These lessons focus on the use of gerunds, participle phrases, infinitives, and so forth. I also use minilessons in grammar when teaching students how to write images.

What Is an Image?

Images, the "scenery" or background to any good story, enable readers to "see" or become mentally engaged with the story. Writing that incorporates images is similar to incorporating backdrops in a film. The following basic rules to writing images can help set the tone and mood of a story:

1. A good literary image shows instead of tells. Students should use their senses to create images. In particular, taste and smell can evoke past experiences and make for very powerful images. To practice writing images, I bring a bag of jellybeans, pass them out, and have students describe the taste or smell of the jellybeans. Students must focus on describing the taste of a specific jellybean out of a bag of 40 flavored jellybeans. Examples of student images included the following:

> Chocolate pudding jellybean: The jellybean reminds me of curling up late on a rainy night and drinking cocoa while watching an old movie on television.

> Yellow and white jellybean: The jellybean reminds me of a comfortable movie theater, and it tastes like the warm popcorn my family and I eat when we see movies at the movie theater.

Teachers can bring in scented candles, perfume (sprayed on paper), or other items that have an interesting odor. Sometimes, I use my own cologne, and the images that it evokes in my students are always surprising to me. Students have associated my cologne with the smell of their grandmother, their mother going out on a special occasion, or a perfume department, but never of me.

2. When it comes to writing images, try to have students avoid using a traditional sentence structure. For example, students often begin sentences with *the*, which is a routine, predictable, and nondescript word. To avoid overusing *the*, simply flip the sentence and start with a clause. The sentence "The red fox jumped over the sleeping dog" could be flipped to "Over the sleeping dog jumped the red fox." Students also can focus on using phrases as an interesting way to start a sentence. Teachers can help students learn how to use participle, infinitive, and gerund phrases to create an image. Following are some examples:

> Running quickly, the red fox jumped over the sleeping dog.

> To avoid the sleeping dog, the red fox jumped over him.

> Jumping over the sleeping dog was the fox's favorite activity.

Images are a useful, practical way to teach new grammatical terms, as well as literary devices such as metaphor, simile, and personification. (See lessons in chapters 2 and 3 for specific examples of how to teach grammar and literary devices.)

Once a week, I have all students write at least two complete sentences for an image. Because beginning writers sometimes tell the reader rather than show the reader, I have students write a second sentence to "show why," which helps them transition to using figurative language. (In order to understand where figurative language may be helpful in a story, the plot scaffolds provided in this book have specific areas listed where writers should provide images and descriptive settings.) For this assignment, students describe a subject, such as a picture, sound, smell, or something to taste or feel, and create a picture with words or "paint a mental image" on paper. Intermediate students should complete this assignment as homework so they have time to reflect on and recall what was covered in class that day. I briefly meet with students individually to discuss their images and make comments and corrections, and then students rewrite the images in their individual Image Books, or journal of images. As I correct the images, I read them aloud to allow the writer to *hear* what he or she has written. I also have found this to be a good proofreading technique.

Writing images can be done at the elementary level as part of a weekly writing program. Even kindergarten or first-grade teachers can incorporate it into their curriculum by scaffolding an image. For example, a first-grade teacher might bring in a large red stuffed crab as the weekly image subject for students. First graders or kindergarteners who are just learning to write can be given a template with specific blanks to fill in (e.g., Looking as _____ as a _____ , that _____crab is_____.).

Kindergarten students can dictate their answers for the teacher to write. First graders can pick a word from a word bank created through class discussion of what the crab looks like. Images like the one above can be copied in large print on a worksheet, leaving room for pictures if so desired. Students or teachers can paste the completed sheets in their Image Books, which can be used as a writing portfolio and passed along with students as they advance from grades K–5 in elementary school. Middle school teachers can also pass Image Books from grades 6–8. Students can choose to use these images later as story starters and, after time, they become almost like diaries or photo albums because they invoke memories of past experiences.

3. Students should avoid using clichés such as "blue as the sky" or "white as snow." Clichés are overused descriptions that no longer make the reader actively form a mental picture. Words such as *pretty, ugly, bad, good, boring,* and other vague terms should be avoided because these terms are subjective—that is, what may be pretty to the writer may not be pretty to the reader. Following are some examples of images in which students focused on avoiding clichés (students number, title, and date their images):

#7 Sound 9/28/04

Reminding me of an alien war, this sound is as sharp as a roller coaster de-railing. Then the sound reminds me of aliens remorsing the dead after a long war.

#2 Tolkien drawing 10/19/04

This hobbit hole looks like the inside of a barrel. When I look at it, it reminds me of dolls in a dollhouse.

#6 Theme Dinner 11/16/04

Our theme dinner was as dark as if we were playing on the ocean floor. Hanging from the ceiling, the golden leaves glittered like metallic seaweed in the sun.

After practicing these rules, student use images to set a tone or mood for their stories. For example, three students wrote the following images using the plot scaffold "Guess Who Moved in Next Door?" based on the story Beowulf, to help set the mood:

Example 1

In the deepest part of the swamp where the water was colored red from blood, the sound of snapping bones filled the underwater cave where Grendel and his mother lived.

Example 2

In the fen Grendel and his mother are having breakfast, eating what smelled like a dead chicken. They are gnarling at it as blood is gushing from it like a fountain.

Example 3

In the fen, a nasty and gross place, Grendel and his mother are having breakfast. A sound as hideous as screeching bats came from their house.

Each of the three students set the tone and mood for their stories by using appropriate images that employ the sense of smell, sight, or sound. The third student told his reader that the fen was "nasty" but gave evidence for it by adding the screeching bat noise. Using images to "dress" the scenery is similar to adding costumes to dress characters.

How Do Students Create Interesting, Relevant Characters?

As previously mentioned, plots generally follow a basic format and there are a few basic plots, but characters, similar to the setting, help make each plot unique. For example, in the basic plot in which hero meets monster, faces monster, and kills monster, the character Beowulf is quite different from the character Jason from *Jason and the Argonauts* (Osborne & Osborne, 1988). Beowulf, a man who takes matters into his own hands, literally rips off Grendel's arm, while Jason, a flatterer, cons Medea, King Aeetes's sorceress daughter, to help him kill the dragon and steal the Golden Fleece. Both men get rid of the monster, but their characters determine how they will act and accomplish the task. Their character traits, flaws, or strengths make how they face problems different in each story. Jason is insincere, so he may use flattery or lies to achieve the goal of taking the Golden Fleece. Beowulf believes in solving problems by depending on his own personal resources. He may choose always to face danger on his own and neglect to realize that the help of others might be necessary to solve a problem.

Each character in a story, much like in a play, has a different "voice," and plot scaffolds help students to write dialogue that gives their characters purpose rather than having nondescript characters and trite, irrelevant dialogue that adds no movement to the plot. This is why the plot scaffolds take on the format of play scripts. Students must create lines for their characters to speak. By reading aloud lines, moving, and becoming familiar with characters, students understand the focus and purpose of the story and can later turn their verbal expressions and gestures into print. Consequently, students are able to better choose words to help paint a picture of what the reader would see if he or she were "watching" the story. Before students write their stories, I use what I call the "Fred and Mary" strategy to help students write interesting dialogue. Students should create dialogue for the characters Fred and Mary by following these steps:

1. Write the lines. (Remember to space dialogue or go to the next line and indent when you change characters.)

2. Add some movement. (What are the characters doing?)

3. Add some scenery (images).

4. Put your characters in costume. (What are the characters wearing or what do they look like?)

I tell students to think of writing dialogue in a story as writing lines in a play or movie. We use the following lines as a starting point:

Fred: There is a dog.

Mary: It is a big dog.

Fred: It bit me.

Students recognize that the dialogue sounds pretty flat. Reading lines from a script can be dull because the reader cannot see the actors or the action. To help readers visualize what is going on, I have students add stage directions or add movement to the script. I also have students give the characters some expression with more exact dialogue.

Fred: (calls out to Mary) There is a huge bulldog coming this way!

Mary: (turns to Fred) It is a gigantic bulldog with fangs and a blue tail. I think it is glaring at us. Do you have a gun?

Fred: (looking down in disbelief) Too late. I think the creature just took my hand off. Ouch!

The dialogue is improving, but the scenery is missing. I have students add some images so readers know where the characters are and then put the dialogue into story form. In addition, I encourage students to use descriptive language when characters talk to one another—for example, students often overuse the word *said*. Finally, I remind students to dress the characters in costumes that match the setting.

The final version of the dialogue read as follows:

> While exploring the dense jungle on planet Xenon, Fred, flipping back his space helmet visor, calls out to Mary, "There is a huge bulldog coming this way."
>
> Turning both of her heads in his direction, Mary quickly responds in a high squeaky voice, "It is a gigantic bull dog with sharp fangs and a blue tail. I think it is glaring at us. Do you have a gun?"
>
> Jumping forward at light speed, the rabid creature leaps at Fred and then quickly retreats into the tall purple vegetation surrounding them. "Too late," Fred sighs, "I think the creature just took my hand off. Ouch!" Fred shrugs his shoulders, "Guess I will just have to grow another hand."

Once students realize that creating dialogue in this way is not intimidating, they become eager to participate and to continually revise and rewrite the story's ending until they are satisfied that the plot says what they want it to say.

How Should Students Be Evaluated?

This book provides practical, hands-on strategies for assessment. Currently, under standards-based curricula, evaluation must include a triangulation of informal, constructed, selected, or performance assessment to determine mastery of a learning standard. In *Making Classroom Assessment Work*, Davies (2000) supports a broader form of assessment that includes a triangulation of evidence. A triangulation of data involves looking at more than one piece of student work in order to determine competency level.

Davies (2000) offers the following suggestions for assessing literacy competence: observing student reading skills, skills of written expression, and listening and speaking skills. These suggestions address current language arts curriculum standards in that evaluation should be measured as a series of short, frequent assessments. Until this time, most assessment had been based on students showing mastery of a subject through passing a test that involved giving correct selected responses. Under current national language arts standards, students are strongly encouraged to self-assess and reflect. Using plot scaffolding techniques that encourage rehearsal, dialogue, and imaging allows for reflection.

For example, when my students study Beowulf, they attempt to answer the "big idea" question, What are a hero's traits? They also answer specific, daily questions, such as What does Beowulf do when he hears about King Hrothgar's problems? Is Beowulf rewarded for his services? or What does Beowulf do with his reward? Answers to these daily, factual questions become a type of informal assessment because it is a quick means of determining whether or not students understand the story line. Factual questions such as these also can be used for selected-response, text-explicit assessment. Students need to understand text-explicit facts before they can answer implicit or evaluative questions and support those answers with evidence from the story. Students also need practice in answering selected responses because most standardized tests are based on this kind of assessment. To assess my intermediate students' understanding of Beowulf, they read the story, act it out, and write an essay on Beowulf as a hero. Individually, students also write a short story based on the plot scaffold "Guess Who Moved in Next Door?" This short story writing not only assesses students' story comprehension but also allows them to analyze it on an evaluative level in order to write from a different viewpoint. In terms of reading comprehension, three levels of understanding are addressed: (1) implicit, (2) evaluative, and (3) explicit. Implicit understandings are those meanings found in a story—which could have more than one interpretation—but require factual evidence from the story for validation. Evaluative understandings refer to how the ideas in the story fit in with the reader's own personal experience. Does the reader agree or disagree with what the story is saying? Explicit understanding refers to knowing the actual facts of the story. (These three levels of understanding are the bases for the Junior Great Book series concepts of Shared Inquiry; see www.greatbooks.org). In addition, writing the short story is a form of constructive assessment because students must construct meaning from what they have read.

Writing a story and acting it out are performance-based assessments. Using a rubric, I evaluate the stories that students write. Evaluation also should include student conferences and self-assessments (Davies, 2000). During the writing process, I meet with students at least twice to review their rough drafts. I check the completed plot scaffolds and read aloud the first part of the story. Together, we assess what is good about the story and what needs to be clarified.

Self-assessment occurs at the end of each play project. I videotape the performances, let students watch the videotape, and then students evaluate themselves using a class-generated rubric that includes a list of elements students believe are important. This process gives students an opportunity for self-assessment and reflection. I usually find that students often are more critical of themselves than I am because as the producer of a work, they are more aware of each mistake and often express a desire to change some part of their performance or revise their work. I believe that students' critical tendencies are a result of plot scaffolds being more process based, which is a positive move toward the realization that writing is organic, alive, and has the potential to change with time and experience.

Self-assessment rubrics include categories such as the following:

- speaking clearly,
- body language,
- remembering lines,
- speaking with feeling
- costume, and
- personal comments (e.g., Did you do anything extra to help this group project?).

As previously mentioned, products also should be included in assessment, and these products might include writing portfolios, test scores, notebooks, and project assessments (Davies, 2000). For example, I keep students' stories in student writing portfolios. I also give short, text-explicit tests after we have read and discussed a story. In addition, I check image rough drafts—that is, two sentences describing an image—on a weekly basis before students transfer them to their Image Books, which are assessed at the end of each quarter. Each writing scaffold is a part of a larger theme unit, and project assessment may include a play we create, a debate, or one of the further elaboration ideas included at the end of some lesson plans in chapters 2 and 3.

What Is the Format of the Plot Scaffold Lessons?

Designed to fit the practical needs of teachers with time constraints, the sessions are roughly 45 minutes to an hour per session over a series of five to seven days. These time frames allow for frequent rehearsals, or rewrites, of the story and, therefore, provide more opportunities to internalize ideas and learning strategies. In order to fit the needs of different class sizes, the scaffolds have many characters whose parts might be deleted or added. To make the task appropriate to the learning environment, plot scaffolds are designed to account for the many different learning styles and ability levels that teachers must face daily. The last line for each character is left blank, and there is just enough of what each character felt or expressed to allow predictions of what that character might say for his or her last line. This gives ownership to the learner and some structure for the teacher, such that the teacher can take more of a collaborative rather than evaluative role. Each story presents a conflict, which the students, either as individuals or as a group, need to resolve in order to complete the plot, because the scaffold was meant to be just that—a support for emerging ideas and solutions to the problems presented. Teachers can determine whether or not students internalized specific literacy strategies by using the recommended rubrics located in Appendix A.

First, the teacher hands out copies of the plot scaffold and has students read it aloud, each taking parts. Next, students get up and move with the parts, discussing how the story would look acted out on stage. Then, as a class the script is read together, with each student taking a different role. Allow students to read other parts if desired, which allows students to hear different possibilities for a character's voice, motivation, and tone. Also allow students to incorporate props. According to one teacher who used the plot scaffolds with her students,

> A lot of them wanted to switch parts; they didn't want the same parts. And then we went back through it and tried to find some parts where they wouldn't be in the same scene. And we were going to throw some parts out. The kids decided no, we want all the parts, and we want to play all the parts. Then when it came right down to it, Josh was left with a male and female part or something like that. He is very shy, but very artistic. I didn't know how he would react because he is not very outgoing. And he just nodded his head; he's not very outgoing. He decided that to act more like a female, he would need to look more female. So he just grabbed some red yarn that was sitting out, stuck it on his head, styled it up a little bit. So he started hamming it up a

little bit; he even had a long T-shirt on that day, and he curtsied to everybody and everything. It really allowed him to come out, and everybody had a good time with it.

By following this format, students at lower reading levels and ESL students have the opportunity to hear lines read more than once, which allows them to internalize words and have more fluency later when they read or write.

Finally, students can begin to write their lines on the plot scaffold or script. Figure 1 is an example of a page from the plot scaffold "Guess Who Moved in Next Door?" Notice in the example the places where students are to add lines or dialogue. Also notice that the door has become a character in the story and speaks. Figure 2 is an example of a completed version of "Guess Who Moved in Next Door?" The student's responses are in bold, and note that her writing is not grammatically correct at this time. As previously mentioned, grammar is focused on during rewriting. At this time, it is important for students to get their ideas down on paper. In fact, sometimes writers get hung up on grammar rules and experience a type of writer's block that prevents them from thinking fluently. Basically, I focus on letting students' creativity flow.

When students rewrite a scaffold, they practice flexibility and elaboration. Some students write adjectives next to nouns they wish to describe. Some write lines next to the character. I also have students write stage directions, which we later add to the dialogue to "see" how they look on stage or on paper. Initially, we put the stage directions in brackets and then later transfer them to dialogue in a story. Student also can add more characters if needed. After a number of rewrites or "rehearsals," the scaffolds begin to take on an originality that is reflective of the students who are writing and the teacher who is facilitating.

The next step after acting out the plot and filling in the dialogue is to write the first draft of the story. Figure 3 is an example of a first draft from that same student's earlier scaffold. The draft still has grammatical and spelling errors (*wreaked* instead of *reeked*). These errors will be corrected by the final draft, but the sixth grader who wrote it did add some descriptive images (for a monster/horror story) and has spaced the dialogue rather than running it all together. The student also added movement to her characters. In a later draft, in addition to correcting grammar, this student also will add "costumes" to her characters—that is, the student will note what the characters are wearing to make the characters more believable. For example, one student added that Grendel was wearing "bone and skull pajamas" and his mother was wearing "her new evening gown made of real snake skin."

If there are time constraints, students may write their final drafts from the completed scaffolds instead of writing a first draft. Beginning and younger writers who may feel overwhelmed by rewriting rough drafts can use the completed plot scaffold—which includes students' additional dialogue, images, and changes—as a first draft. However, if using the plot scaffold as a first draft to produce a finished work, the teacher needs to constantly monitor the final draft in order to ensure its quality. Checking the students' work after every few paragraphs or after every page is a good idea so beginning writers can correct mistakes before possibly making more of them.

For intermediate writers, once the first draft is completed, have students write the first page of the next and possibly final draft. (As with the first draft, the next draft

Figure 1
Sample Page From "Guess Who Moved in Next Door?"

Characters:

Beowulf	Queen Wealhtheow
Grendel	14 Warriors
Grendel's Mother (SHE)	Door of Hall Heorot
King Hrothgar	Narrator/Writer
Unferth	Servants One and Two

Narrator/Writer: In the fen, Grendel and his mother are having breakfast. (Write an image that describes this situation.) _____ _____

Grendel: Mom, what was all that noise next door last night? I couldn't get my beauty sleep!

Mother: I know, my little bone cruncher. It must be the new neighbors with that gaudy house. After dark, they should be more respectful of our quiet little swamp. Honey, take your elbows off the table when you are gorging.

Grendel: Mom, can I go visit them tonight? I promise to make them be quiet.

Mother: Yes, mommy's baby, you go along and be a good monster tonight. Oh...and bring me home a snack, dear.

Grendel: Yes, mom. (Grendel goes toward Heorot. Write an image that describes this situation.) _____ _____

Narrator/Writer: King Hrothgar and his men are feasting. Grendel knocks at the door. (Write an image that describes this situation.) _____ _____

Door of Heorot: (How might the door react? Think of the door as a character in the story. Would you fall or faint when Grendel knocks on you?) _____ _____

Grendel: Hey guys. My, my, if you all don't look good enough to eat! Excuse me if I help myself.

People in the Hall: (What would they say? Make their lines.) _____ _____

Grendel: It was nice visiting you. I have to go home to my mom now. (Grendel leaves. Write an image that describes this situation.) _____ _____

Narrator/Writer: (Describe the scene of Hall Heorot the next day. Two servants are discussing the noise in the hall last night.) _____ _____

Figure 2
Completed Example of "Guess Who Moved in Next Door?"

Characters:

Beowulf	Queen Wealhtheow
Grendel	14 Warriors
Grendel's Mother (SHE)	Door of Hall Heorot
King Hrothgar	Narrator/Writer
Unferth	Servants One and Two

Narrator/Writer: In the <u>reaking</u> fen, Grendel and his mother are having <u>gory</u> breakfast. (Write an image that describes this situation.) <u>which was leftovers of the lost people from the road last night.</u>

Grendel: Mom, what was all that noise next door last night! I couldn't get my beauty sleep? <u>(He whined as he beat his fists on the table)</u> <u>Can't you tell?</u>

Mother: I know, my little bone cruncher. It must be the new neighbors with that gaudy house. After dark, they should be more respectful of our quiet little swamp. Honey, take your elbows off the table when you are gorging.

Grendel: Mom, can I go visit them <u>those wretched people</u> tonight? I promise to make them be so quiet. <u>You'll never know they're there.</u>

Mother: Yes, mommy's baby, you go along and be a good monster tonight. Oh...and bring me home a snack, dear.

Grendel: Yes, <u>my favorite</u> mom. (Grendel goes toward Heorot. Write an image that describes this situation.) _____

Narrator/Writer: King Hrothgar and his men are feasting <u>on a wonderful feast of cherries and turkey, meat and gravy</u>. Grendel knocks at the door. (Write an image that describes this situation.) _____

Door of Heorot: (How might the door react? Think of the door as a character in the story. Would you fall or faint when Grendel knocks on you?) <u>Fall down and goes ahh, its you why are you here?</u> _____

Grendel: Hey guys. My, my, if you all don't look good enough to eat! Excuse me if I help myself.

People in the Hall: (What would they say? Make their lines.) <u>Warriors-Your ugly and you're a freak and go away you scary beast.</u>

Queen Wealhtheow: <u>Warriors, stay and fight.</u>

Grendel: It was nice visiting you. I have to go home to my <u>sweet mommy</u> mom now. (Grendel leaves. Write an image that describes this situation.) _____

Narrator/Writer: (Describe the scene of Hall Heorot the next day. Two servants are discussing the noise in the hall last night.) <u>organs and guts hung from the chandelier and ceiling, puddles of blood forming in hall and the air was icey and silent.</u>

Student additions are underlined.

Figure 3
Story First Draft Based on "Guess Who Moved in Next Door?"

In the fen, that had a wreaking scent of road kill with a mix of body odor, Grendel and his mother are having a breakfast only suitable for someone from the underworld. Their meal wreaked of rotting eggs!

"Mommy, what was that awful noise last night? I could not even get my beauty sleep that every good monster, that is cute, needs to get!" Grendel whined while he beat his green and bumpy fists on the table, while his mother retied his robe.

"I could hear that awful noise inside my room too. I think it is to our misfortune we have new neighbors. They should be more respectful of our comfy little swamp. Honey, take your elbows off the table while you are gorging."

"Mommy, can I go visit those wretched people tonight? I promise to make them be so quiet you'll never know they're there." Grendel snickered at the thought.

"Yes, my sweet baby, of course, just bring me home a little snack."

"Yes, my favorite mommy." Grendel said sliding down from his old creaky chair. He headed towards the exit of the cave where the swirling and bubbling water lay.

Meanwhile, at Hall Heorot, King Hrothgar and his men are eating a wonderful feast that included ham and beef. Little did they know, Grendel is advancing toward the door. Just as Grendel was about to pound on the door, the door squealed and dodged Grendel's blow. Then the door quietly moved aside so Grendel could get in. Grendel trudged in, leaving a thick, green and gritty slime behind him.

"Hello my friendly new neighbors! Mind if I join you at dinner?" Grendel growled as he moved quickly towards them.

The people in the hall all screamed with fright. They backed away quickly and then started yelling at Grendel to go away. You could hear, every few minutes, someone say something directly like "go away", "get out", "go bug someone else you ugly beast", or "run away".

After picking a few of the tastiest and fattest looking people and stuffing them greedily into his green and yellow mouth, where then you could see his yellowish-brown teeth stained red from the blood of the people. He said loudly and happily, "It was nice eating you, but I'll just take some to go. My mom likes extra crunchy ones." Grendel said out loud to himself. He swiftly grabbed two skinny people from the tight bundle that had formed. He went home to the smelly fen quickly.

may contain too many grammatical errors to be considered a final draft. If a paper has too many mistakes, I consider it to be a second draft, not a final draft.) To save time, all grammatical errors should be corrected before the final draft is written. To reduce redundancy issues, I set a page length at this point, as well as read the first page of each student's next or final draft to ensure that they understand how to use proper spacing with dialogue. Sometimes it helps to remind students to "keep it like a script." For those students who are using a computer and possess good word-processing skills, writing the final draft is a relatively easy step of polishing previous drafts. They may have completely changed the original plot scaffold, but it still needs to make sense. For example, if the original scaffold has an American West or "Old West" setting, and the student changed the setting to a place under the ocean and changed the characters to fish, then the resulting new story still needs to have the appropriate additions or deletions to make sense to the reader.

To incorporate multiple sign systems (Harste, Woodward, & Burke, 1984)—such as dance, art, and music—within the lessons, teachers can choose students' best lines to make a class script and then act out the play. Students' best lines are the most unique and different lines in comparison with the original plot scaffold (however, they still need to tie into the dialogue or action).

Plot scaffolds allow teachers to become facilitators of learning as they "sit near" students and use multiple assessments that include informal, selected, constructed, and performance-based formats. Giving style to an author's writing, the "script" format of plot scaffolds acts as a bridge showing how dramatized dialogue and set description can cross into the imagery and dialogue used in narrative text. The scaffolds in this book allow for ownership, appropriateness, support, collaboration, and internalization, which are all key ingredients for active learning in an inquiry approach. Creativity is apparent as students take the scaffolds and elaborate on them using fluency and flexibility to create an original product. Imagination or "pretend" becomes important as students act out the scaffolds that are designed for diverse learning styles. Because plot scaffolds are open-ended, the inquiry approach helps create a more focused, relevant story plot. Memorable stories have problems and conflicts to resolve.

Plot scaffolds allow teachers to become facilitators and give students guidelines for writing. Plot scaffolds are also a way to make otherwise difficult text more user-friendly. Chapters 2 and 3 provide the detailed lesson plans for plot scaffolds that emphasize grammar, creating images and dialogue, and performance.

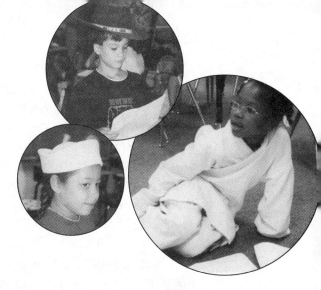

CHAPTER 2

Plot Scaffolds for Beginning Writers

Once upon a time there were two ferrets named Marty and Zelda. Marty was white. My grandmother owns a ferret. Zelda was black and little. Do you like ferrets? They were nice ferrets. Ferrets have teeth. The ferrets lived in ferret town.

"Hi," said Marty.

"Let's go for a vacation," said Zelda.

"OK."

"Sounds good."

"Let's take the car."

"OK I will get my purse."

They got in the car and drove to the store. I like going to the store.

"What do you do with this type of writer, and what if that writer is in the same class as the one who wrote the *Star Wars* story?" inquires the teacher.

"Writers come in several stages. At what stage is this writer?" I ask.

"Stage? What do you mean by stage?" she asks.

In this chapter, I explain the different types of beginning writers and review the plot scaffolds that can be used to match students' different stages of development (see Appendix B for complete versions of these plot scaffolds). I also provide sample lesson plans for using these plot scaffolds and review how teachers can make their own plot scaffolds designed to meet the specific needs of students in their classrooms. Depending on grade level, each lesson plan has steps that take 45 to 60 minutes to complete. Teachers should adjust this time frame as needed to match their students' attention spans.

The specific structure of the following lessons is as follows: Step 1, Determining Prior Knowledge, is done first in order to determine what students already know or believe about the writing topic. Next, students complete Step 2, Acting Out the Plot Scaffold, to complete the story plot, to practice adding characterization and dialogue, and to visualize what the reader might need to see (images) if the story were being read, not performed. These two steps could be done in one lesson lasting about 45 minutes to one hour.

The next day students complete Step 2 again and then complete Step 3, Completing the Plot Scaffold, which includes writing dialogue and images onto the plot scaffold. Students are also free to make any changes to the scaffold. This takes about 45 minutes or could be done as a homework assignment.

Step 4, Adding Effective Dialogue, is done after students have acted out and orally shared the images and dialogue written on their scaffolds. Effective dialogue can be added directly to the plot scaffold. Students also can practice placing quotation marks in the correct place for dialogue on the scaffold, which makes for an easier transition to their next or first draft of narrative text. This step takes 45 minutes to one hour. Teachers should check the completed plot scaffolds for the seven elements of plot (see pages 13–14) before students write their first drafts.

Step 5, Expanding the Plot Scaffold, involves writing the first narrative draft from the plot scaffold. Beginning writers may feel less intimidated by the rewriting process if they are allowed to use the completed plot scaffold sheets as their "first drafts." However, they should be encouraged to make all additions and corrections, including grammar conventions, to the scaffold sheets before they write their final draft. They may also change the original scaffold dialogue if it fits their new story. If beginning writers are using the scaffold sheets as their first draft, teachers need to carefully monitor students' final draft writing. When checking to see that students are copying changes correctly as well as spacing dialogue, to catch mistakes before they become repeated errors, it is a good idea to have students show you small sections as they write, rather than wait until the whole story is finished.

Within each lesson I have included a section called Grammar to Improve Style. I want both teachers and students to think of using grammar—the system underlying the formal features of language—as a means to improve their writing style. Using grammar for style isn't just recognizing a gerund phrase or being able to identify an adjective in a sentence, it is knowing how to effectively use word combinations to create an intended reader response.

Further Elaborations are noted for the plot scaffolds and usually include turning the plot scaffolds into performance tasks by having students act them out. Because the plot scaffolds are short and the characters have few lines, they could be performed for an audience after students have one week to practice. Larger productions, of course, would take more time to prepare.

Finally, some plot scaffolds in this chapter and chapter 3 feature an ESL adaptation (see "The Rent"). These adaptations involve using students' native languages, using multiple sign systems, and nonverbal communication. These adaptations may be used with other plot scaffolds, too.

For a better idea of what a complete lesson looks like, the first lesson plan includes the detailed listing of learning objectives and actual rubrics for beginning writers that correspond with the lesson. (See Appendix A for learning objectives and rubrics for the remaining lessons.) The objectives and rubrics are based on the developmental stages of writing noted in the next section. The objectives for each scaffold have been drawn from Georgia's 2004 English/Language Arts Performance Standards, which adhere to national language arts standards. These standards are process oriented and allow for an easy triangulation of data in terms of assessment—that is, assessment is reliant on teacher observation, written product, and student–teacher conversation.

Teachers should choose objectives and rubrics from Appendix A that meet their students' current needs. The rubrics are based on ability rather than grade level because different classes and diverse students have individual needs that may not be considered on grade level. Students should be taught according to their abilities, not just the preconceived ability of a grade level. Thus, teaching and evaluation start from what students know (Courtney, 1989; Dwyer, 1990; Wagner, 1998; Wolf et al., 2005). Based on my experience, students with different abilities can pool their strengths and produce a product, such as a play, provided that each student is honored for his or her own unique contributions. For example, in a performance of "The Rent," one student who was rather shy chose to play the door, which was so well done that he became as important to the plot as the protagonist.

The plot scaffolds in this chapter are placed in order of increasing difficulty—from emergent to experimenting writing ability. However, certain plot scaffolds, such as "Emergency," "Shoot Out at the Bottoms Up Saloon," and "The Rent," also can be used successfully with intermediate writers. Intermediate writers are learning to recognize specific elements in genres such as melodrama or Westerns. Looking at the plot scaffolds from the standpoint of genre makes them useful to more experienced writers. An adaptation may be necessary for pacing as intermediate writers often work faster than beginning writers. As intermediate writers use scaffolds like "Shoot Out at the Bottoms Up Saloon," they can also be encouraged to change the setting. For example, one of my eighth-grade groups once placed the whole story in an undersea setting and all the characters became fish. The story still had the elements of a Western, but the dialogue and imagery fit the new undersea theme. Lessons on comparative literature also may be used to expand plot scaffolds. For example, stories about knights in King Arthur epics (e.g., Johnston, 1979) share many of the same qualities as those of cowboys in classic Westerns like *Shane* (Schaefer, 1949/1975).

I also would like to note that when writing plot scaffolds for young children, I purposefully choose "silly" plots—that is, they may seem silly to an adult, but elementary school humor is quite different from adolescent and adult humor. I have found that first graders are literal minded and they like obvious, concrete jokes. In addition, the plot scaffolds in this chapter do not contain any death or killing, based on the ancient Greek idea of not actually showing death or killing on stage (however, students' descriptive, focused images often make up for this absence). Similar to the rating system used for motion pictures, the plot scaffolds described in this chapter are rated "G."

Types of Beginning Writers

Beginning writers typically experience the following stages of writing development: emerging, developing, focusing, and experimenting (Georgia Department of Education, 2004b). Teachers need to be aware of students' stage of development so they may recognize and work effectively with students at different stages. In the first stage, the emerging writer needs work on topic development, organization, and detail because this writer has little awareness of audience or the writing task and makes errors in grammar or surface features that prevent the reader from understanding the writer's message.

Although the writer has a message, structure is needed in order to make the message known. Typically, the emerging writer's story wanders and has no purpose or ending. (The writer at the start of this chapter is a good example of an emerging writer.)

In the second stage, the developing writer is able to begin developing the topic, and his or her response to writing has the beginning of an organizational plan. This writer has a limited awareness of audience and uses simple words and sentence patterns. The developing writer uses short, choppy, repetitive sentences that have errors in surface features such as spacing, format, and grammar that hinder communication with the reader. For example, once the emerging writer at the beginning of this chapter develops an organizational plan for the ferret story, then he will work on correcting the repetition and the short, choppy sentences, which will lead him to the next stage of development where he can focus on organization and transition.

In the third stage, the focusing writer has a clear topic even though his or her story development is not complete. The organizational plan is loosely structured, but the writer has an awareness of the audience. The focusing writer uses a limited variety of vocabulary and sentence patterns, and errors in surface features interrupt the fluency of communication.

In the fourth stage, the experimenting writer, unlike the emerging, developing, or focusing writer, can write showing a clear topic; however, the development may be uneven because although there is a clear plan with beginning, middle, and end, the beginning and end may be awkward. The experimenting writer, who is aware of the audience, experiments with language and sentence patterns. Word combinations and word choice may be unique, and errors in surface features may interrupt fluency.

Beginning writers often have better success with focus and transition if they build on their own prior knowledge of a subject.

The Importance of Building on Prior Knowledge for Beginning Writers

Writers often write about what they know, and writing plots can be done based on a collaboration of life experiences. Students use movies such as *Star Wars*, other book plots, and their own life experiences to build stories, which is a form of building on prior knowledge. Just as in reading, students and teachers must bring prior knowledge to the writing process or play performance (Booth, 1985; Smith, 1978). Prior knowledge is essential to being a good reader; otherwise, what is being read will not make much sense (Smith, 1978). For example, if a student is reading about a Manx and does not know what it is, then telling the student that a Manx is a type of cat gives meaning to the text. In most cases, the student recognizes a cat, and the teacher's explanation that the Manx has a short, bobbed tail like a rabbit will provide a more recognizable image.

Because of their limited research skills, beginning writers sometimes work best when writing about something they know because their own prior knowledge may aid in topic development, organization of events, and detail. For example, when creating a scaffold about eating out (the idea behind the scaffold, "There's a Bug in My Beans")— something most children have done—students can draw on their own experiences regarding restaurants. Perhaps they have had an experience where the food did not taste good or perhaps they enjoyed being sung "Happy Birthday" while in a special restaurant. Students' actual experiences can be used to make the story believable. Teachers can explore students' prior knowledge by asking questions such as, In formal dining, what is the purpose behind the placement of silverware? How does one behave toward a waiter or waitress? What is tipping? How are food orders taken? In what order (organization) are courses presented? How are restaurants organized? Prior knowledge on the part of the writer helps provide answers to the above questions and set the stage for writing a narrative story about eating out at a restaurant. The inquiry approach can then be used to turn the dining-out experience into a possible plot with conflict (e.g., What if you found a bug in your food?).

The inquiry approach can be further elaborated upon by exploring different characters' viewpoints. What if the person finding the bug is an elderly person who doesn't see well? What if the person is a lawyer? What might be the "catch" or complication to the plot? In plot scaffolds, I purposely exclude children's characters because I want students to imagine what it would be like to be another character and think about how a story character might act and respond to others in a particular situation. This is also a way to explore students' prior knowledge and how it creates stereotypes. Are all lawyers in a hurry to sue? Are all elderly people slow? By becoming different characters and acting the parts, in essence it is like putting on different "masks"; students are less intimidated with writing about someone other than themselves. Sometimes students get attached to a particular part and may be disappointed if they cannot play that part in finished performance, but I tell them to remember, as the writer of a story, essentially you get to play all the parts because you dress the characters, write the dialogue, and organize the plot.

Further, plot scaffolds such as "There's a Bug in My Beans" have to be flexible and allow for the possibility of different numbers of students with a variety of reading levels. The characters in this first plot scaffold include waiters, cooks, an elderly couple, an insect, bug spray, a health inspector, and an artist (among others). All the characters were given strong personalities on which to build, and I left the last lines of this short plot blank to let my students determine the dark moment and resolution (Figure 4 shows these elements). Students first use prior knowledge to complete the scaffolds and help with characterization but later may explore more "what if" situations such as, What if the restaurant owner could not speak English? What if a can of bug spray could speak? or What might the story be like if the setting and characters changed?

Making Predictions

In addition, plot scaffolds that provide students with dramatic situations in which they must decide the outcome teaches prediction skills because the writer or reader must decide what will happen next (Wright, 1985). Students, as story writers, must determine how characters will react, what they will say, and how the story will end. In this context, such scaffolds, in their dramatic treatment, provide for reflection and abstract growth, which are needed to improve critical thinking (Verriour, 1985). Students must use higher-level thinking skills, such as inference, in order to complete the plot scaffolds.

Figure 4
Page From "There's a Bug in My Beans"

Old Lady: Albert dear, do you have your glasses? I forgot mine. I can't see too well, but it looks like one of my string beans is taking a walk off the plate.

Old Man: Yes, Martha dear, your beans are most surely taking a little stroll. You would think they would be dead after being cooked.

Bug: Buzzzzz....hummmmm, goooood beans....lovvvve hum.

Old Lady: Glory be! Albert dear, my beans aren't walking. There's an ugly, slimy bug in my beans! Do something! Oh my goodness. I think I'm going to faint.

Old Man: Waiter! Waiter!

Waiter: You rang?

Old Man: My wife just found an awful, dirty bug strolling away with her beans.

Waiter: (What would you say? Write your own line.)

_____

_____

Old Man: (What would you say? Write your own line.)

_____

_____

Old Lady: (What would you say? Write your own line.)

_____

_____

Creating Voice

Using the open-ended plot scaffold as a frame to build on, we complete the story line as students read and reread the lines. The students complete the lines that are intentionally left blank, and we continually revise the lines so the plot makes sense. During their rewrites, students listen carefully to one another, often re-creating lines to fit the story. For example, one student, interested in the U.S. Confederacy, spoke with a southern accent and learned to write and speak using this dialect. He enjoyed writing lines because he was able to create his own character based on his prior knowledge of U.S. history and his ability to mimic an accent, which made him truly involved in the lesson because his interests were creatively integrated. Writing about what he knew helped this student to organize and develop his story plot. Students bring prior knowledge to literacy in order to make it relevant. Because drama occurs in the first person, present tense, students must know who their characters are and what they did earlier. They learn to create a character from the clues provided within the scaffold (Wright, 1985). Students learn to use prior knowledge, which is essential to being an effective reader (Smith, 1978). Further, by writing about what they know and what interests them, students find authentic reasons to read and write because the characters they create have "voice." Voice means stance. Characters in a story should have both extrinsic and intrinsic reason for their dialogue and actions. Dramatizing scaffolds allows for what Heathcote (Heathcote & Herbert, 1985) refers to as the "mantle of the expert." Heathcote believes that letting students have power over story plot lets them acquire the mantle of the expert, which is important to becoming an active learner. In writing a narrative story, having voice is synonymous with becoming the expert; the story, to have style, portrays the writer's feelings, thoughts, and often personal opinions and beliefs. "Constructivist theory posits that human beings do not simply soak up another person's meanings. Rather they actively create their own" (Wagner, 1998, p. 16). Eastman (1970) believes that writers do not begin with a complete message within themselves but that writing is a discovery of outlook, a way of wrapping language around an experience in order to convey it to an audience. Through repeated practice, students learn about story and dialogue and how it is sequenced to make sense. They use their imaginations and become different characters, exploring voices and actions unlike their own. By exploring different characters with different feelings, students begin to learn how to use empathy as a writing skill. There are several studies that show that drama allows for the fostering of empathy (Buege, 1993; Gourney et al., 1985; Schonmann, 1996). While performing a scaffold, students must convey to an audience meaning through voice inflection and emotion. Emotional exploration gives more depth to the characters that students will create, making the characters more memorable. (Emotionless characters are pasteboard and easily forgotten.) In the search for meaning, building plot scaffolds is a collaborative experience, while silent reading is a private one (Bolton, 1985; Booth, 1985). Unlike silent reading, performing a scaffold as a literacy activity is a group effort, and each member of the group must support one another to make a finished product. Therefore, as Wagner argues, "As participants experience the perspectives of various roles, they not only see the world from other viewpoints and develop empathy, but they also enlarge their understandings" (p. 9). Beginning writers, who often need more concrete examples, benefit by acting out the characters in a story to give them feeling. To keep readers' attention, good writers create characters that their readers react to on an emotional level (Knight et al., 2004).

Creating Images

To create props or scenery for the written images in their stories, students draw on their knowledge of print and art. In a very collaborative manner, students' repeated practice or "rehearsal" develops skills such as patience and reflection needed for rewriting. Students frequently will get up and walk around acting like their characters, making them come to life. Often good writers will imaginatively "have lunch with" the characters in their stories, talking about what might happen next, allowing their characters to lead the plot (Scarborough et al., 2003). Writing and reading a story go far beyond the simple decoding of print. Instead of a bestseller becoming a movie, when using plot scaffolds, think of a play becoming a book so you remember to include images of important things in the story the reader must be able to "see" in order to understand what is happening in the plot. I have used these plot scaffolds with many classes, and each time they are completed, different stories emerge because students bring their own experiences, interests, and interpretations to the basic story line.

PLOT SCAFFOLD FOR "THERE'S A BUG IN MY BEANS"

As a summer school student teacher, I was given the task of finding a play for my first graders to perform, but I found most of the plays in print were too long and difficult, and irrelevant to my students' experiences. I decided to write my own play but have my students complete it. As a result, "There's a Bug in My Beans" came about as collaboration with my first-grade students and was based on my own experience while student teaching and working part time at a Mexican restaurant. Revolving around finding an insect in one's food while dining out, I thought this plot might be a relatively easy topic my first-grade students would find amusing because they, like many children, could relate to issues pertaining to food, such as taste, texture, and so forth.

LEARNING OBJECTIVES

Because of the concrete, silly humor in "There's a Bug in My Beans" (see Appendix B), typically first- through third-grade students or emerging writers enjoy the plot. Emerging writers need to focus on topic development, organization, and detail; they often have a message to tell but need a structure to make it known. In addition, teachers can choose to use the objectives for the developing or focusing writer (see Appendix A) if they correspond with their students' abilities. Table 1 shows the learning objectives for this lesson.

PROCEDURE

STEP 1

Determining Prior Knowledge

Using the inquiry approach previously mentioned, discuss with students the following three questions pertaining to plot:

- What if?
- What is the catch?
- What then?

Apply these questions to the plot scaffold:

- What if you found a bug in your food while eating at a restaurant?
- What could be the catch to finding the bug?
- What might you do then?

Hand out copies of the plot scaffold to students and read it aloud with them. Do not read aloud the stage directions or plot directions. Read the plot scaffold as if it were

Table 1
Learning Objectives for Emerging Writers

Listening/Speaking
- Adapts or changes oral language to fit the situation by following the rules of conversation with peers and adults.
- Listens to a variety of literary forms, including plays, stories, songs, movies, videos, and so forth.
- Follows two- and three-part oral directions.
- Recalls information presented orally.
- Interprets the meaning of a question in order to give an appropriate response.
- Communicates effectively when using descriptive language; relating experiences; and retelling stories read, heard, or viewed.

Writing
- Uses examples from literature to create individual and group stories.
- Uses correct spelling for frequently used sight vocabulary.
- Communicates ideas by using the writing process:
  Prewriting—Generates ideas.
  Drafting—Focuses on topic, uses prewriting ideas to complete first draft.
  Revising—Expands use of descriptive words.
  Editing—Begins each sentence and proper noun with capital letter, uses correct spelling, appropriate punctuation, and complete sentences.
  Publishing—Shares writing with others.

Reading
- Increases vocabulary to reflect a growing range of interests and knowledge.
- Uses word order and sentence structure to read.
- Increases sight vocabulary (instant recognition).
- Reads with fluency and expression.
- Recognizes EXPLICIT main ideas, details, sequence of events, and cause–effect relationships in fiction.
- Recognizes IMPLICIT main ideas, details, sequence of events, and cause–effect relationships in fiction.
- Identifies main characters.
- Identifies characters' actions, motives, emotions, traits, and feelings.
- Draws conclusions and makes predictions and comparisons.
- Demonstrates comprehension when reading a variety of literary forms including drama.

Adapted from the Georgia English/Language Arts Performance Standards (2004a).

a play script. Assign students parts for the first reading, and tell them that the last line is blank and will be supplied by them. Allow students ample time to think about and reflect on this. Students may help one another and suggest ideas. They will need to think about what a waiter, an old man, or an artist might say. Next, allow students to switch parts and read the plot again. This should take about 20 minutes.

STEP 2

Acting Out the Plot Scaffold

Allow students to get up and act out the script. Encourage them to change their voices, become the characters, and think about the setting and props. Talk about what kind of restaurant this might be and restaurant etiquette. Discuss what the characters might look like and wear. Students enjoy switching parts (I have found that many times boys do a great job playing the part of a woman). At this point, teachers or students can begin filling in the plot scaffold with lines and images provided by students. If students are not able to write (this might include kindergarten or first-grade students who are just learning letter formation), work with them as a group and write the lines on the board for students to copy onto their plot scaffolds. If necessary, teachers may also write dictated sentences onto scaffolds. Kindergarten teachers may wish to have their students only perform the scaffolds because writing them may not be developmentally appropriate for this age group, which typically does most language arts activities orally.

STEP 3

Completing the Plot Scaffold

Have students simply read the plot scaffold two more times to ensure that students who have reading difficulties have had enough repetition for sight word recognition and meaning, and then have students write in their own lines and finish the script. As previously mentioned, do not emphasize grammar or spelling at this time because it is more important for students to get their ideas down on paper. (However, students should be able to read them back to you. If not, then you need to write their dictated lines. Because emerging writers often make errors in grammar or surface structure that can prevent the reader from understanding the message, dictated stories are a good strategy.) Students should complete this task individually and write their own lines for each character on the plot scaffold, which becomes the student's rough draft. This step may be continued as a homework assignment in order to give students more time to reflect on what they want to say. Students also may begin to create images on the lines provided on the plot scaffold. I generally allow two days for writing the rough draft.

STEP 4

Adding Effective Dialogue

Next, discuss with students how to write the dialogue for the story by adding costumes and movement to the characters. (This idea of simple costumes can be added to any scaffold to help students actually see their characters in the physical sense.) For example, teachers can use the Fred and Mary strategy in chapter 1 (see page 18) to create effective dialogue. Remind students that because the characters in written text cannot be seen, this step is necessary to writing a clear, descriptive story. Review the rules of punctuation for dialogue as well. Students can practice placing quotation marks around the dialogue on the hard copies of the plot scaffolds, which reminds them to put the same marks around dialogue when they write their stories. Students may change the original scaffold dialogue if they wish. Remind students that because they are now the "narrator" of the story and telling the story (in third person), they do not need to say something like, "The narrator said, 'We are inside a restaurant.'" Simply say, "We are

---

Figure 5
Sample for Creating Effective Dialogue

We are inside an elegant restaurant, and six tables are set for dinner. It is a French restaurant with food as tasty as McDonalds. It is evening, and there are several people in the Cuccamonga Restaurant eating big dinners, including an unwanted visitor, a bug. An old man and his wife, who are very hungry, are eating their dinner when they hear a weird sound.

"Buzz....Buzz....Buzzzzzzzz....yum yum...Beans," hummed a huge, green bug as he flew into the plate.

"Albert dear, do you hear something odd?" asked the old lady in the flower print dress.

"No, Martha dear, just a buzzing noise in my ear. There must be something wrong with my hearing aid," replied her husband as he tapped his hearing aid on the marble table, making a sharp metal rapping. "Stupid Machine! I need a new computerized hearing aid."

---

inside a restaurant." Figure 5 shows the changes one student made to the plot scaffold to add effective dialogue. For emerging writers, this activity may be collaborative with the teacher writing the plot scaffold on the board or large paper as students offer suggestions and dialogue.

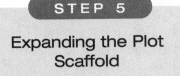

STEP 5

Expanding the Plot Scaffold

Next, have students share their plot scaffolds (which have become like rough drafts) with one another and peer edit or make suggestions for changes. The teacher acts as a second peer editor and checks all plot scaffolds to make sure they have been filled in and the lines make sense. Have students identify the elements of plot: Is there a hook to the story? Does it grab the reader's attention? Does the story have backfill that adds to the plot? Does the story have a recognizable, interesting problem? The plot scaffolds in this book all include problems, but students should have a clear understanding of the main problem in order to add complications, action–reaction, and a dark moment. For example, the dark moment of "There's a Bug in My Beans" occurs just before Bug Spray appears. Bug Spray, or any of the other characters in the story, can provide the resolution, but a resolution to the problem needs to be evident.

Finished group stories may be printed on large chart paper, or they may be photocopied so students can have their own books to illustrate and read, thus creating student-generated books. If time is an issue with completing the final draft, teachers can break it into small segments and have students copy one to two pages of the rough draft script each day. Another option is to have students finalize two or three pages and then summarize the remainder of the play in their own words and provide an ending for the story. This allows students to work at their own paces but complete the story within a specific time frame.

GRAMMAR TO IMPROVE STYLE (NOUNS AND VERBS)

Teachers can choose to give students a word bank before having them write lines or images. This word bank should be student generated and include nouns and verbs that relate to restaurants, cooking, food, and any other topic that students think pertains to the plot scaffold. In addition, teachers can create a list of adjectives and adverbs next to this list of nouns and verbs so students have some good descriptive words. For developing or emerging writers, teachers also can choose to introduce simile and metaphor by providing students with examples of both. For example, the Bug Spray character in this plot scaffold is an example of personification, or making an inanimate object come to life. Teachers can use lines from the plot scaffold to illustrate examples such as the following simile based on one student's lines:

We are inside a restaurant and three or four tables are set for dinner. <u>It was a French restaurant with food as wonderful as going to eat at McDonalds.</u>

FURTHER ELABORATION (OPTIONAL)

Act out the play.

EVALUATION

Using the evaluation form in Table 2 (see also Appendix A), the Beginning Writer Rubric, I first have students rate themselves, and then I fill in whether or not I agree with their evaluation. Including the performance, the total possible score for this project is 100 points. If the performance is not done, simply use the 85-point rubric and divide all point scores by 85 to get a percent score. For example, a point score of 66 would receive 77%. However, the most important result should not be this score but how students show progress in individual writing scores during the entire year. Reading, listening, and speaking skills pertain to writing skills because all interact and enmesh with this literacy activity.

Teachers may choose to have students become involved in the assessment process by creating their own checklists. See Appendix A for instructions.

PLOT SCAFFOLD FOR "THE RENT"

This plot scaffold, "The Rent" (see Appendix B), was developed when I taught third grade in an inner-city Catholic school. At the time, an undercurrent of worry expressed by several third graders in my class was about paying the bills and what happens when this does not occur. Because paying bills is a universal, real-life issue, I decided to build on students' prior knowledge and incorporate this issue in the format of a melodrama. Thus, "The Rent" poses questions about financial responsibility in the style of a Victorian melodrama, complete with sign holders for audience participation. Because it is a melodrama, there is a hero, heroine, and villain, with many plot twists based on characters' choices.

Table 2
Beginning Writer Rubric

Literacy Skills	Standards	Student Evaluation	Teacher Evaluation	Comments
Listening/Speaking	Spoke clearly	1 2 3 4 5	1 2 3 4 5	
	Followed directions	1 2 3 4 5	1 2 3 4 5	
	Remembered information	1 2 3 4 5	1 2 3 4 5	
Reading	Read fluently	1 2 3 4 5	1 2 3 4 5	
	Made predictions by filling in the scaffold	1 2 3 4 5	1 2 3 4 5	
	Read with expression	1 2 3 4 5	1 2 3 4 5	
	Understood the story	1 2 3 4 5	1 2 3 4 5	
	Increased vocabulary	1 2 3 4 5	1 2 3 4 5	
Writing	Filled in the scaffold (prewriting)	1 2 3 4 5	1 2 3 4 5	
	Wrote complete rough draft	1 2 3 4 5	1 2 3 4 5	
	Wrote finished product	1 2 3 4 5	1 2 3 4 5	
	Used descriptive images	1 2 3 4 5	1 2 3 4 5	
	Wrote dialogue correctly	1 2 3 4 5	1 2 3 4 5	
	Grammar:			
	Used complete sentences	1 2 3 4 5	1 2 3 4 5	
	Used appropriate punctuation	1 2 3 4 5	1 2 3 4 5	
	Corrected spelling	1 2 3 4 5	1 2 3 4 5	
	Shared ideas with others	1 2 3 4 5	1 2 3 4 5	

Listening/Speaking _____ / 15 points

Reading _____ / 25 points

Writing _____ / 45 points

Total score _____ / 85 points

77–85 = 90%

68–76 = 80%

60–67 = 70%

51–66 = 60%

Literacy Skill	Standard	Student Evaluation	Teacher Evaluation	Comments
Performance	Body movement	1 2 3 4 5	1 2 3 4 5	
	Artwork	1 2 3 4 5	1 2 3 4 5	
	Voice	1 2 3 4 5	1 2 3 4 5	

Performance _____ / 15 points

LEARNING OBJECTIVES

This plot scaffold is appropriate for developing or focusing writers (see Appendix A) because it has a clear, strong organizational plan and topic.

PROCEDURE

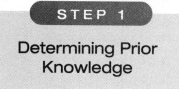

STEP 1

Determining Prior Knowledge

Discuss with students the following plot questions:

- What if you had to pay rent money?
- What if the catch was one of the people in your house had spent the rent money?
- What would happen to you then?

Hand out the plot scaffold to students. Explain to them how Victorian theater was interactive and called for audience participation. For example, if the hero entered, someone in the audience would hold up a sign with the word *Hooray* on it, and the audience would respond by saying the word and cheering. In my classroom, we created signs with words such as *Boo*, *Hiss*, *Ah*, and *Hooray* to show to the audience so they would respond in that manner when characters entered onstage. Later, students can use these signs to help them create images or to engage reader response or elicit empathy. For example, if the villain were coming onstage the audience might say, "Hiss!" If the villain was being introduced in the story, the writer might write the following:

> Slinking into the room, the dastardly villain, who smelled like an unwashed dirty-dog blanket, approached the two helpless girls.

Assign parts to the students for the first reading, with students not having parts acting as the audience and participating by making the sounds for *Hiss*, *Boo*, and so forth. Everyone participates, no matter how large or small the task. Just as in a real reading task, the engaged reader responds cognitively and emotionally to print. In a Victorian melodrama, the audience watches to respond to the playwright's signs just as the reader watches for signs in the text. This example can be used to teach sociocognitive literacy skills because literacy is a combination of writer, text, and reader (Ruddell & Unrau, 1994). Literacy is a very interactive process of meaning making.

Remind students that the last lines of the plot are left blank for them to supply an appropriate response based on their character. There are also blank spaces for images or setting, which will be added later. Allow students time to reflect on the lines they would like to add, and for the first reading, allow them to work with others in the class to help create responses. This step should take 20 to 25 minutes.

STEP 2

Acting Out the Plot Scaffold

Choose parts for a second reading and change students' parts so they can explore different character interpretations. Allow students to get up and act out their characters. Encourage students to change their voices, become the characters, and think about appropriate props and setting. Talk about the meaning of the audience participation signs and how this can be turned into images that set the tone for the story. For example, when the hero enters, a sign calls for audience cheering. Students can use the sign to create an image such as the following:

Narrator/writer: The hero enters. <u>Like a white knight, he stood ready to help poor Mayflower and Annabelle.</u>

The physical cheering sign has been used to create an image that might cause the reader to cheer "mentally." Thus, a sign for the audience becomes a mental image for the mind's eye to understand, and a concrete idea has become print based.

Completing the Plot Scaffold

Once students write their lines and images in the lines provided, the plot scaffold becomes a working first draft of a story. For beginning writers, it takes about two days for this process, and for intermediate writers, it takes about one hour or one class period. Remember that students are the narrators of the story, so it can be written in first person.

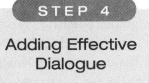

Adding Effective Dialogue

Students turn the plot scaffold into narrative format, focusing on dialogue spacing and punctuation. To help with this process, students can write small descriptions and movements (stage directions) next to the characters on the script to help them make the transition to dialogue in story text. Placing the quotation marks in the correct place for dialogue is also helpful so students can practice placing them correctly.

Expanding the Plot Scaffold

After adding dialogue and images on the scaffold, teachers need to check it for completeness and consistency of plot. Students can still act out the plot scaffold, taking turns reading the different character lines they have chosen as well as the images. If students are having trouble describing the characters, I sometimes supply simple props and costumes, such as hats, so students have something to actually see. It is a strategy that helps students realize that characters in stories need descriptions like costumes or the reader cannot visualize them. Students then write a first draft, making the transition to narrative-style text.

When they finish, they can exchange first drafts to receive input from peers. I often have my students write comments on sticky notes about the papers they are reading. The sticky notes are placed on the paper being read so when the writer gets the draft back, he or she can decide which notes or comments are useful. In the case of "The Rent," I ask students to make sure the papers they are reading have a hook and to check for necessary backfill. For example, have Mayflower and Annabelle always fought over the chores? Why does the grandfather like to read the paper? Check for complication, action–reaction, and an exciting dark moment (usually the train scene). The resolution should solve the rent problem. Killing off the main character is not an option. This may eliminate the problem, but it doesn't really solve it.

ESL

"The Rent" is useful especially for developing dialogue, both verbal and nonverbal, among ESL students, perhaps because the basic plot of "hero saves heroine" is common to many cultures. One strategy for using a plot scaffold is to allow an ESL student to speak in his or her native language. For example, while teaching gifted middle school language arts, one very limited English-speaking student was placed in my class because the school did not have an ESL program. Perhaps because I allowed her to speak her lines in her native language, she interacted well with the class while using "The Rent." In fact, she took the lead role of Mayflower, and the rest of the class made up lines to match hers. For example, when she said the line: "My hero, I'll marry you!" to the dog in her native language, the student playing Annabelle responded in a pleading voice, "You always get to marry the dog. I never get to marry the dog. You always get to speak Chinese. I never get to speak Chinese." Thus, the student was validated for her own voice and language while also becoming part of a group of English speakers. (She also later taught them some words in her native language.) And although her English speaking ability was very limited at the time, her ability to listen to and understand English was being developed as she attended to the play and watched for her cue to enter. Finally, because the repetitive nature of rehearsing for a performance allowed her to repeat her English lines, she could learn written and spoken words along with corresponding body movements, gestures, and inflections.

GRAMMAR TO IMPROVE STYLE (VERBS)

Similar to "There's a Bug in My Beans," this plot scaffold can be used to teach students to recognize nouns and verbs, but because of the dramatic use of the signs, this scaffold calls for more active, vivid verbs that may elicit a stronger emotional response from the reader. Verbs, more than adverbs or adjectives, make writing dynamic. Often, developing and focusing writers are comfortable with verb forms of "to be" and need to begin moving away from this dependence by using more active verbs to improve their simple word choices and sentence patterns. The following examples show how students can replace linking verbs with action verbs in order to express their ideas more clearly and forcefully.

> Mayflower feels scared whenever Mr. Snake comes in the room. (using linking verb)
> Mayflower screams as Mr. Snake chases her around the room. (using action verbs)

In addition, this plot scaffold can be used to emphasize the use of the active, present tense as a better writing technique so the action is more engaging for the reader. Although this might be regarded as a more advanced writing skill, I feel that good writing habits are easier to develop if started early. The following example illustrates the effectiveness of this type of change:

> Mr. Snake boldly confronted Mayflower and her family, stepped back, and asked her to marry him instead of paying the rent.

> Mr. Snake boldly confronts Mayflower and her family, steps back, and asks her to marry him instead of paying the rent.

FURTHER ELABORATION (OPTIONAL)

Perhaps because of its basic, universal plot and audience participation, "The Rent" often blossoms into a full-scale, elaborate production. It begs to be acted out and makes for an easy play to perform for Parent–Teacher Association meetings or other school functions where classes are asked to perform. A play also draws parental support because all students are needed for the show to be successful. In terms of practical classroom considerations, "The Rent" has doubles of all main character parts in case a student is unable to make it to a performance: There are two villains, the villain and Peabody; three possible heroes, the Hero, sheriff, and Spot; and two heroines, Mayflower and Annabelle. In addition, multiple sign holders can add voice and movement to their parts, and students enjoy playing the train as well. In some productions, the dog has been changed to a horse, depending on students' animal preferences. If a student is absent, his or her part can be ad-libbed, a strategy that teaches students to think quickly and adapt to new situations (rather like the real-life skill of managing a job interview).

"The Rent" also lends itself to a Victorian theme dinner, which I have developed as a kind of literacy celebration. In addition, I often use the theme dinner as part of a bigger theme unit on Victorian England. Theme units are designed to cover the art, literature, music, dance, dress, and food of a particular time period, which helps account for multiple sign systems and multiple intelligences. The Victorian theme unit culminates in a large dinner or banquet that can be held at school, a community center, or, more daring, in a teacher's home (I still remember having 70 "Romans" dining on the white carpet in my living room). This is a great way to break the barrier between teacher and parents. Parents, students, and interested parties can come costumed in the time period being studied or as book characters from literature. During one Victorian theme dinner, students came dressed as characters from *Alice in Wonderland* (Carroll, 1865/2002) and *The Adventures of Sherlock Holmes* (Conan Doyle, 2003). Students researched appropriate recipes and served authentic foods at the banquet. They also brought artwork, which included dried flower arrangements and student silhouettes. We played games, such as forfeits and blind man's bluff, which were mentioned in *A Christmas Carol* (Dickens, 1843/1986). (Many of the ideas for this event came from my own "prior knowledge" growing up in San Francisco, California, USA, and attending the yearly "Dickens' Faire.") The theme dinner ended with a version of "The Rent" followed by dancing simple yet vigorous reels much like those mentioned in the scene of Fezziwig's warehouse from *A Christmas Carol*. Students learn that it is just as exciting to dramatize print as it is to turn drama into print.

EVALUATION

The Beginning Writer Rubric and the Intermediate Writer Rubric can be used with this scaffold (see Appendix A); however, note that the Intermediate Writer Rubric emphasizes character motivation and the recognition of multiple word usage that is usually evident in satire.

PLOT SCAFFOLD FOR "EMERGENCY"

"Emergency" (see Appendix B) is a satire about problems in the U.S. healthcare system and, in particular, with the paperwork and bureaucracy associated with hospitals. Satire is a form of criticism of certain practices of people and society using ridicule and contempt. A satirist uses wit to target the weak points of specific practices, often provoking laughter from an audience. Irony and exaggeration may be used also. This scaffold is also a humorous look at soap operas, which are complicated story plots with twists and constant action–reaction. Soap opera writers in particular must write good hooks to keep their viewers coming back each day. "Emergency" deals specifically with the use of hook and action–reaction. Both beginning and intermediate writers enjoy this scaffold: Beginning writers enjoy the campy slapstick humor, and intermediate writers enjoy the satire and plot twists involving major characters.

LEARNING OBJECTIVES

This scaffold is appropriate for developing, focusing, experimenting, and engaging writers. In addition, for extending writers, teachers should focus on the use of satire, and how—unlike simple slapstick humor—it relies on the schema of one's audience or reader. That is, humor only "translates" if both the reader and the writer share the same cultural background or knowledge of the events, which is why jokes often fall flat or do not translate well into other languages or cultures.

PROCEDURE

STEP 1

Determining Prior Knowledge

Discuss with students the following plot questions:

- What if you needed to go to the emergency room?
- What if you had to wait a long time in the waiting room but didn't feel well?
- What if the catch was you did not have medical insurance?
- What if the catch was your mother is in a hurry and the doctors are slow?
- What happens to you then if they needed to operate?
- What if the doctor in charge had no self-confidence?

Note how each question naturally leads to another question, which is a way to plan out plot twists or action–reaction.

Hold a class discussion about hospitals in order to determine students' level of prior knowledge. How many students in the class have been in a hospital, waiting room, or walk-in clinic? What was it like? How much did it cost? What do hospitals smell like? Hand out copies of the scaffold to students, have them choose parts and read them aloud. Students may change parts for a second reading. Talk about how the plot twists when one emergency leads to another. How is it similar to the soap operas on television? How are hooks used? Do books with many sequels, such as the Harry Potter series by J.K. Rowling, have hooks and twists to their plots? Why do writers use hooks and action–reaction? What makes readers want to return and keep reading the story? All of the discussion topics can be brainstormed as students think of ideas for new twists to the plot.

STEP 2

Acting Out the Plot Scaffold

Have students take turns playing different parts and acting out characters. Then, have students think about what kinds of scenery, props, or costumes might be appropriate.

STEP 3

Completing the Plot Scaffold

Have students complete the plot scaffold by adding images and dialogue to the story. Students may alter the original scaffold to incorporate new material if necessary. For example, the Patient does not have to have a sore toe; it can be another problem. (Because elementary school students usually delight in taking their shoes off in class, this part, although silly, generally remains in the plot scaffold. Amusing socks, painted toenails, and strange shoes all add to the images students create.) Students can create new illnesses for the Patient as long as the symptoms remain consistent throughout the story. Plot twists can be silly, but they need to make sense and be consistent. I also instruct focusing and experimenting writers to tell their readers more than once about important details in a story. Due to short-term memory parameters, readers may "lose" the image if it is not repeated.

STEP 4

Adding Effective Dialogue

Students turn the plot scaffold into narrative format, focusing on dialogue, spacing, and punctuation. To help with this process, students can write brief descriptions and movements (stage directions) next to the characters on the script to help them make the transition to dialogue in story text. Putting words that pertain to dialogue like *said*, *replied*, *whispered*, or *groaned* on the plot scaffold next to the characters helps students think about how characters sound when they talk. How a character talks can be a reflection of his or her personality or the plot situation. Placing quotation marks in the correct place for dialogue on the scaffold is also helpful so students can practice placing them correctly, and it makes for an easier transition to their next or first draft of narrative text.

Expanding the Plot Scaffold

Check students' completed plot scaffolds, and have students exchange them for peer review. After peer review, students should make revisions directly on the plot scaffold and then write a rough draft, adding proper spacing, dialogue, images, and punctuation. Teachers check for the seven elements of plot (see pages 13–14), and pay particular attention to the resolution. Because focusing writers need to work on completing plot development, or solving the plot's dilemma, they should avoid using resolutions in which they do not solve the problem. For example, students should not kill off the main character to solve the problem. Inexperienced writers often choose this easy way out to finish a plot when they have "written themselves into a corner." Further, I do not accept *deus ex machina* endings (i.e., God stepping in to fix the ending) or endings such as "It was all a dream" or "Tune in next week." Likewise, "Tune in next week" is not a satisfactory cliffhanger unless the writer actually plans on writing and presenting the next chapter to readers the next week.

When good writers create story worlds, they need to create consistent rules for these worlds in order to keep the "suspension of disbelief"—when a reader or viewer accepts the story world and its rules in order to make the story more believable. For example, readers or viewers accept that Superman has superhuman strength but that he is susceptible to Kryptonite. If Kryptonite suddenly were no longer fatal to Superman, readers might lose belief in him. Author Stephen King makes his readers comfortable with his small town, everyday settings and then effectively adds unexpected plot twists, something out of the ordinary, such as dead pets coming to life in *Pet Sematary* (King, 1983). However, King makes his plots believable and consistent by enforcing certain rules—for example, the pets are bound by the plot rule of having to be buried in a certain cemetery. Plot twists need to twist the story—not break it. The following examples of plot twists were created by students for "Emergency":

Doctor Ron is really trying to take over the hospital.

Nurse Able has always wanted to be a karaoke singer and is trying to raise money for her own karaoke bar.

Doctor Ben gets amnesia and must be helped by the patient's mother, his long lost sister.

Using the man-in-the-tree analogy (see pages 12–13), students also can think of all the things that could go wrong with the patient, which is a way of "throwing rocks at the man in the tree." This adds complication as well as action–reaction to the plot.

Holding conferences is an informal assessment that can be used to check for effective dialogue and plot. During a conference, teachers can check the finished rough draft by having the student read aloud his or her draft. Students also can read aloud the draft to the class while each classmate writes a suggestion or comment regarding the story on a note, which is given to the writer after the story has been read. I recommend that writers use at least two of the suggestions, adding that the best changes to incorporate are those that have been noted by more than one person, which generally means the writer has missed something. For beginning writers, this activity is best done orally and in a small group. If time is a factor, intermediate writers can do this in groups of four to five, because telling all the stories to the class will take a few class periods. However, it has been my experience that having four or five students read aloud each day can be done in a 20-minute time span. This time frame keeps most students focused.

Then, students should rewrite their finished drafts. At this time, review the importance of handwriting. Just as a good oral storyteller must use clear enunciation and body language, students must write stories that are easy to decode and read. Students find it interesting that the post office hires numerous people simply to read hand-addressed envelopes and that millions of letters are lost each year due to illegibility. In addition, because most standardized writing tests require handwritten responses, if the evaluator cannot read what is written, the writer's score will suffer.

GRAMMAR TO IMPROVE STYLE
(PARTICIPLE AND APPOSITIVE PHRASES)

For experimenting writers, I use the images in stories to teach students about phrases, such as participle and appositive phrases. Images that include the use of participle phrases to describe them typically are stronger, more focused images. The use of appositive phrases helps writers add elaboration to their work: Experimenting writers have shown they understand plot organization but need more varied language and sentence patterns. Focusing writers may also benefit from learning to add phrases at the beginning of sentences because these students need to expand their sentence patterns. I find that if students use a specific type of phrase in a story, they begin to see that use as a good writing technique. Perhaps on a more practical note, because intermediate students often are required to recognize types of phrases on standardized tests, learning how to add them to stories helps them to recognize phrases later during formal, standardized assessments. The following examples illustrate how appositive phrases can be used to include more detail:

> Endlessly tossing in her sleep, the helpless teenager, Nora, is as terrified as a fly being chased by a fly swatter.
>
> Doctor Ron's devoted nurse, Nurse Able, gazed at him with adoring eyes.

FURTHER ELABORATION (OPTIONAL)

Once the story is written, it may be returned to a play format for performance. For beginning writers, "Emergency" can be a way to explore how hospitals work. (Students often find that putting on hospital gloves is not as easy as it looks.) For intermediate writers, "Emergency" can be developed into an elaborate soap opera, or it can be used to begin a unit on healthcare.

One of my favorite productions included a third grader playing the part of Doctor Ben; he wore a large pair of hospital scrubs that his father had worn in the delivery room at the time of his birth. Performing plot scaffolds is a way to involve parents in helping to find costumes and props, helping with filming, and even participating as the audience. In addition, another production of this scaffold resulted in an hour-and-a-half musical called "The Old and the Waiting." We were able to incorporate multiple sign systems as students worked on transferring the metaphors or meanings in the story from print to music. Students even decided that the elevator needed mood music (the hospital set got very elaborate). In the elevator, a live band played such favorites as "We Hate Ron" or "Bedpan Blues" depending on the user's moods. The audience was served gelatin snacks in the shape of leeches during intermission. (Because the class had just finished a unit on the Middle Ages, prior knowledge regarding leeches entered the plot.)

EVALUATION

Use the Beginning Writer Rubric or Intermediate Writer Rubric, depending on the stage of writers in the classroom (see Appendix A).

PLOT SCAFFOLD FOR "SHOOT OUT AT THE BOTTOMS UP SALOON"

Set in the American West or "Old West," this scaffold (see Appendix B) addresses the problem of name-calling and fighting. The hero in "Shoot Out at the Bottoms Up Saloon," Good Guy, cannot tolerate name-calling. Many small children can relate to the harm caused by this type of bullying, so Good Guy's flaw has relevance to them and makes for a good evaluative discussion. Is Good Guy's flaw really a character flaw or is it caused by the circumstances in the story? Can heroes learn to control flaws such as short tempers and maybe even use them to their advantage? Do heroes become more heroic when they face their limitations, either mental or physical, and exceed them? A flaw can be the result of not adjusting to a physical limitation, such as Achilles' heel or Superman's intolerance of Kryptonite. In some retellings, the hero Beowulf has poor vision, but he makes the most of this physical flaw by actually "seeing" where other people are only "looking." Thus, overcoming a physical flaw can become a strength. Odysseus has the mental flaw of hubris (i.e., too much pride), and only by acknowledging that he is human, not above the gods, does he finally make it home.

LEARNING OBJECTIVES

This scaffold is appropriate for focusing and experimenting writers because the emphasis in this unit is on developing extrinsic and intrinsic character traits.

PROCEDURE

STEP 1

Determining Prior Knowledge

Discuss the following plot questions:

- What if someone tried to pick a fight with you?
- What if the catch is that person is very popular?
- What do you do when the person insults you?

Hand out copies of the plot scaffold to students. First, ask what they know about the Old or Wild West. Where was the Old West, and what was this time period? What were the people like? Were they all gunfighters? What made the Old West "wild"? Next, read aloud the scaffold and assign parts to students. Students who do not have lines for the first reading may offer suggestions for characters' last lines. Read the scaffold again, and allow other students the opportunity to play a part and add their voice. Then, discuss what the setting might look like. This should take about 30 minutes.

Acting Out the Plot Scaffold

Read the scaffold again, and allow students to get up and act out their characters. Discuss what kind of props might be needed in the story. What would the characters wear? As previously mentioned, sometimes I bring in hats or simple costumes for students to wear while acting out their characters so they can see what kind of images can be used to describe these characters before they write about them.

Completing the Plot Scaffold

Next, have students complete their scaffolds by adding dialogue and images. Students should try to include images that allow the reader to hear, see, and smell the Old West. In addition, students should treat the setting like a character in the story (Scarborough et al., 2003), which will help give the background a vivid description and tone. In fact, the setting can motivate and influence other characters' decisions. For example, in one version of "Shoot Out at the Bottoms Up Saloon" students decided that because the bar only served milk and soft drinks, the fight scene should involve drinking straws. Characters in the play tore off the ends of the paper wrappers on the straws and fired them at each other by blowing on one end of the straw. Paper flew all over, making the bar "messy," so a character briefly mentioned in the story, Good Guy's Mother, became an active participant. She came in after the bar fight and made them all pick up the mess. All the characters groaned but obeyed "Mother" and tidied up the saloon.

STEP 4

Adding Effective Dialogue

Dialogue in this plot scaffold should be charged with emotion because the plot involves anger and hurt feelings. Students should avoid the use of nondescript words such as *said* and brainstorm a list of more dynamic verbs for the dialogue such as *exclaimed*, *muttered*, or *insinuated*. In addition, students should put the characters in appropriate attire for the era (no zippers or tennis shoes) and add movement to characters as they speak. Finally, there is an optional fight scene, and it should be written so readers can see and hear the action. The following example illustrates this point.

Now things were really going to get wild. Everyone had an attitude. They began to eye the drinking straws on the dusty tables. Sensing trouble, the bartender nervously picked up the glasses.

Bad Guy, his black hat pulled down over his face, growled at Good Guy, "You don't deserve a horse that eats fish heads, you should ride a cow."

"What! Well your girlfriend looks like a cow," yelled Good Guy as he shoved off Bad Guy's hat.

"Cow! Who said I am a cow!" screamed a ruffled Miss Glitter as she stomped, shaking the pink tassels on her red lizard cowgirl boots. The rest of the people in the bar stepped back as the plump Glitter's eyes blazed. She grabbed a handful of drink straws.

STEP 5

Expanding the Plot Scaffold

Have students exchange scaffolds for peer review and then hold brief conferences with students once their scaffolds are complete. Students should write their first drafts in narrative format using the completed scaffold as a guide. Note that the main character should have an intrinsic flaw that drives the plot. The seven elements of plot should be present (see pages 13–14), and students should focus on including backfill and complication regarding the character's flaw.

After writing their first drafts, students should engage in peer review for feedback. Teachers also need to check first drafts for grammar and style. This feedback can be given in small stages for younger students or beginning writers. It is easier to catch mistakes in the early stages of writing a rough draft, before they are repeated throughout the entire story. Most mistakes occur as students begin to write dialogue. They often forget to indent, use quotation marks, or give their characters movement or costumes so readers can see characters as they speak. The teacher should ensure that stories have a beginning, middle, and end and pay particular attention to closure. Teachers can divide the story into four days and check the beginning of the story the first day (Monday), the middle on the third day (Wednesday), and the ending on the fourth day (Thursday).

Emerging writers, with limited skills in actually writing down sentences, may work slowly or feel intimidated by the length of the story. In order to meet the needs of diverse learners such as these writers, I allow them to summarize the end of the story. For example, if a student is working on writing a first draft and only has progressed to the third page of a scaffold and time is an issue, the student can summarize the story in his or her own words and write this as the ending to his or her draft. This is an effective strategy in light of the time constraints that students experience during standardized writing tests. Students learn to summarize and finish a project within a set time frame.

GRAMMAR TO IMPROVE STYLE (METAPHOR AND SIMILE)

Discuss the use of metaphor and simile in writing images that will be used in the story. Grammar for style is not simply a matter of recognizing metaphors and similes as a formal feature of language; it is using these features to improve writing style. Students need to remember that the reader cannot see what is happening on stage, so the action needs to be explained. Telling (i.e., simple description) does not work as effectively as showing (i.e., explaining how something feels, smells, and so forth) because telling does not have as great an emotional appeal. Telling does not "hook" the reader as well as showing through images. Metaphors and similes make strong images.

> Looking like a dust-covered old goat, Good Guy's horse waited patiently by his side. (simile)

> Five men sat playing cards around a table that King Arthur might have used. The men were not knights, but the white feather, worn on each man's hat, recalled medieval heraldry. (metaphor)

Metaphor and simile can be taught to any level writer. Even kindergartners can compose sentences that contain images with the words *like* or *as*, or explain how some object reminds them of a specific smell, sight, sound, feeling, or touch. Learning to compose sentences that include metaphors and similes also touches on grammatical skills because the sentences must be complete thoughts. Often students forget to write a complete sentence with both a subject and verb when writing images, especially when they try to start the sentence with a phrase or clause.

FURTHER ELABORATION (OPTIONAL)

Students can use their "best" lines in a performance of this plot scaffold. In addition, students can use this same plot scaffold but situate it in different settings. For example, in one production students changed the setting to an underwater environment and then changed the characters to fish. They also changed the dialogue to make it fit with the undersea theme. (The production involved beach toys, towels, and water pistols.) Placing a story in another setting—in a sense, treating the setting like a character with a costume—also is plot-development strategy. What the setting "wears" can determine the action in a plot.

For practice with small-group collaboration, divide the class into groups of four or five and have them fill in the scaffolds. Learning to work within a small group is a valuable real-life skill. In small groups, students can again read aloud the scaffolds and add movement. Have group members act out different roles in front of the class. See how many different types of main characters and minor characters emerge from the plot scaffold. Do all students see the same thing happening in the plot? Discuss the idea of stereotype and how writers can avoid it. This plot works well for looking at stereotypes, especially those dealing with gender. One way to avoid stereotype is to create the main character with a different "flaw" or problem. If all the plot scaffolds are very similar the first time students complete them, have them try the strategy of changing the main character's flaw or problem to see how the plot changes from there.

One interesting story that developed from this plot scaffold involved changing the main character to a female. The team who created this plot made the female character, the ranch's owner, independent and capable. In the story, she has to take her cattle to market via a cattle drive, and a male character helps her. In stereotypical fashion, he wants to marry her. She replies with the question, "I don't know if I have to do this?"

However, the question seems to be a statement about following a norm that may not fit an individual's needs. She ends up marrying him, but there was an element of doubt voiced by the characters around her. Perhaps the team's (a number of gifted females) concerns about being caught between two worlds, career and family, were able to emerge as a result of this lesson. I have noted as students collaboratively build plots, reflections on societal beliefs and taboos begin to surface. Teachers can take advantage of these situations by leading class discussions that focus on the origins and need of such beliefs. The class then can discuss the advantages and disadvantages of these beliefs.

EVALUATION

Use the Beginning Writer Rubric or Intermediate Writer Rubric, depending on the stage of writers in the classroom (see Appendix A).

PLOT SCAFFOLD FOR "JUST SLEEPING"

"Just Sleeping" (see Appendix B) is a plot scaffold for a mystery; therefore, the emphasis in this lesson is on how to write important, relevant details or "clues" for readers to use to solve the mystery. Writing relevant clues aids students in paying attention to detail. Beginning writers often incorporate details into story that are irrelevant or do not help advance the plot.

LEARNING OBJECTIVES

Because of the attention to detail it requires, "Just Sleeping" can be used with developing, focusing, and especially experimenting writers who need to work on smoothing out plot development. Although "Just Sleeping" is primarily for beginning writers, it can be used with intermediate writers as an introduction to detective story writing.

PROCEDURE

STEP 1

Determining Prior Knowledge

Discuss the following plot questions:

- What if you were at a very expensive, high class party?
- What if the catch is someone is murdered at the party?
- What do you do then to find the murderer?

Hand out copies of the plot scaffold and assign parts for students to read aloud. After reading the play once, it becomes evident that no one really dies. The victim in the play is "just sleeping"; however, it is important to leave a trail of clues about what happened to the victim because all characters in the story must supply their own lines about their role during the supposed murder. The detective character can ask questions that determine which clues are important. Students should switch parts, read the plot scaffold a second time, and create new clues and questions for the detective to ask.

STEP 2

Acting Out the Plot Scaffold

After reading the plot scaffold aloud a few times, have students take turns playing roles and acting according to what is said in the story. Because the main characters have strong personalities, their character traits should dictate how they move and respond when questioned by the detective or one another. By incorporating emotion, students will add depth to the characters. Discuss the setting of the story and how the characters would be dressed. Is it a costume party? What time of year is it? Is the house old or in disrepair? All of these factors could possibly determine the motive behind a specific character's actions. Discuss the concept of motivation, both intrinsic and extrinsic. What makes a character act one way or another?

STEP 3

Completing the Plot Scaffold

Have students complete the plot scaffold with their own character lines, settings, and images. Teachers should check scaffolds to ensure that they are completed, but students should not exchange scaffolds with their peers at this time. Instead, have students begin to write their first drafts. Students can include "red herrings" or clues that look significant but, in fact, are not. They make interesting plot twists and keep the reader guessing.

STEP 4

Adding Effective Dialogue

Instruct students that emotion, evident in the dramatization of the plot scaffold, should transfer to the written page. In addition, dialogue should contain clues that help the reader solve the mystery, but students should avoid having the detective simply tell the solution to the mystery for its resolution. The detective can summarize the solution, but the writer should show—not just tell—the story.

Remember to have students make notes about dialogue directly on the scaffold. Noting words that pertain to dialogue like *wondered*, *yelled*, *implored*, or *whined* directly on the plot scaffold next to the characters helps students think about how characters sound when they talk. Students also can read aloud these suggestions or treat them like stage directions while acting out the plot scaffold. How a character talks can be a reflection of his or her personality or the plot situation. Placing quotation marks in the correct place for dialogue on the scaffold is also helpful so students can practice placing them correctly, and it makes for an easier transition to their next or first draft of narrative text.

STEP 5

Expanding the Plot Scaffold

After students have completed their first drafts, allow them to share their drafts with a peer except for the ending. Instead, the peer should attempt to solve the mystery by telling the writer which character "did it" or committed the crime. Then, students can decide if the trail of clues was too easy, too hard, or made sense. Were the red herrings too obvious? Did they help keep the reader guessing? Did the mystery have a strong hook? Can the reader recognize the climax of the story, or is it confused with action–reaction? Students should make any necessary changes to their first drafts to "smooth" out any problems. Finally, students write their final drafts.

Because classrooms include diverse learners with different ability levels, teachers may choose to have students write a final draft from a completed plot scaffold. Teachers need to monitor students' work constantly for quality though. All first drafts, whether actual plot scaffolds or first drafts made from scaffolds, should be corrected before they can be used to make final drafts of a story.

GRAMMAR TO IMPROVE STYLE (ADJECTIVES AND ADVERBS)

Because clues and details are so important to a mystery, students need to pay attention to their word choice. Students should work on creating images that are specific. It may be helpful to make a list of words that are vague such as *pretty, stuff, nice, beautiful, thing, sound*, and so forth. (This is a good opportunity for a minilesson on grammar terms such as adjective and adverb and how their degrees are used [e.g., positive, comparative, and superlative] and often change spelling.) Following is an example illustrating the importance of word choice.

> The butler's jacket had stuff on it. (vague)
>
> Humphrey's jacket, normally spotless, was covered in a light dusting of chocolate cookie crumbs. Detective Finder glanced over at the still body. Were those crumbs near the left shoulder? (more specific)

FURTHER ELABORATION (OPTIONAL)

Choose one mystery and turn it back into a play. Act out the play for another class and let them figure out the mystery just before it is solved. This is a good way to exercise higher level thinking skills such as prediction and deduction, as well as finding context clues for implicit and evaluative questions.

EVALUATION

Use the Beginning Writer Rubric (see Appendix A).

PLOT SCAFFOLD FOR "THE BOOK FINE"

"The Book Fine" (see Appendix B) is a good introduction to persuasive or thesis writing because students must, similar to lawyers in court, prove a case. A lawyer's opening statement to the jury is similar to a thesis introductory paragraph because a brief introduction, with some hint at further evidence to come, is stated. While sitting on a real jury, I was impressed by the "hook" used in the prosecuting attorney's ominous first sentence, "Nothing good happens after midnight." I remember thinking that it was a wonderful first line to an exciting story—I wanted to know more.

Just as a lawyer presents the evidence during a trial, so does a persuasive writer present evidence in the body of a thesis paper. Students must learn to support their thesis statements with evidence that persuades the reader to accept their case, and they also need to include characters (in a sense, witnesses) whose actions and dialogue reinforce an underlying argument.

Closing arguments in a trial case are much the same as the closing summary in a persuasive paper. Lawyers even use images. Sitting on the same jury previously mentioned, the defense attorney made the analogy of the case needing more evidence, just as a board, if not nailed down in two places, can spin instead of staying fixed. Including images adds clarity to persuasive arguments. Being able to effectively use persuasive writing becomes more important as students enter high school. Standardized writing tests in high school and the current Scholastic Aptitude Test (SAT) essay requirement emphasize persuasive writing using literary evidence.

LEARNING OBJECTIVES

Objectives listed for developing, focusing, and experimenting writers are appropriate for this scaffold.

PROCEDURE

STEP 1

Determining Prior Knowledge

Discuss the following plot questions:

- What if someone accused you of a crime?
- What if the catch is that you need to go to court to answer to these charges?
- What would happen in your case?

Discuss courtroom proceedings with students in order to find out how much prior knowledge they have of the U.S. judicial system. Review the following legal terms and positions.

Judge: Presides over the court and passes sentence. A judge decides innocence or guilt if a jury is not present.

Jury: Twelve people chosen to decide innocence or guilt. They listen to the arguments of both sides and then must reach, in private, a unanimous decision.

Prosecution: Argues that the defendant is guilty.

Defense: Argues that the defendant is innocent.

Bailiff: Swears in witnesses and helps to keep order in the court.

Court Recorder: Records, in writing, all that is said in the courtroom.

Witness: Person called on to give testimony about the case. Testimony is any spoken evidence regarding the case.

These are simple definitions; however, depending on students' capabilities, teachers can have them research the terms more thoroughly. In addition, if a student or teacher knows a lawyer or judge, the teacher could invite these guests to the classroom to answer questions about the U.S. court system. For example, when my intermediate students put Medea on trial for the murder of Creon (based on *Medea*, Applebaum, 1993), a real lawyer advised them on the strength of their case. When reading *Macbeth* (Shakespeare, 1994d), placing Lady Macbeth on trial for accessory to murder is also an exciting exercise in rhetoric.

After a discussion on the court system, hand out copies of the plot scaffold to students and assign parts. Have students read the scaffold aloud, adding lines. Do this twice, and allow students to take turns reading the parts.

STEP 2

Acting Out the Plot Scaffold

Discuss how the plot might change depending on whether the defendant Ralph Ransom is guilty or innocent. Have students act out the scaffold while reading the lines of the play. Read one version in which Ralph is guilty and another version in which he is innocent. Discuss what constitutes believable evidence (i.e., factual or tangible evidence, not hearsay or secondhand accounts) and how the characters might act depending on Ralph's innocence or guilt. Look at both sides of the issue. Allow students to add more characters or witnesses or change lines to accommodate more students, if necessary.

STEP 3

Completing the Plot Scaffold

Next, have students add lines and images to complete their plot scaffolds. Allow students to review one another's papers, but pair students so one student is attempting to prove Ralph innocent and one student is attempting to prove him guilty. This allows students to see both sides of an issue more effectively. Have students decide who has the better or stronger "case" and then make any necessary changes to their scaffolds to make their cases stronger.

After the teacher ensures that all lines have been completed and they make sense, students may write their first drafts.

STEP 4

Adding Effective Dialogue

Persuasive speech is central to this play, and the characters require dialogue to sway the reader. However, students should be sure to present accurate evidence in both the opening and closing statements, which results in more convincing arguments.

Students can add words that pertain to dialogue like *asked*, *stated*, *objected*, and *agreed* directly on the plot scaffold next to the characters to help students think about how characters sound when they talk. How a character talks can be a reflection of his or her personality or the plot situation. Placing quotation marks in the correct place for dialogue on the scaffold is also helpful so students can practice placing them correctly, and it makes for an easier transition to their next or first draft of narrative text. After all scaffolds have been checked for completion and grammar has been corrected, have students write their narrative drafts.

Expanding the Plot Scaffold

Students should engage in peer review again with a student with the opposite verdict. If there are not enough opposing views, have students who have very different plots share their drafts. Try to avoid having students "piggy-back" or copy one another's ideas by verbalizing the rule that once an idea has been used by one student, it cannot be used by another student. Teachers should check students' drafts for hook, problem, backfill, complication, action–reaction, dark moment, and resolution (see pages 13–14).

GRAMMAR TO IMPROVE STYLE (PUNCTUATION)

In this plot scaffold, the bailiff character does not use appropriate courtroom language and also confuses words (which are evidenced in the spelling of these words). Discuss how grammar and appropriate word usage are extremely important in law. For this particular scaffold, teachers can incorporate minilessons on punctuation and how the placement of punctuation marks can change meaning. For example, the placement of punctuation in the following example changes the meaning of the sentence because in one sentence a woman is helpless without a man, and in the other sentence, it is the man who is helpless when he does not have a woman.

A woman, without her man, is helpless.

A woman—without her, man is helpless.

FURTHER ELABORATION (OPTIONAL)

Act out this play for another group or class. Have them act as a jury and decide if the defendant is guilty or innocent.

EVALUATION

Use the Beginning Writer Rubric or Intermediate Writer Rubric, depending on the stage of writers in the classroom (see Appendix A).

How to Create Your Own Plot Scaffolds Based on Genres

To write a plot scaffold for use in your own classroom, first remember that plot scaffolds are not complete stories. They should be only three to four pages because a set story length helps prevent students from rambling. Teachers should leave spaces between the characters' dialogue to make the scaffold look like a play script. Teachers also should provide blanks or lines to write on so students can complete the scaffold and use it as a rough draft, plan, or outline. This format makes it easier for students to keep their place during oral reading and to provide completed scaffolds that are clear and easy to copy. Allow students to cross out words or change preexisting dialogue in the plot scaffold (another good reason to leave spaces between the characters' lines). For beginning writers, keep the lines short and full of high-frequency sight words, but also include a few more difficult common vocabulary words. Remember that students will be repeating these words several times, which will help students, especially ESL students, practice vocabulary pronunciation and comprehension.

It also is important for teachers to ensure that the plots have a problem to solve, so the plot should be scaffolded only to the point of making the question or problem evident. Do not provide a resolution, which, as previously mentioned, is referred to as gate keeping. I write to the point of the climax or dark moment in the story because, at that point, there is enough material for beginning writers to build on and for intermediate writers to simply turn the dark moment into another action–reaction to keep the story going longer if they desire.

In addition, I find that making a list of characters allows me to think of the problems that might arise between or because of them. This is an exercise I have my own students do when we create group stories. It allows us to come up with the questions that drive the plot.

All literary genres have certain unique elements. A literary genre is a specific writing style and a way of classifying literary works into specific categories. The plot scaffolds in this chapter are based on literary genres. For example, a mystery deals with the solution of a fictitious crime or the unraveling of fictitious secrets. A melodrama has a simplified moral universe composed of stock good and evil characters. The plot has an episodic form and traditionally the villain poses a threat, the hero or heroine escapes, and the whole story has a happy ending.

To create a plot scaffold for a genre—for example, science fiction—first decide what characters are needed and then let their characteristics, problems, or jobs drive the plot. Science fiction is based on the impact of actual, imagined, or potential science, and usually is set in the future or on other planets. Characters for a typical science fiction story might include astronauts, scientists, computer technicians, or aliens. Teachers can use different genres to explore issues such as stereotype and diversity. Do all heroes have to be male or save the girl? Are elderly people really forgetful? In addition, science fiction must have an element of real science or it is not true science fiction. Science fiction stories do not have wizards or magic; that is considered fantasy. Writers can cross genres by combining science fiction and fantasy, but students need to know they are "mixing" much like an artist does with colors when painting. Knowing the primary and secondary colors of writing gives writers more control over their art.

Finally, teachers should choose a rubric that corresponds with students' stage of writing development (see Appendix A), or have students help create a rubric that will measure their ability and success. Triangulate your evaluation by assessing student achievement in listening, writing, and reading. If the scaffold is acted out, include elements of nonverbal communication (e.g., Was the actor believable?).

Figure 6
Revised Student Writing Sample

At exactly twelve o'clock midnight, a squirrel crept silently out of its white-flowered tree that looks as if it was covered in snow. This tree makes up the squirrel's empire. A few moments later, across the road, a ferret slowly emerged out of trailer fourteen, which makes up the ferret's rebel base.

Back at the squirrel's base, Darth Squader was reporting in to Lord Squithus.

"All was quiet at Ferret Central," Darth Squader reported in a voice like that of someone who gives you nightmares about turning into a robot.

Figure 6 shows the developing work of the beginning writer from the example that opens this chapter. The writer uses dialogue and images and appears to be more than just an experimenting writer. The image for Darth Squader's voice conveys dread to the reader; the writer shows the reader how Darth Squader sounds as he speaks his lines. The beginnings of sentences vary, which helps hook the reader into thinking something sinister is about to happen. The writer uses more active, descriptive verbs like *emerged* or *crept*. Now the dialogue and images help advance the plot.

Now that I have explained how to create plot scaffolds based on genres, in chapter 3, I will focus on using preexisting stories to develop plot scaffolds. Intermediate writers often have difficulty understanding more complex text. Incorporating the plot scaffold strategy with more complex text will provide students with a means to understand this material.

Plot Scaffolds for Intermediate Writers

As they flew, their furry tails flapped in the wind like boat sails. They flew just like all the other super heroes you've heard of. They held their paws in front of them and straightened their bodies as best they could, and flew in the direction of their paws.

"Now my fur is all screwed up like it was this morning when I woke up!" yelled Zelda, as they landed on a small ledge about 200 yards from the ground. They came to a large steel door and stopped moving.

"Oh great, they have a security system," said Marty sarcastically. He picked up a rock with his small claws and threw it at the door.

"Quit it stupid!" said Zelda, trying as best she could to whisper, "You'll give away where we are!"

"Hey, look," said Marty, peering through a small hole to the left of the huge steel door. The door was as tall as both the ferrets and just as wide, in the shape of a square.

Behind the small hole was a terrifying sight. The penguins had a cage hung over a pit of lava about ten feet wide. The penguins were chanting and walking in a circle around the pit. Every two steps the penguins took, they would slowly spin in around in a circle, then walk two more steps. Their changing sounded exactly like the song the evil flying monkeys from "The Wizard of Oz" sing. They had the cage suspended in the air by a big yellow crane.

"Oh my God!" shouted Marty, "Those posers! They stole that song from 'The Wizard of Oz'! How did they get a crane in there?"

"I can see where this writer is getting some of his ideas. His writing seems beyond emerging, developing, focusing, and experimenting," notes the teacher while examining the student's rough draft.

"He is an engaging or extending writer," I state.

"Do engaging and extending writers use scaffolding in the same manner as beginning writers?" asks the teacher.

"In many ways they do, but these writers, mostly found in middle school, are capable of extending their writing to include historical fiction, persuasive formats, satire, and research writing," I explain. "Based on my experience, I have found that persuasive writing and satire are appropriate for middle school students who are becoming more vocal and firm regarding their beliefs."

This chapter provides explanations of these types of writers and presents plot scaffolds and strategies for meeting those needs while continuing to focus on the seven plot elements (see pages 13–14).

The plot scaffold lessons in this chapter are similar to the format of chapter 2. However, Step 1 often includes various reading strategies because students at the intermediate level are moving away from simply decoding print to finding meaning in print. They are learning to read and write in a more critical manner. And, in Step 5, Expanding the Plot Scaffold, intermediate writers should write a first draft and then a final one. This is important because intermediate writers are moving toward becoming engaging and extending writers, which requires more elaboration, reflection, and revision in their writing. Intermediate writers should be encouraged to make the story more original, and the revision process for the first draft can address this issue. To help with the revision process, it is helpful to include Grammar to Improve Style during Step 5. This step may take three or more class periods of 45–60 minutes depending on how many draft revisions the teacher feels are necessary in order to meet instructional goals. Intermediate writers should be capable of writing their drafts outside of class, and class periods can be used for teacher and student conferencing or peer editing.

Again, an ESL adaptation is featured with one plot scaffold (see "Wolf Kids"). ESL adaptations such as this one involve using students' native languages and cultures; adaptations may be used with other plot scaffolds, too. Because the emphasis in this chapter is on using mythology and legend as plot scaffolds, students can have opportunities to explore ESL students' native stories, legends, and myths. By sharing stories, students from different cultures can find commonalities, and communication may become easier once people realize they have similar ideas or folk wisdoms. Exploring the differences can also be exciting as well as provide writers with new settings, plot twists, and character motivation.

The order of the scaffolds in this section is not in degree of difficulty but by Norse, Greek, or Roman story origin. Because Norse, Greek, and Roman legends and mythology contain violence, it is appropriate to include violence in these plot scaffolds if teachers wish to maintain the original story lines.

Types of Intermediate Writers

Although several of the plot scaffolds in this chapter may be used successfully with developing, focusing, and experimenting writers, the main emphasis in this chapter is using them with engaging and extending writers. Engaging writers develop their story topics clearly, with a focused beginning, middle, and end. They engage the reader's interest with an effective use of varied language and sentence patterns. For example, the student who wrote the example that opened this chapter uses satire in his comments about *The Wizard of Oz* (Fleming, 1939), which is characteristic of engaging writers. In addition, the student incorporated movie references like *Superman* (Donner,

1978)—topics with rich, vivid images—in his writing and used these topics to elaborate his text. Engaging writers also use organization to sustain the writer's purpose and move the reader through the piece.

An extending writer has all the qualities of an engaging writer but has a better grasp than an engaging reader of how to create images and novel language. By examining how this is accomplished successfully in literary works, these writers can become more proficient in using their own experiences to reach a broader audience. Good writers often use successful writers as role models (Scarborough et al., 2003).

Finally, for both engaging and extending writers, the errors they may make in surface structure do not interfere with meaning. Both engaging and extending writers need more practice in engaging and sustaining the reader's interest through the use of creative and novel use of language and the effective use of varied sentence patterns.

Use of Legend, Mythology, and Existing Literature

Besides using real-life experiences and literary genres, such as mystery or science fiction, to create plot scaffolds, teachers also can use legends, mythology, or existing stories. Mythology is a rich source for scaffolding because the themes behind their plots are timeless (which is evidenced in adaptations to film of stories such as the Iliad, the Odyssey, or Jason and the Argonauts). Many of the stories based on mythology and legend are as relevant and interesting to us now as they were hundreds of years ago. For example, stories such as the Odyssey reveal the human condition and a human search for answers to questions about death, pride, or the journey home. Further, stories such as Arabian Nights are simply good examples of how hook and action–reaction are used to keep the reader's interest.

Mythologies are reflections of a culture's worldview (Campbell, 1989; Meade, 2002); they can be found worldwide and include oral traditions from all continents. Storytelling is an oral tradition. Only in the last two centuries and then only in English has reading a story come to be identified almost exclusively with the interpretation of written material (Levison, 1983). Reading or "giving counsel, taking charge, explaining the obscure" (Levison, 1983, p. 49) are all forms of active communication, which is an active language process in which a writer communicates to his or her reader like an oral storyteller to his or her audience. The reader or listener must be actively "thinking" in order to comprehend the message that the storyteller wishes to convey (Smith, 1978). Thus, teaching writing using legends, myths, and existing stories as plot scaffolds allows the power of several literacy components to work in the service of communication.

Some educators may argue that Beowulf may be too sophisticated or frightening for children. However, scaffolding the story can make this literature more user-friendly to children. Also, myths and legends such as Beowulf are a part of a cultural heritage for English speakers. The ideals behind the story, such as how leaders protect their people and how to face one's fears, are all as relevant today as they were in the fifth century. For example, Beowulf's character is evidenced in the character Bilbo from *The*

Hobbit (Tolkien, 1966). Bilbo shows many of Beowulf's traits of sacrifice, service, and generosity. Both characters also face similar dangers: They both face monsters who live in damp places, deal with dragons, and go on an adventure in the service of others. Creating new stories based on existing stories has been done by many good writers.

PLOT SCAFFOLD FOR "GUESS WHO MOVED IN NEXT DOOR?"

I use "Guess Who Moved in Next Door?" as a prereading or postreading strategy in conjunction with *Beowulf: A New Telling* (Nye, 1968). Scaffolding myths and legends such as Beowulf allows students to explore the theme behind the story without having to struggle through the Old English language barrier. Allowing students exposure to the story of Beowulf before translating it helps students to understand and even enjoy it. I have used the plot scaffold "Guess Who Moved in Next Door?" with my sixth-grade students, who respect the story for its message rather than being bogged down by the language.

LEARNING OBJECTIVES

Objectives listed for experimenting, engaging, or extending writers are appropriate for this plot scaffold. Experimenting writers can experiment with language and sentence patterns, but their scaffolds should be checked closely for surface features that interrupt fluency. Because experimenting writers may have awkward story beginnings or endings, they should also pay particular attention to the use of hook, problem, backfill, complication, action–reaction, dark moment, and resolution. Teachers should have these writers label these elements on their rough drafts to ensure that their plots are complete. Engaging writers also should work on the use of varied language and sentence patterns, especially using participial phrases to begin sentences. Extending writers can explore larger issues that may arise when looking at Beowulf from Grendel's viewpoint, such as environmental factors and ownership (e.g., Who owned the fen, or swamp? What problems arise when humans build in wildlife habitats?).

PROCEDURE

STEP 1

Determining Prior Knowledge (and Various Reading Strategies)

Hand out copies of the plot scaffold and read it aloud. Allow students to act as the characters and decide the ending of the story. After the reading, the teacher also can create a list of selected-response questions to determine students' factual understanding, such as

- What is a fen?
- Who was Grendel?
- Why do these people have such strange names?

If this plot scaffold is used as a prereading strategy (that is, prior to reading the epic poem), teachers can supply the answers to these questions as backfill. Or teachers can choose not to reveal the correct answers and have students present their own ideas to complete the story and make it their own.

Next, discuss the following plot questions:

- What if you had a dream to build a beautiful house?

- What if the catch is you built the house on land inhabited by a monster?

- What would happen if you decided to live in the house?

After reading or telling the story of Beowulf (there are many shorter editions of the story that can be found in collections of Nordic myths and legends [e.g., *Timeless Myths*, Lewis, 1980; *World Tales*, Shah, 1979; *The Golden Treasury of Myths and Legends*, White, 1964]), teachers can use the scaffold as an evaluative tool to determine students' understanding of the myth. The scaffold also can be used to explore in depth various ideas such as the heroic ideal or the ecological issues that arise when humans move into a wildlife area. Who has what rights? The story of Beowulf raises these questions, and students may find other open-ended questions ripe for debate. Thus, this scaffold can be used as a prereading or postreading strategy.

This plot scaffold also can be used as a metacognitive reading strategy. Simply pass out the scaffold, assign parts, and have students act it out—but stop at critical points in the story and ask students to put down the scripts and predict what happens next. For example, teachers could stop at the point where Beowulf grabs Grendel's arm and ask students what they think happens next. Allow students to make some predictions but use clues in the story to make them. Then, reveal to students what actually happens in the poem—Beowulf tears off Grendel's arm and then Grendel runs back to the swamp and bleeds to death. This type of metacognitive reading practice allows students to practice prediction skills necessary to a higher level reading ability (Readence et al., 1981; Wright, 1985). A metacognitive reader is actively engaged when reading text just as a writer is actively engaged when creating text.

STEP 2

Acting Out the Plot Scaffold

Have students take turns playing the characters and acting out the plot. Remember, it is not necessary to read aloud the stage directions or plot scaffold instructions; read this scaffold as if it were a play script. What parts would be helpful to describe using images? What would people see in terms of scenery if they were the audience watching this play or movie? As a group, go through the scaffold and decide on places for a good "camera angle." Which story parts need to be seen? Are extra scenes needed? Can a scene be dropped? For example, some scenes from the book *The Fellowship of the Ring* (Tolkien, 1956), such as those concerning the four hobbits meeting Tom Bombadil in the Old Forest, were dropped from the movie version. Have students brainstorm other incidents in which changing a book to a movie alters the story. Why is this done? Why can't movies depict all the scenes found in a book? How long would the movie be if all scenes were included? Do movie directors change a book's plot line in order to give the story a different message? How might the editing and changing of an existing story be an example of an extending writing strategy?

Completing the Plot Scaffold

Have students complete the scaffold by adding dialogue and images. Check this draft of the story to make sure it answers the plot's initial questions. Read aloud one or two of the scaffolds or have students review one another's stories.

Because of the setting and the inclusion of monsters, *Beowulf* has certain elements of a good horror story. For example, the setting is a dark, gloomy swamp, or fen; Grendel, a monster, eats people; and after he is killed, another monster, his mother, jumps out of the swamp. These elements add complication to the plot. Students need to be aware of how to establish complications in their writing before action–reaction can take place so the hero can take an action that elicits a reaction. The action–reaction and the climax should leave the reader surprised but still make sense.

Teachers also should check students' scaffolds to ensure that they have included the seven plot elements (see pages 13–14).

Adding Effective Dialogue

Review with students how to write the dialogue for the story by adding costumes and movement to the characters. Using the Fred and Mary strategy (see page 18) to create dialogue also is effective with intermediate writers. Remind students that the characters cannot be "seen" when it is in written text, so this step is necessary to writing a clear, descriptive story. Review rules of punctuation for dialogue, too.

Expanding the Plot Scaffold

Next, have students revise the scaffold into a story. Then, have students review one another's papers. Students can perform the peer review by actually marking their partner's paper while reading it or making comments on sticky notes and attaching them to the paper. Stress to students that their criticism should be constructive. As mentioned in chapter 2, I do not require students to make all the changes that their peers suggest, but they should make at least two. These two changes should be circled on the rough draft or sticky note and attached to the rough draft when it is turned in with the final draft.

GRAMMAR TO IMPROVE STYLE (PARTICIPLE PHRASES, GERUND PHRASES, AND PERSONIFICATION)

Writing good descriptive images or figurative language can help students set the tone for this "horror" story. Students can use the scaffold to rewrite images using participle and gerund phrases, which help them create more descriptive images and vary their sentences. The following example illustrates the effect of incorporating a participle change:

Grendel sat in the shadows and watched the fourteen warriors waiting for him where the front door of the hall should have been (he had knocked it down the night before). He laughed as he saw their tiny swords and their puny little spears.

Crouching in the shadows, Grendel watched the fourteen waiting warriors where the Hall's front door should have been (he had knocked it down the night before). Laughing, he saw their tiny swords and puny spears.

Students also can focus on incorporating personification—making an inanimate object or animal take on an almost human personality—at this stage. In "Guess Who Moved in Next Door?" the door is a good object to be personified. Therefore, to help students recognize personification, the door becomes an actual character in this scaffold. Following are some examples of how the door "speaks":

Door of Heorot: (How might the door react? Think of the door as a character in the story. Would you fall or faint when Grendel knocks on you?) <u>Trembling, the normally strong door of Heorot shuddered and groaned as it felt Grendel's claws rake across its oaken planks.</u>

Meanwhile, at Hall Heorot, King Hrothgar and his men were having a wonderful feast that included ham and beef. Little did they know, Grendel was advancing toward the door. Just as Grendel was about to pound on the door, the door squealed and dodged Grendel's blow. Then the door quietly moved aside so Grendel could get in. Grendel trudged in, leaving a thick green and gritty slime behind him.

In addition, students can attempt to personify a specific setting in the story, such as Grendel's mother's pool:

Beowulf dived in, and the pool could feel some of its water being plunged down further, and it felt a tickling sensation. When Beowulf dove in, he could feel the warm water smack his face and he could taste the gross water on his lips. It tasted like a year old egg that had been saved.

FURTHER ELABORATION (OPTIONAL)

Students can choose the best lines (or this can be done by the teacher) from the plot scaffolds and perform "Guess Who Moved in Next Door?" Again, this activity incorporates listening and speaking skills, body movement, and art.

In addition, to introduce the idea of comparative literature, I have students compare the Nordic hero Beowulf to the Greek hero Jason. Students are always surprised at how the Greek ideal of the handsome young man may have some "holes" in it when it comes to heroics. Students also compare Beowulf to Bilbo in *The Hobbit*. Students examine similarities in terms of setting, major and minor characters, and events. For example, Bilbo travels on a journey, like Beowulf, in a company of 14. In the stories, both characters obtain a gold ring, and a cup is stolen from a dragon. In addition, Gollum, like Grendel, lives in a damp cave. There are many other similarities as well, which helps clarify for students how writers use and reinvent preexisting stories (in fact, Tolkien translated medieval literature, including Beowulf).

EVALUATION

Use the Intermediate Writer Rubric (see Appendix A).

PLOT SCAFFOLD FOR "THAT APPLE"

Based on the events leading up to the Iliad, the plot scaffold "That Apple" (see Appendix B) is the story of what caused the Trojan War. The myth is rich in message and theme. Problems found in "That Apple," like not being asked to a party, in this case a wedding (an age-old dilemma); a beauty contest where the participants "cheat"; and the problems of one's wife leaving (or, based on the original story's time period, stealing someone else's property), are all subjects addressed by Greek Trojan War legends. The plot scaffolds "Beware of Gifts" and "Are We Home Yet?" continue this story (see pages 70–76 and 76–78).

"That Apple" can be used as an introduction to Greek mythology and gods and goddesses (in fact, "That Apple," "Beware of Gifts," "Are We Home Yet?" and "Wolf Kids" are part of a unit on Roman and Greek mythology). It is important for students to have a basic understanding of Greek and Roman mythology because many classic plays, books, and stories are based on those plots, themes, and characters.

LEARNING OBJECTIVES

Because of its simple vocabulary and sentence patterns, "That Apple" is appropriate for focusing writers. It also is appropriate for experimenting writers, who should focus on the seven plot elements. Engaging writers can focus on using emotion to grab readers' attention and creating novel use of language through examining characters' motivation.

PROCEDURE

STEP 1

Determining Prior Knowledge (and Various Reading Strategies)

Hand out copies of the plot scaffold to students. Read it aloud and allow students to act out the characters and decide the ending of the story. After reading, start a list of selected-response questions in order to determine factual understanding and prior knowledge regarding the Trojan War, such as

- Who are some of the Greek gods and goddesses?
- Where did they live?
- What do you know about the Trojan War?

Discussing the answers to these questions can provide backfill to the story of the Trojan War. Students can also practice research skills by collecting information regarding the Trojan War or Greek mythology and sharing it in class with others.

Discuss the following plot questions:

- What if there was a large wedding and everyone was going?

- What if the catch was, you were not invited? In fact, you were excluded on purpose.
- What would you do?

or

- What if you had to judge a beauty contest?
- What if the catch was that the contestants all offer you a bribe?
- What would you do?

Teachers can use this scaffold as a type of anticipation–reaction guide before reading the original version of the story. Students complete the scaffold, read the story on which the scaffold is based, and then revisit their predictions to see how well they predicted the actual outcome. Anticipation–reaction guides help to develop higher-level reading skills, such as prediction, and also allow students to examine preexisting schema (Readence et al., 1981). Schema theory refers to "the process by which we add to (assimilate) or adjust (accommodate) our existing cognitive structure in the face of new or discordant information" (Readence et al., 1981, p. 223). When teachers connect new information to what a student already knows (preexisting schema), it is often much easier for a student to understand a text. Anticipation–reaction guides allow teachers to determine what students know or believe about a subject prior to adding new information.

As a metacognitive strategy, this plot works particularly well because there are many stopping points where the teacher can have students make predictions about the plot's outcome. For example, I ask students which goddess they think Paris finally chooses as the winner of the contest. Students answer by writing a brief explanation, and then I collect the "votes" and tally them. Often, students think Paris chooses Athena because she could make him the smartest man in the world and give him the ability to become rich and marry any beautiful woman he wanted. At this point, students have to critically rethink their original prediction and look back at clues in the text. Ignoring what they, as readers, might believe, instead students have to reread the text and think about how Paris's character might determine his choice. This is a metacognitive reading strategy, too, because students must be actively engaged with text as they read with the purpose of finding reasons for Paris's choice. In a way, students have to "think like Paris," to answer the question. By having students examine Paris's character, they realize that he is, at the time, only a poor shepherd, innocent of the world around him. People often make choices based on what they know. Having lived with Oenone, a beautiful wood nymph, Paris knows beauty, not riches or fame. Engaging and extending writers can explore why people make personal choices. Students at any level can explore the consequences of Paris's choice as they learn the Trojan War story. Once students have been told or have read stories of the Trojan War, they can further explore the plot by using the inquiry approach; for example, students might ask, What if the plot changes and Paris picks a different goddess? Intermediate writers may explore this idea to create their own original story that reflects their personal stances. Changing the plot of a myth or legend—or even a historical event like the U.S. Civil War (writers could choose to have the South win the war)—allows writers to look at more than one possibility for a story. Finally, teachers can tie in one of the story's themes, Achilles' anger, with the main theme of the Iliad, and discuss how anger brings devastation upon Achilles, his friends, and others.

STEP 2

Acting Out the Plot Scaffold

Have students take turns acting as the characters and determine the driving force of the story. Is it character? How do the characters drive the plot? Is it with emotion? What emotions do the gods and goddesses represent? Discuss how writers create believable characters through giving them real emotions and motivations.

STEP 3

Completing the Plot Scaffold

Students should complete their plot scaffolds by specifically focusing on how the characters are emotionally motivated. This can be conveyed through the use of vivid adverbs and adjectives for images and dialogue. Students make any changes to the original scaffold in order for it to fit the ending they have created.

STEP 4

Adding Effective Dialogue

Review with students how to write the dialogue for the story by adding costumes and movement to the characters. Emphasize the emotion in the dialogue when students are reading aloud the scaffold and discuss how the emotional quality can be written in text. Remind students that the characters cannot be "seen" in written text, so include any movement the character might make that clarifies motivation or intent. Review rules of punctuation for dialogue, too.

STEP 5

Expanding the Plot Scaffold

Check students' completed scaffolds for dialogue and images, have students engage in peer review, and then have students use the scaffold as a guide for writing their first drafts. After writing their first drafts, have students use a highlighter to show the first word of each sentence and identify each word that is an article or simple pronoun such as *the*, *a*, or *it* . Have students count how many times they have used dull or vague words to start sentences. Students can practice flipping sentences or rewriting them so they include better, attention-grabbing words to begin their sentences. In addition, students can practice using vivid adverbs, such as *angrily* or *desperately*, to play on the readers' emotions and set them up for what is to come.

After students have written their first drafts, teachers or students, who are acting as peer editors, check for the seven plot elements (see pages 13–14). It should be evident in each student's story that events go from bad to worse because of anger. In this plot scaffold, one character's rage leads to more people becoming upset, a result of action–reaction. One dark moment occurs when King Agamemnon discovers that Paris has eloped with Helen; however, because the scaffold is meant to be a cliffhanger that leads to the rest of the Trojan War stories, students' final stories may contain a summary of what occurred after Helen is stolen.

GRAMMAR TO IMPROVE STYLE (ADVERBS, ADJECTIVES, AND APPOSITIVE PHRASES)

Because this scaffold focuses on emotional motivation, vivid adverbs and adjectives can help the writer's style. Brainstorm a list of adverbs and adjectives that describe emotions such as love, hate, jealousy, pride, and disappointment. In addition, students can work on sentence variety by including metaphors and similes within appositive phrases, which aids in avoiding beginning sentences with *like* or *as*. Following is an example of an image of love that includes an appositive phrase:

> Love, as dangerous as the golden apple Discord threw upon the table, was about to catch Helen unaware as Cupid drew his bow and aimed.

FURTHER ELABORATION (OPTIONAL)

Have students act out the plot scaffold. To address multiple sign systems or different learning styles, I have students videotape or "film" the story. Shoot scenes several times to allow students to see their performances, reflect on them, and improve them. In addition, you can choose to use a specific set or scenery. For example, one group of students filmed scenes in the woods near our school. Students were able to see more effectively how the backdrops of a movie are like the images in a book. In addition, simple special effects help to create visual images—for example, turning the video camera off and having characters walk off the set gives the effect of someone "disappearing" once the film is rolling again. Finally, if necessary, students can add additional gods or goddesses to the plot scaffold to help accommodate larger groups or classes.

EVALUATION

Use the Intermediate Writer Rubric (see Appendix A).

PLOT SCAFFOLD FOR "BEWARE OF GIFTS"

"Beware of Gifts" (see Appendix B) is based on the Greek legend of the Trojan Horse. Greek legends and myths, as well as those in many other cultures, often include stories about how a trickster plays on his or her adversary's desires, sets up the adversary for a fall, and ultimately wins. African stories of Anansi the Spider are a good example of this format. Anansi uses tricks to take advantage of others. In one situation, he keeps all the tasty yams to himself by telling his dinner guest, a turtle, to wash his hands first before joining him. It takes the turtle so long to get his hands clean (because he has to walk on them) that Anansi is able to eat all the yams himself. After all, according to Anansi, cold yams are not very good to eat. Clever tricks are often viewed by readers as sign of intelligence and resourcefulness, and perhaps that explains why the story of the Trojan Horse still holds readers' interest today.

"Beware of Gifts" can be used to introduce the topic of writing a research paper on the Trojan War because questions such as Did the Trojan War really occur? naturally arise from the plot. It also can be used as an introduction to the genre of historical fiction, for which extending writers may use to further explore language. Historical fiction includes fictional characters that take part in actual historical events and interact with people from the past. When writing historical fiction, writers need to know accurate historical references in order to create believable settings, dialogue, and events for the reader similar to how students, when writing a research paper, need to know historical facts to support their theses.

LEARNING OBJECTIVES

This plot scaffold is appropriate for experimenting, engaging, or extending writers. For experimenting writers, "Beware of Gifts" can be used to develop a clear beginning, middle, and end to their stories, which can be accomplished by specifically focusing on the seven elements of plot. Engaging writers should focus on including vivid images and varied dialogue, and extending writers can go a step further and write a persuasive research paper.

PROCEDURE

STEP 1

Determining Prior Knowledge

Discuss selected-response questions in order to determine students' factual understanding and prior knowledge regarding the Trojan War, such as

- What was the Trojan Horse?
- Who built the horse?
- What happened when the horse came into the city of Troy?
- Was the story of the Trojan War based on fact? Did it actually happen?
- Who was Heinrich Schliemann? Did he really find Troy?
- Can myths and legends have bases in historical fact?

As previously mentioned, teachers should ask such questions as students read aloud the scaffold, so students can practice metacognitive strategies and become more active, engaged readers.

STEP 2

Acting Out the Plot Scaffold

Hand out copies of the plot scaffold to students. Have them act out the parts and then switch parts to explore new angles on character development. Students explore the following questions: Does tone of voice and body stance determine character? What parts of the story would an audience need to see? What needs to be described using images?

STEP 3

Completing the Plot Scaffold

Students complete the scaffold by adding lines and images. In order for extending writers to complete this scaffold and turn it into historical fiction, students need to research the Trojan War and know the basic facts of the story. (Yes, the Greeks won the war by coming out of the wooden horse and burning Troy.) However, in order to make the story more interesting to the reader, the characters' descriptions need to be detailed, match the time period, and enhance the story setting. Students may need to add fictional characters and have them take part in the actual historical events if their new plots require these characters so the story makes sense. Students also may choose to include themselves in their stories and write from the first-person perspective. Students can explore the following questions, which will aid in characterization: How would it feel to be a character during that period? What might the soldiers have been thinking while waiting in the wooden horse? Thus, this scaffold also aids in helping students practice writing from another point of view.

Steps for writing the first draft of historical fiction follow similar guidelines: Students add dialogue and images, but the images must be historically accurate. Clothing, weapons, animals, and so forth must be believable and accurate when writing historical fiction.

STEP 4

Adding Effective Dialogue

When students add to a section of dialogue from the plot scaffold (see Step 5), they need to ensure that the images are historically accurate. Adding effective dialogue includes checking for appropriate descriptions to match the time period. Remind students that the characters cannot be "seen" in written text, so they should include any movements the characters might make that clarifies their motivation or intent. Review rules of punctuation for dialogue, too.

STEP 5

Expanding the Plot Scaffold

Students write their first drafts in narrative form. Students have the option of writing in first person if they are telling the story from the viewpoint of a character who is actually there at the time of the war.

"It's been ten years outside these walls," sighed proud King Agamemnon as he gazed at Troy. "Anyone have any ideas on how we, the mighty Greeks, can finally win this war?"

Having been around Agamemnon, who was not the brightest tactician, I knew I, Odysseus, would have to come up with a plan or it might be another ten years before I saw my wife, Penelope, again. "Maybe we could pull the tricky Greek Gift strategy," I proposed.

Most often, the dark moment occurs when the Greeks are hidden in the wooden horse and are about to sneak out.

Finally, ensure that students' stories have a good hook, which also can be done effectively using dialogue.

GRAMMAR TO IMPROVE STYLE (DANGLING MODIFIERS)

To make this scaffold come alive, have students write it in the present tense and use active verbs. Using gerunds, participles, and infinitive phrases also can improve the writer's style, but make students aware of dangling modifiers. When a sentence begins with a participial phrase, a gerund, or an elliptical clause (i.e., one in which essential words are missing), students should ensure that the phrase or clause logically agrees with the subject of the sentence.

> Example: Participial Phrase
>
> Incorrect: Stashed away on the ship for many days, the sailors decided to open the bag.
>
> Correct: The sailors decided to open the bag that had been stashed away on the ship for many days.

> Example: Infinitive Phrase
>
> Incorrect: To appreciate the full value of Circe's gift, all previous gifts should be examined.
>
> Correct: To appreciate the full value of Circe's gift, Ulysses needs to examine all her previous gifts.

FURTHER ELABORATION (OPTIONAL)

After reading "Beware of Gifts," have students list a series of questions for further investigation. Then, students can use these questions as a starting point for writing a research paper. My students use a model or guide when writing their research papers, which they have now affectionately named the "Guinea Pig Paper." The model for the Guinea Pig Paper has sections that serve as a scaffold for writing a research paper (see Appendix C). The research presented in the Guinea Pig Paper is fictional but, because of its serious tone, students, and sometimes other teachers, mistake it for an actual study. The Guinea Pig Paper is a good example of how a writer's style and voice can persuade a reader into believing an idea.

In addition, the Guinea Pig Paper serves as a helpful scaffold for science projects or social studies papers. For example, my students have used the model to research science and social studies questions about *Alice in Wonderland* (Carroll, 1865/2002). They do experiments to answer questions such as, How do people react to smells? (from the chapter "Pig and Pepper") or Would people try to fit in if they were uninvited and treated rudely? (from Alice's "Mad Tea Party").

Figure 7 shows the model being used as a scaffold to research the Trojan War. Boldface print illustrates specifically how students adapted the model.

Figure 7
Guinea Pig Paper Model With Notations

Research Question

Why did the Inca Indians keep guinea pigs? **Students would write a question from the Trojan War story such as "Was there really a Trojan Horse?"**

Review of Literature

Archeologists have found many drawings of guinea pigs on temple walls in the jungles of Peru, and there are many theories as to why the Incas kept guinea pigs. Guinea pigs can still be found in Peru and have been there for thousands of years. Today we keep guinea pigs as pets or use them for lab experiments. The Incas may have had other uses for them. **Here students must, in a brief paragraph, give some background on the Trojan Horse. In the next three paragraphs, students write a literature review with each paragraph acting as a summary of a particular article on the Trojan Horse. This reinforces summary skills.**

One theory by Whitworth (1968) states that the Incas kept guinea pigs as a type of watchdog. He points out that most of the temple drawings show guinea pigs in small cages hanging outside of what are obviously shops and houses. Guinea pigs would squeak when an intruder approached and warn their masters. "Other societies such as the Chinese use a similar type of alarm system when they hang cages of crickets outside their shops and homes" (Whitworth, 1968, p. 186). When the crickets stop chirping, an intruder must be present. Guinea pigs are practical and eat less than dogs. There is no evidence that the Incas kept large dogs. Guinea pigs were one of the first alarm systems.

Another theory by Sims (1998) states that guinea pigs were kept as a food source. Evidence for this are the mounds of literally millions of guinea pig bones found outside most Inca ruins. Like rabbits, guinea pigs breed rapidly and would prove an excellent food source. "Guinea pigs taste like chicken" (Sims, 1998, p. 333). Sims has also noted that the pictures on temple walls show very large guinea pigs, some as big as ten pounds. This huge South American guinea pig may have become extinct due to disease as guinea pigs are notorious for getting viruses easily, and that is why they are used in labs today (Sims, 1977). Guinea pigs could have been a food source for the Incas.

Yet another possibility is that guinea pigs may have been raised for their fur and skins (Myers, 1944). Guinea pigs have very warm, soft fur that comes in a great variety of colors. Their skins could be used for leather products such as belts or shoes.

Myers also found a necklace made of hundreds of tiny guinea pig feet, but as this is the only one ever found, "...guinea pig feet as a form of jewelry may be not a wide spread use of the animal" (Myers, 1935, p. 99).

Analysis

There are four theories for guinea pig use, and they do not seem to have much in common with each other. They could have been used as watchdogs, a food source, for clothing, and for jewelry. It is true that some societies keep small animals as watchdogs. These animals, like the Mexican Hairless, are very small and bark at intruders to scare them away. As a food source, guinea pigs might be edible, but it would take many of them to make a meal. Their fur is soft and long and might have been used like we use rabbit skins today. Decorating oneself with guinea pig feet may have been a fad just as today we have fads like wearing owl-dropping jewelry. All four theories do not seem to have much in common.

(continued)

Figure 7 (continued)
Guinea Pig Paper Model With Notations

Here students analyze their data from the literature review and look for themes.

Methodology (Depending on one's project, this section is optional. This is the section for research study design.)

In order to test the theories on guinea pig use this researcher will raise guinea pigs for ten months in order to find out how fast they breed. The researcher will also then eat guinea pig and serve it to other people to determine if it is edible. The researcher will also attempt to make clothing and jewelry from the remaining skins and feet.

Students write how they might actually do a study to test whatever theory they have derived from their analyses.

Conclusion

The most likely explanation seems to be that guinea pigs were kept as a food source. As watch dogs, guinea pigs would not scare someone away because they cannot attack. Besides, they only squeak when they want food so the intruder would have to be bringing them their dinner. Guinea pigs could not be used for clothing because it would take over 200 skins to make a small coat (Whitworth, 1968). This is not practical when making clothing, and their skins are too thin to make good soles for shoes. The guinea pig necklace mentioned by Myers seems to be an isolated incident or perhaps just a one-time use. The most practical use of guinea pigs appears to be as a food source for the Incas. The evidence which might prove this are the mounds of guinea pig bones found outside temples, and the fact that guinea pigs do taste good. This researcher has raised and eaten guinea pigs herself and finds that, indeed, they taste like chicken. The Incas used guinea pigs for food.

Here students write their conclusions about the Trojan Horse, answering the question about its existence.

Sources (APA)

Borman, W.C., Hanson, M.A., Oppler, S.H., and White, L.A. (1993). Role of early Incan people in food production. *Journal of Applied Foodstuff, 78,* 433–449. Retrieved October 23, 2000, from Psycarticles database.

Hammond, T. (2000, July 14). *New resources for the giant guinea pig* [Msg 311]. Message posted to http://groups.yahoo.com/group/visualcognition/message/31 (Message posted to online forum or discussion group)

Myers, M. (1935, October 29). Jewelry in the ancient world. *Journal of Anthropology, 2,* 67–99. (magazine article)

Myers, M. (1944). New Coats. In *The new encyclopedia Britannica* (Vol. 26, pp. 501–588). Chicago: Encyclopedia Britannica. (entry in an encyclopedia)

Sims, N.L. (1998). *It tastes like chicken.* Washington, DC: American Psychological Association. (one-author book)

Whitworth, S. (Ed.). (1968). *The new Grove dictionary of animals* (6th ed., Vols. 1–20). London: Macmillan. (encyclopedia or dictionary)

EVALUATION

For historical fiction, use the Intermediate Writer Rubric (see Appendix A). For research papers, use the rubric and learning objectives listed with the Guinea Pig Paper (see Appendix C).

PLOT SCAFFOLD FOR "ARE WE HOME YET?"

This plot scaffold (see Appendix B), based on *Homer: The Odyssey* (Rieu & Rieu, 1991), is the story of Ulysses and his journey home. Students can apply the story's life lessons to their own situations to better understand the universality and purpose of mythology. Passed on to succeeding generations, mythology contains cultural wisdom for human survival. Therefore, to complete this plot scaffold, students can think of themselves as Ulysses and describe what might have happened to him. Thus, students' stories may become autobiographies that document their own journeys, which works well for intermediate writers who are at the stage where they are becoming self-aware and interested in exploring who they are.

LEARNING OBJECTIVES

This scaffold is appropriate for engaging or extending writers. Engaging writers will approach the scaffold as an opportunity to use varied language. Extending writers may choose to extend the themes found in this scaffold into an exploration of their own life experiences.

PROCEDURE

STEP 1

Determining Prior Knowledge

Hand out copies of the plot scaffold, read it aloud, and have students switch parts and act out the script. Another way to build on extending writers' prior knowledge, instead of using the scaffold as a narrative story to be completed, is to use it as a means of connecting Ulysses' travels with students' lives. This can be done verbally and then in writing later. Students can match each of Ulysses' adventures with one of their own "adventures." Students can explore whether they learned the same lessons as Ulysses and can recognize that myths contain cultural wisdoms that are relevant today.

For example, an extending writer made the following comparison:

On his voyage Ulysses learned that he shouldn't keep secrets from his crew. When Ulysses landed on Aeolus's island, he was given a bag of the North, South, and East Winds. When he received the winds, he didn't tell his crew what was in the bag. His crew became curious and opened the bag letting the winds escape. I can relate to this problem because I can't keep secrets from my friends. I tried to not tell a friend that someone had said something about her. When my friend found out that I had known, she was mad. Because of this I lost the trust my friend had in me, and this is why you shouldn't keep secrets from your friends or crew.

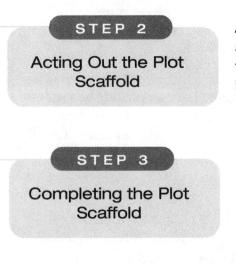

Allow students to take turns playing the characters and acting out the plot. Have students brainstorm what parts of the story need to be described with images for the reader.

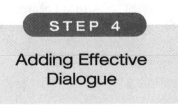

For engaging writers, have them read the plot scaffold, complete the lines, exchange the scaffolds with their peers, and write their rough drafts. Students should focus on novel use of language and effective use of varied sentence patterns. Students can create novel dialogue by changing the setting of the story. For example, I saw a novel, thought-provoking version of the Odyssey with Ulysses as a female character and the story set in outer space.

STEP 4

Adding Effective Dialogue

Review with students how to write the dialogue for the story by adding costumes and movement to the characters. Remind students that the characters cannot be "seen" in written text, so they should include any movement the characters might make that clarifies their motivation or intent. Also, students may wish to incorporate words that pertain to the dialogue, such as *replied*, *muttered*, or *ordered*, next to characters' names on the scaffold. Notes regarding to whom the character is speaking or any facial expressions can also be made on the scaffold itself. These tasks save time when students write their first drafts. Review rules of punctuation for dialogue, too.

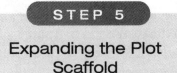

Students should identify and label the seven elements of plot (see pages 13–14) on their rough drafts because sometimes as students create a novel plot, they become distracted by adding details surrounding the setting and the elements become blurred. Teachers should check students' rough drafts for the seven elements of plot, make suggestions for revision, and then have students write their final drafts.

Students also learn to recognize allegory, which is a figurative work in which a surface narrative carries a secondary, symbolic or metaphorical meaning. Ulysses, in many ways, is a kind of "Everyman" in the journey through life. For example, from the Ciconians he learns the lesson that appearances can be deceiving. The Ciconians look like "fat sheep, ripe for picking," when in fact they retaliate and kill many of Ulysses' men. Another example is from the incident with Scylla and Charybdis in which Ulysses learns to take the middle path, or if this is not possible, pick the lesser of the two evils on either side of the path.

GRAMMAR TO IMPROVE STYLE (GERUND, PARTICIPLE, AND INFINITIVE PHRASES)

"Are We Home Yet?" is full of action, so sentences should have an exciting quality, not dull beginnings. As in previous lessons, emphasize using gerund, participle, and infinitive phrases to begin sentences and avoid using dull sounding sentence starters like *the*, *so*, *a*, or *then*.

FURTHER ELABORATION (OPTIONAL)

Experimenting writers will enjoy the plot scaffold on an explicit level—that is, as an adventure story full of exciting events, monsters, narrow escapes, and reaching one's goal. Working on a text-explicit level enables experimenting writers to map out the seven elements of plot. Then, students can brainstorm elements in good adventure stories and write more adventures for Ulysses. Students also can rewrite the story using a different setting. (For example, the film *O Brother, Where Art Thou*, Coen & Coen, 2000, is an adaptation of the Odyssey set in the 1930s Depression era in the United States.)

"Are We Home Yet?" may also be written using a different time period and then turned into a student-made film or play.

EVALUATION

Use the Intermediate Writer Rubric (see Appendix A). This scaffold also can be used as a postreading evaluation tool for checking students' understanding of the Odyssey.

PLOT SCAFFOLD FOR "WOLF KIDS"

I wrote "Wolf Kids" (see Appendix B) based on Romulus and Remus and the founding of Rome, at the request of some elementary school teachers who wanted to try using a plot scaffold for their Roman theme unit with gifted students but felt that the plot scaffold "Tyrant?" was too sophisticated for them. Thus, "Wolf Kids" was designed with dialogue and humor similar to "The Rent" and "There's a Bug in My Beans." The emphasis is on the theme of sibling rivalry because the myth deals with two children who are raised by a she-wolf who has trouble dealing with their constant bickering and fighting.

Although the story of Romulus and Remus is not based entirely on historical fact, the ending is factual (i.e., the founding of Rome). Thus, "Wolf Kids" can be considered a loose historical fiction or legend, if students are writing with the goal of retelling the story.

The teachers who used "Wolf Kids" found that the format allowed their students to think of other possible endings to the story. Although the teachers believed that creativity was essential to the gifted program, ironically, creativity became an issue with this scaffold. The dilemma arose when the teachers tried to assert their idea of the "right" ending to the story of Romulus and Remus. Historically, Romulus killed Remus, but the students, who were not aware of this, wanted Romulus and Remus to make up and work together. Therefore, in order to avoid possible confusion regarding the objectives for this plot scaffold when completing plots that are based on preexisting stories, teachers should decide if they want students to use the plot scaffold as a means to write new fictional stories or as a means to evaluate students' knowledge of the facts surrounding this myth. It is appropriate to use the plot scaffold for either purpose, so teachers need to decide if their role will be evaluator or facilitator. I have included plans for both options.

LEARNING OBJECTIVES

This plot scaffold is appropriate for emerging, developing, and focusing writers. Emerging and developing writers can work on topic development, and focusing writers can pay particular attention to using a variety of words and sentence structures to convey meaning.

Factual Use of the Scaffold: If the objective is to have students write a story with an ending based on the actual legend of Romulus and Remus, the teacher should have students research the end of the story (after determining students' prior knowledge) or the teacher could choose to simply explain it to students because the ending is not included in the scaffold. Teachers also can explain that Romulus killed Remus and founded Rome, although these events are not a proven historical fact, but rather, part of a legend. In addition, teachers should note that the part of the story in which the twins are raised by a she-wolf is legend.

Narrative Use of the Scaffold: If the objective is to have students create new stories, teachers hand out copies of the scaffold, assign roles, and read aloud the scaffold—but do not supply the factual ending to the legend. Instead, students can create their own endings based on what they think might have happened. Students can explore alternative endings to the story by answering the following constructed-response questions. They can provide examples from their own lives to support their answers.

- What happened as a result of the two brothers always fighting?
- Is fighting always bad, or does it ever lead to something good?
- What is the purpose of anger?
- What if the setting were in Africa? Would the wolf be a lion? What customs would be different? Are there any African tales that are similar to Romulus and Remus?

Because a limited number of tales are found at every time and place in the world (Shah, 1979), it is possible that students might find an African tale similar to Romulus and Remus—for example, there are over 300 versions of Cinderella (Shah, 1979).

Thus, the focus here is on the many endings the story might have based on the personalities a writer might choose to give each character.

PROCEDURE

STEP 1

Determining Prior Knowledge

Before handing out copies of "Wolf Kids," ask students selected-response questions to determine their prior knowledge about ancient Rome such as

- Where is Rome?
- Do you know any facts about the Roman Empire?
- Who founded Rome?

Then, hand out copies of "Wolf Kids" to students, assign roles, and read aloud the scaffold.

STEP 2

Acting Out the Plot Scaffold

Whether they are writing creative narratives or historical fiction, students now act out the scaffold. The teacher assigns roles, and students may act out the scaffold more than once in order to let different students take different roles. Then, as students read and act out the plot scaffold, discuss what the scenery would look like and what kinds of costumes the character would be wearing in order for the reader to believe that he or she is in Rome. One of the biggest problems I face when I have students write historical fiction is that they often include modern devices and ways of doing things. For example, the ancient Romans did not go to the shopping mall every day, eat spaghetti, or constantly buy new armor. In addition, weaponry is often misused. In order to write good historical fiction, it is necessary for students to research the time period to find out how the people lived, what they ate, and what type of technology they used. In fact, good writers often write about what they can research because it gives more credibility to their writing (Scarborough et al., 2003). Write about what you know or what you can research is the advice I give my students.

STEP 3

Completing the Plot Scaffold

Students complete their scaffolds and pay particular attention to imagery and historical context. All dialogue and images should be completed.

STEP 4

Adding Effective Dialogue

Review with students how to write the dialogue for the story by adding costumes and movement to the characters. Remind students that the characters cannot be "seen" in written text so they should include any movement the characters might make that clarifies their motivation or intent. Also, students may wish to incorporate words that pertain to the dialogue such as *replied*, *muttered*, or *ordered* next to characters' names on the scaffold. Notes regarding to whom the character is speaking or any facial expressions can also be made on the scaffold itself. These tasks save time when students write their first drafts. Also remember that characters should be wearing ancient Roman costumes if the story is going to be historically accurate. Finally, review rules of punctuation for dialogue, too.

STEP 5

Expanding the Plot Scaffold

Next, students use their completed plot scaffolds as a guide to write their first drafts. As they write, students are still free to make changes, and often students wish to add another character at this point. It is also useful to have students act out the plot scaffolds again and take turns reading aloud their images. The teacher and other students may make informal comments during this process. After the first draft is complete, teachers need to check the draft for the seven elements of plot (see pages 13–14) and to ensure that the story is historically accurate (if historical fiction is the focus), grammar is correct (especially for dialogue), and the images make sense.

ESL

"Wolf Kids" is also an opportunity for ESL students to share any stories from their native culture that may be similar to the story of Romulus and Remus; a plot involving two fighting brothers is common to many cultures. Sharing or comparing stories provides a way for ESL students to incorporate ideas from their culture into the plot scaffold for class performance.

Lines in "Wolf Kids" can be translated into an ESL student's native language so the student may act out the plot scaffold in class. As previously discussed in chapter 2, it is possible to incorporate multiple languages into a plot scaffold. For example, my middle school language arts students, along with ESL students, rewrote *A Midsummer Night's Dream* (Shakespeare, 1994a) and changed the setting to Peru. The fairies were changed to Inca gods and goddesses, and the dialogue contained Spanish words. This allowed ESL students to take a leading role in creating the play. In addition, changing the setting of a scaffold to match ESL students' countries and cultures allows students to share cultures and languages in the regular classroom setting.

Another strategy is to first perform the scaffold in English and then in another language. For example, one of my classes created a simple plot scaffold based on the Pyramus and Thisby (act 5, scene 1) play within Shakespeare's *A Midsummer's Night Dream*. This class included English-speaking students and a Japanese student who was living in the United States while her father was in the country on business. The play was presented first in English, and the setting matched what might have typically been seen in a traditional Shakespearean production. Then, the play was presented again in Japanese. In this production, Pyramus and Thisby committed *seppuku* rather than suicide, the character Moonshine became the Rising Sun, and Ninny's Tomb was transformed into a Buddhist Shrine. The cast even wore kimonos. The ESL student helped with the pronunciation of the Japanese script while English speakers helped her pronounce English for the more traditional production. My English-speaking students also learned that body language was often a better means of expressing the meaning behind the Japanese words they could not easily pronounce. Thus, both ESL students and English-speaking students learned lessons in nonverbal communication—and they both could relate to the common themes found in the play. Like the play we created from Pyramus and Thisby, "Wolf Kids," with its short, simple lines and common themes, can be translated easily into other languages.

GRAMMAR TO IMPROVE STYLE (ADJECTIVES, PREFIXES, AND SUFFIXES)

Because this plot scaffold has historical fiction elements, teachers should focus students' attention on descriptive adjectives that enable the reader see, feel, smell, hear, and taste the time period. Because this story takes place in Rome, teachers may wish to take the opportunity to explain how many Latin words, especially prefixes and suffixes, are found in the English language (e.g., *de*—down, *dis*—away, *com*—together, *post*—after, *pre*—before, *inter*—between; see also Thompson, 1998, an excellent source for improving vocabulary through decoding Latin and Greek stem words in English). My students enjoy creating new words using Latin and Greek stem words, and then adding them to their stories. (For example, my eighth-grade students created the word *Megathermagyn*: *Mega* meaning large, *therma* meaning heat, and *gyn* meaning woman). In fact, William Shakespeare is said to have created 2,000 words now used in English and he "used nouns as verbs, as adverbs, as substantives, and as adjectives—often in ways they had never been employed before" (Bryson, 1990, p. 64). Teaching students to create images by using adverbs as adjectives or adding new suffixes or prefixes allows them to draw on their creativity as they realize the open flexibility found in the English language.

FURTHER ELABORATION (OPTIONAL)

I have ended this unit with a theme dinner, which is similar to a Renaissance fair: students present their stories, fictional or factual, as plays; share artwork they created; wear Roman costumes; and prepare and eat authentic Roman food in the manner of the ancient times. (See chapter 4 for a discussion of formats for preparing literacy celebrations such as the Roman theme dinner.)

Engaging and extending writers can choose to explore whether or not such an occurrence could happen in the wild and write about it using the model of the Guinea Pig Paper (see Appendix C).

EVALUATION

Use the Beginning Writer Rubric (see Appendix A).

PLOT SCAFFOLD FOR "TYRANT?"

"Tyrant?" (see Appendix B), based on the assassination of Julius Caesar, can be used to explore issues in history or political science. It also can be used as an introduction to Shakespeare's *Julius Caesar* (1994c). Often, students are intimidated by Shakespeare's language (although teachers may view the language as a series of excellent, descriptive images). However, I have found that knowing the text-explicit plots of his stories can make students more comfortable looking for text-implicit messages. Text-explicit messages are facts stated directly in the text. Text-implicit messages are implied by the writer and not stated directly. By presenting Shakespeare's plays as plot scaffolds and helping students recognize their plots on a text-explicit level, engaging and extending writers are able to create their own plays using Shakespeare's plays as scaffolds.

The format of this lesson is similar to the lesson for "Wolf Kids"; teachers can choose to focus on historical fiction or narratives with alternative endings.

LEARNING OBJECTIVES

"Tyrant?" is appropriate for engaging and extending writers. Engaging writers work on effective language use to persuade readers into believing their viewpoint: Either Julius Caesar was a dangerous tyrant about to destroy citizens' personal freedoms, or he was a reformer, attempting to reorganize an ineffective Roman government. Extending writers may take the question a step further and compare the issues in "Tyrant?" with current political trends. Does history repeat itself?

Factual Use of the Scaffold: If the objective is to have students write a story with an ending based on actual facts about Julius Caesar, the teacher should have students research the end of the story (after determining students' prior knowledge), or the teacher can simply explain how Caesar was assassinated by his friend, Brutus, and a mob of senators on the Senate steps in Rome. This ending is not included in the scaffold. Hand out copies of the plot scaffold, have students take parts, read it aloud, and then discuss the events surrounding Caesar's death as it really happened.

Teachers may also choose to have students create an ending that would be relevant to today's political and social system. What would happen if a U.S. president acted like Julius Caesar? Would the senators kill him? Would he be impeached? How is assassination viewed today compared to ancient Rome? Was Abraham Lincoln or John F. Kennedy assassinated for the same reasons as Julius Caesar? How is the Roman Republic similar to the republic in the United States? Backfill in this story is very important for understanding character motivation and story line. How the writer presents backfill in "Tyrant?" may persuade the reader whether to believe Julius Caesar was a possible dictator, a concerned citizen trying to save Rome, or both. Shakespeare's *Julius Caesar* presents a similar plot.

Narrative Use of the Scaffold: If the objective is to have students create new stories, teachers hand out copies of the scaffold, assign roles, and read aloud the scaffold, but do not supply the factual ending to the legend. Instead, students can create their own endings based on what they think might have happened when Caesar went to the Roman Senate. Students can explore alternative endings to the story by answering the following constructed-response questions:

- What happens when people get too greedy?
- When might a best friend betray you?
- Will Caesar take care of Cleopatra?
- How will Caesar's wife, Calpurnia, react to Cleopatra?

PROCEDURE

STEP 1

Determining Prior Knowledge

Discuss the following plot questions:

- What if your country is doing very well and the current leader has solved many economic problems?
- What if the catch is that the leader may enjoy the power, become the sole ruler of the country for life, and take away certain civil rights, like voting for representatives?
- What should the citizens do?

STEP 2

Acting Out the Plot Scaffold

Have students choose parts and act out the scaffold, which usually makes the story easier to understand. I have found that having students act out or watch Shakespearean plays rather than simply read them makes it easier for students to understand the story. Reading a play script can often be flat and lifeless unless it is acted out (because it is not written as a novel, the characters are not "dressed" and readers are not "told" how characters are speaking).

STEP 3

Completing the Plot Scaffold

Students complete the plot scaffold by adding dialogue and images. How to complete the scaffold depends on teachers' individual instructional goals. Writing across the curriculum is a current goal in many schools, and this scaffold can provide a means of meeting the goal of crossing language arts into social studies; thus, students would write a historical piece. Or teachers can choose to have students write an alternative ending to "Tyrant?" or change the viewpoint of the story. Could this story be told from another character's viewpoint? What would the story be like if Cleopatra or Brutus were telling it? Because of the numerous characters within the scaffold, students may choose to write in the first person from any character's viewpoint. For either option, check completed scaffolds and have students exchange stories as well.

STEP 4

Adding Effective Dialogue

Review with students how to write the dialogue for the story by adding costumes and movement to the characters. Remind students that the characters cannot be "seen" in written text, so they should include any movement the characters might make that clarifies their motivation or intent. Also, students may wish to incorporate words that pertain to the dialogue such as *replied*, *muttered*, or *ordered* next to characters' names on the scaffold. Notes regarding to whom the character is speaking or any facial expressions can also be made on the scaffold itself. This saves time when students write their first drafts. Also remember that characters should be wearing ancient Roman costumes if the story is going to be historically accurate. Review rules of punctuation for dialogue as well.

Effective dialogue also should help to make the seven plot elements (see pages 13–14) more vivid. For example, during the dark moment, the main character should react and speak as if this were the most desperate time in the story:

> Walking confidently up the senate steps, Caesar appeared unaware of the grave danger about to explode. Calmly he remarked, "My fellow Romans, Greetings. I know you are pleased to see me today, and I am so happy to be with you."
>
> Like a snake about to strike, yet keeping the crowd of Senators near him like a shield, Casca moved cautiously toward Caesar, " I don't think you will be pleased today, but Rome will be happier once we are finished with the task at hand."

STEP 5

Expanding the Plot Scaffold

Students use their plot scaffolds to write their first drafts. The historical setting is important to this story, and images should portray ancient Rome. Images, which help set the tone or mood of a story, should help support character motivation. For example, in Shakespeare's *Julius Caesar*, the characters describe a horrific storm that takes place during Caesar's assassination. As a reflection of people's deeds, the weather acts as a character in the story, and students can choose to personify the weather in their versions of "Tyrant?"

Next, teachers should check students' first drafts for correct grammar and to ensure that the plot makes sense. Students also should include the seven elements of plot and identify and list each element on their rough drafts. Students should make any needed corrections and write the final draft.

FURTHER ELABORATION (OPTIONAL)

Students can perform this plot scaffold as a play.

EVALUATION

Use the Intermediate Writer Rubric (see Appendix A).

How to Write Plot Scaffolds Based on Existing Literature

For me, writing plot scaffolds based on current literature began as a way to match classic literature to the reading level of the class I was teaching. It was also a practical way to overcome the obstacle of having appropriate resources for my students. For example, one school year I had 30 students, one textbook, and no money in the budget for more books. Because reading aloud the textbook was going to take too long to be efficient, I used the plot scaffold as a time-management strategy.

In addition, plot scaffolds can even be created based on picture books. Often the plots within picture books like *The Polar Express* (Van Allsburg, 1985) or *Crocodile, Crocodile* (Nickl & Schroeder, 1976) can be used and expanded on by beginning or intermediate writers. Having pictures helps writers see the images for the story. Using drawings and photographs in picture books to illustrate stories is also a primary literacy strategy that helps students understand how mental images are created in the reader's mind. This is an especially helpful strategy in kindergarten and first grade, when students are still learning handwriting and moving toward creating print. Kindergarten and first-grade students can also draw a picture to illustrate their images and stories.

For example, a teacher might use the picture book *Working Cotton* (Williams, 1992), write the beginning lines, and have students complete the rest. The plot scaffold might read as follows:

Daddy: Shelan, time to wake up. Time to work.

Shelan: But Daddy, the sun's not up.

Daddy: I know. We gotta start working.

Shelan: (What would you say?) _____

Daddy: (What would you say?) _____

Teachers can choose to include Shelan's family members and, to accommodate bigger classes, incorporate the other field laborers as characters. Then, teachers could create dialogue for these characters—for example, they could talk with Shelan's family or they might create a song to sing while they work. Then, as students work on creating stories based on the scaffold, teachers and students together can compare the workings of cotton fields a century ago with today. Students can build images in the story using the information that they discover about this time period and the African Americans who worked the cotton fields. In addition, students can study the music and dance of the time and incorporate this into stories or performances based on their plot scaffolds.

Through these efforts, writing and its connection to students' lives becomes rich, complex, and multidimensional. When plot scaffolding is used as a way for students to understand the essential elements of story—character, setting, motivation—it also becomes a vehicle for them to understand the essential elements of living. Fictional stories often are a reflection of incidents that occur in real life. As students experience the events in stories, they may find solutions to problems or events in their own lives. With a caring and thoughtful facilitator, students can participate in the drama of other people's lives, opening doors for new conversations that may lead to deeper understandings.

Chapter 4 explores how to open larger doors and include more participants in the conversation. In this next chapter, we will look at how plot scaffolds can be used to meet the demands of standardized testing and the current call for more performance-based assessment.

CHAPTER 4

Building on the Plot Scaffold Strategy

any educators are familiar with the saying that the educational "pendulum" seems to swing back and forth. That is, educational programs go back and forth in their approaches to learning. For example, at one time phonics programs, with their emphasis on skill and drill, seemed to have been the most popular method for teaching reading and were regarded as "the way" to teach reading until researchers like Goodman (1996) expanded the term *reading* to include using cues from text.

> As readers use cues from the linguistic text, they bring their knowledge and beliefs about the world to bear on making sense. They "guess" what's coming, making predictions and inferences; they are selective about use of text cues and they monitor their "guesses" for contradictory cues. Effective reading, then, is not accurate word recognition; it is getting to meaning. And efficient reading is using just enough of the available cues, given what a reader brings to the reading, to make sense of text. (pp. 7–8)

Then, the whole language approach, with its emphasis on meaning rather than decoding, found favor among educators, and skill and drill was enhanced to include constructive strategies to aid in comprehension.

Currently, however, standardized tests emphasize selected and constructed responses while national standards include performance-based tasks and informal assessment. Thus, the pendulum seems to be swinging from side to side. How can teachers plan for standardized tests and still include performance-based tasks? How can teachers cover "both sides" of curriculum demands?

I believe that the demands can be met by realizing that both sides are valid. Why can't reading be taught using whole language *and* phonics? Why do educators have to choose one way or the other? Consequently, this chapter illustrates how plot scaffolds can work to meet both standardized test needs and performance needs. I present evidence to prove that plot scaffolds can be used to raise students' standardized test scores and as an effective performance-based assessment.

In chapters 2 and 3, I have presented the lessons for using plot scaffolds and strategies for writing. In this chapter, I expand on the strategy by explaining how ideas found within the scaffolds can be used to create a schoolwide writing mentor program designed to raise standardized writing scores.

Dealing With Current Educational Issues

In light of high-stakes testing and the No Child Left Behind Act of 2001 (2002), many schools feel pressured to meet legislative demands and close the reading and writing achievement gap—that is, raise test scores. In some schools, such as my own Title I school, this gap may appear wider, but creative strategies that are cost and time efficient may be the solution. Modifying and expanding my plot scaffold writing strategies can help to foster students' creativity and provide a means to raise standardized reading and writing test scores. When it comes to successful reading and writing test scores, the key may lie in creativity rather than skill and drill (Fisher & Frey, 2003). Fisher and Frey (2003) confirm findings that students today are given more writing assignments, mostly in the form of independent writing prompts, and then teachers evaluate the writing prompts, but writing scores haven't changed as a result. However, Fisher and Frey's studies found that achievement gains were noted when students were asked to refine their writing over several drafts. When writing instruction included more creative strategies, such as interactive and generative models, struggling students made greater gains. Research shows that progress was made toward closing the achievement for poor or minority students "usually through pull-out programs characterized by drill and practice with a paraprofessional" (Haycock, 2001, p. 11). However, this approach reached its potential to raise test scores in the early 1980s, so now most of the remaining achievement gaps are found when students must apply basic skills to higher-level problems, such as analyzing texts: "These higher order abilities aren't simply amenable to improvement through drill under the direction of a paraprofessional, especially for those students who are struggling anyway" (Haycock, 2001, p. 11). We need to bolster the skills of classroom teachers to raise the level of challenge in regular classrooms while supporting their efforts toward providing for diverse students.

In addition, because schools are being held accountable for mandated tests such as state writing assessments, responsibility for these tests rests on the entire faculty, not just language arts teachers. Teaching writing skills must be a collaborative effort. For those schools with large minority populations or economically disadvantaged students, the achievement gap may seem to be an insurmountable obstacle unless teachers, students, and administrators work together. Literacy needs to be a schoolwide effort and not restricted to language arts classrooms. For example, in my school the focus was on making all teachers aware of how good writing works, and they were put in situations in which they taught small groups and did not have to give grades. In reality, a standardized writing test was used to help encourage all teachers to become teachers of writing.

Developing a Schoolwide Writing Mentor Program

Currently, in the state in which I teach, students take the state writing test in third, fifth, eighth, and eleventh grade. The middle school where I taught typically receives incoming sixth graders who are at a third- or fourth-grade level in writing ability. Because these students must leave the middle school writing at the eighth-grade level, in order to close the achievement gap, students will have to progress five years instead of three years in their writing ability growth. These students must be at grade level in order to achieve in high school, because of the high probability that they will not do well if they lack proficient literary skills (Fisher & Frey, 2003). As cited in several studies (Bean, 2002; Dreher, 2003; Stewart, Paradis, & Ross, 1996), children who have not developed proficient literacy skills by approximately 9 years old are highly likely to struggle with reading throughout their educational career and perhaps for the rest of their lives (National Assessment of Educational Progress [NAEP], 2003). By its very nature, middle school bridges the gap between elementary and high school because high school readers are expected to be able to acquire information through textbooks and other reading materials. If these students leave elementary school reading below grade level, then how can they be expected to comprehend information found in higher level textbooks that typically focus on content areas?

Data from NAEP (2003) also indicate that

- nearly 60% of adolescents can comprehend specific factual information (which means 40% cannot), yet less than 5% of those adolescents are able to extend or elaborate the meaning of the materials they read.

- the proportion of fourth graders reaching the basic achievement level rose from 84% in 1998 to 86% in 2002. The proportion reaching the proficient level rose from 23% to 28%. The average score increased from 150 to 154 (the NAEP writing scale for each grade ranges from 0 to 300 points, with the average score set at 150 in 1998).

- the percentage of eighth graders reaching basic achievement was virtually unchanged at 85%, while the proportion at or above proficient increased from 27% to 31%. The average score climbed from 150 in 1998 to 153 in 2002.

- the percentage of 12th graders reaching basic achievement fell to 74%, compared to 78% in 1998. The proportion reaching proficient was virtually unchanged at 24%, while the average score of 148 showed no significant change.

Adolescents could write effectively with sufficient detail to support main points. However, "Instruction for adolescents typically focuses on teaching content, science, math, literature, etc.—and does not focus on teaching students how to read and write effectively" (NAEP, 2003, n.p.).

In an effort to close the literacy gap, the middle school developed a writing mentor program, an effort to focus on collaboration and team effort, in which every teacher, despite their area of expertise, met with 5 eighth-grade students to help tutor them in writing skills. This program—which my principal was instrumental in facilitating—focused on using students' natural strengths rather than imposed, teacher-driven expectations. However, many teachers felt out of their element and were anxious about having to teach writing to eighth graders, especially the math, science, and physical education teachers. If teachers were uncomfortable, how could they effectively help students? However, I saw this situation as an opportunity to help teachers feel both relief and confidence about teaching writing by giving them short, useful strategies to teach small groups of writers. Teaching the strategies to the small groups enabled teachers to practice specific writing strategies before presenting them in their own classrooms and determine if a strategy was useful.

After reviewing the district's scores for the state mandated writing test, I realized that 70% of the scoring rested on content and style. Only 30% of the test was on mechanics. Traditionally, however, the district had emphasized helping poor writers learn to write by focusing on writing grammatically correct sentences. Based on my experience working with gifted learners and ESL students, I felt it would be better to help all writers learn to write using their creative strengths. Standardized tests could, in fact, be used as a vehicle for allowing students "voice." Giving students voice is like giving them what Heathcote refers to as the "mantle of the expert," a key to success (Heathcote & Herbert, 1985). Allowing students to tell their own stories makes for more creative writing, and allowing students to bring their own diverse experiences to their writing helps give the task meaning (Hiebert, 1991). Thus, we could use students' creativity, which raises students' higher level thinking (Gardner, 1990; Sternberg, 1997), to improve their writing scores. Because teaching students to think creatively and communicate clearly is universal to all academic subjects, the reluctant teachers I mentioned earlier, who did not feel prepared to teaching writing, had an active interest in learning to improve students' writing skills.

Effectively Managing Time

Because time is often the most important factor in determining whether or not a teacher will use a program, I convinced the administration to reduce the number of mandated meetings between the mentor and mentees, or teachers and students, from nine to five. The meetings were to be only 15 to 20 minutes and take place during each teacher's planning period on predetermined dates. Before streamlining the meetings, they had occurred randomly whenever teachers could grab enough spare time to meet with their writing mentees. However, I believe that knowing when something is expected and being able to plan for it are crucial to implementing a program effectively.

Prior to each scheduled meeting between mentors and mentees, I give the teachers a brief, 10-minute presentation of a creative writing strategy that they can present to their mentees. The program did not include hour-long, after-school inservice training sessions, which I feel often create passive resistance on the part of teachers because of limited free time and attempting to balance home life and school life (Robbins & Alvy, 2003). The program attempts to avoid teacher burnout, which can occur when the stress of having to do yet "one more thing" becomes a perceived reality. Just a brief "how to" with a hook was the format of these five presentations, which were then incorporated as part of a regular faculty meeting agenda. The presentations were always scheduled on faculty meeting days that occurred just before a writing mentor meeting day so the strategies would be fresh in teachers' minds.

Over the course of three months and prior to the writing test, each teacher is given handouts (see Appendix D) that cover four different writing strategies; these strategies are based on those used with plot scaffolds. The handouts give a brief description of the goals to accomplish in each 20-minute meeting between mentors and mentees and should be presented in sequential order. They can be adapted to meet the needs of standardized test requirements. For example, if the standardized writing test requires students to write in a persuasive rather than narrative format, the writing mentor meeting objectives could be changed to meet the new demand. The teachers used their planning time to meet with students. In addition, students were made aware of when and where they were expected to meet their mentors.

Overview of the Meetings

Of the five meetings, meeting one is designed to inform students how they will be evaluated and how to use a simple scaffold, such as a graphic organizer, to help focus and direct their writing. Because most standardized tests are timed, organization is a key factor in helping emerging, developing, and focusing writers stay on task and have a clear plan for writing. Meeting two is designed to make students aware of how to use images in their writing to give the reader a clear picture of their feelings and ideas. Writing images in standardized tests is often regarded as a higher-level skill, but beginning writers also can learn to include images. Meeting three emphasizes teaching writers to vary word choice and sentence structure. Thus, the meeting focuses on the strategy of "flipping" sentences in order to avoid "dull" and common sentences. Also, students use the Fred and Mary strategy (see page 18) to create dialogue and "dress" the characters they use. Meeting four, the last meeting before the standardized test, is designed to emphasize the appearance of students' written work (which I relate to an enticingly wrapped present under the Christmas tree). Presentation is an important part of showcasing students' work. Finally, meeting five is a time for teachers to share test scores with students and celebrate their success.

The Results

Using plot scaffolding techniques on standardized writing tests has resulted in a rise in writing test scores in the middle school where I taught. Figure 8 shows the tests results for the last six years. The 1999–2000 scores reflect the period prior to implementing the writing mentor program. In 2002–2003, scores at the top level increased from 12% to 26%. The low level decreased from 4% to 0%. Based on these results, all students were writing at or above grade level—a reason for celebration at the school. Thus, the plot scaffold approach to teaching writing content and style had "standardized test" validity. In 2003–2004, the school's writing score was 92% with 74% on target and 18% exceeding target. Although not at 100% for 2004, the score still exceeded the state's average, and the scores for style and content/organization continued to be almost twice as high when compared with some of the more economically affluent schools in the district. It should be noted again that style and content/organization scores equal 70% of this standardized testing instrument.

Since the writing mentor program was implemented in the middle school in 1999, each year the student population is reviewed to target students' needs for the upcoming school year and make slight "tweaks" in the program. This same process should be used in every school that chooses to adopt this program: Look at the writing

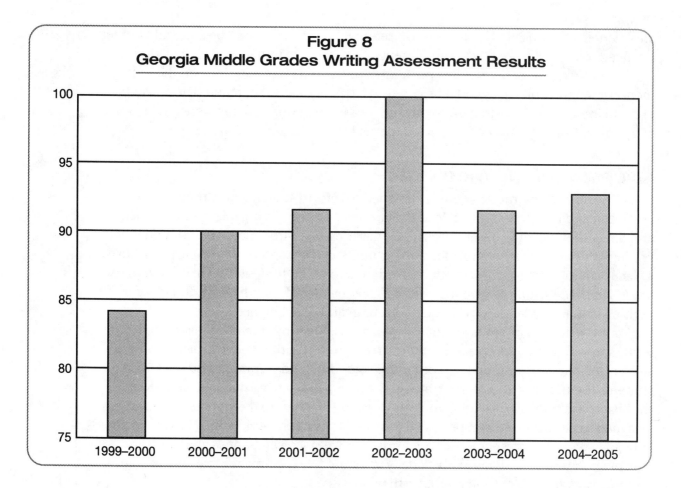

Figure 8
Georgia Middle Grades Writing Assessment Results

test scores for your school, see where students need work, and go for the higher-level thinking strategies that enable a student to use creativity. It is important that educators do not wait until students are in the eighth grade to prepare them for standardized writing tests. The schoolwide writing test practices in the school also include the sixth and seventh graders because it gives them an opportunity to practice for the test and makes all teachers aware of what their mentees are going to need to know. In addition, the writing mentor program can be adapted for elementary-age students as well. Implementation for elementary students is not that different. Five writing mentor meetings occur prior to a standardized writing test, like the Georgia Fifth Grade State Writing Assessment. All elementary teachers and administrators at the school are involved in mentoring small groups of students. This is very beneficial for K–4 teachers because it gives them a better understanding of what they need to do in their own grade levels to prepare students for becoming competent writers when they leave elementary school. Teachers are made more aware of the standards fifth graders have to meet. Because all elementary school teachers are responsible for teaching language arts, the writing strategies they learn during the presentations can have a direct effect on all grade levels, not just fifth grade.

Strategies chosen for specific presentations can also be incorporated into monthly creative writing projects. For example, while learning to write images, all of the students at the elementary school wrote stories about taking a monster to lunch. They wrote stories using the inquiry approach:

- What if I took a monster to lunch?
- What would be the catch? (The monster might eat the table, might have bad manners, and so forth.)
- What happens then?

Although each year teacher attrition is a factor at the middle school, the writing program has continued to do well. This may be because the program emphasizes students' creativity rather than individual teacher's experience in teaching writing. The program relies on all teachers, regardless of area of expertise, becoming facilitators of writing. The ratio of mentor to mentee (1 to 5) also provides the adult attention each student needs. Students are often placed with a teacher who is not their regular classroom instructor but who fits their particular individual needs or personality. Every member of the school staff takes the role of a writing coach in a team effort to help close the achievement gap in literacy. Teacher encouragement and attention play a large factor in students wanting to do well on the test. The writing strategies used are not graded exercises but are viewed by students and teachers as techniques to help them write creatively and showcase their unique abilities to test evaluators. Further, these strategies, which are new to teachers outside of language arts, allow teachers to feel comfortable. Teachers also can enjoy being the facilitator rather than the evaluator, which reduces teachers' and students' stress.

Further, with the current slating for the addition of an essay to the SAT, these same plot scaffold writing strategies that are practiced in middle school also can be used in high school. In the writing section, students must clearly show appropriate examples to support their ideas. Appropriate examples can be in the form of an image, which students have learned to create to engage the pathos of the reader. Students must also "display consistent facility in the use of language, demonstrating variety in sentence structure and range of vocabulary" (College Entrance Examination Board, 2003, p. 10). Students can demonstrate these skills by flipping sentences and using vivid, interesting language—two strategies that will show students' creativity. In addition, writing personal narratives allows students to use their voices. Finally, in order to obtain a high score on the SAT writing component, students will be required to "effectively" and "insightfully" address the writing task (College Entrance Examination Board, 2003, p. 10). *Insightfully* implies higher-level thinking, or what I refer to as impressionistic literacy.

Impressionistic literacy is a term I created to describe how scaffolding works. In his last years, Monet spent his time painting reflections of the sky upon lily pools in his gardens at Giverny, France. His original idea was to capture impressions of color and light, and he elaborated on this concept, painting over 260 pictures of the same pools at different times. Some paintings depict life-sized water lilies floating on the transparent surface of the water, without showing the pond's banks or horizon line. Only the reflections of trees along the banks and sky above provide reference to anything beyond; yet, with each repetition, his work reflects the fluid enmeshing of design and impression such that we immediately accept that the horizontal surface of the pond is shown on the vertical plane of canvas. Reflecting their ideas through color and texture, impressionistic artists seek to capture and record on canvas their feelings of an event, time, or person. Like Monet's canvas, plot scaffolds are the palettes for teachers to draw on as they capture impressions of literacy. Using the broad questions and situations within each scaffold, teachers can help to create an impression of current student thought as they express their meanings dependent on present knowledge and developed by prediction, empathy, voice, imagination, and reflection. The plot scaffolds are constantly changing through rehearsal and rewrite. Like Monet's many views of the same pond, each reflects different concepts. Teachers, using this sociocognitive interactive model, can become constructive artists of knowledge, playing with combinations of the many diverse ideas learners bring as they seek to elaborate shared meaning. The unique blend of creative drama and writing of scaffolds produces impressionistic literacy.

Perhaps, in a sense, impressionistic literacy might be a move toward a return to myth. Myth as in *muthos* refers to an oral tradition in which there is a speaker and listener or two participants telling a story. In the case of impressionistic literacy, the writer is allowed to tell his or her "own" story, and what makes the storytelling so powerful is the intimate relationship that occurs when one person speaks to another about what he or she feels or has experienced. Telling stories keeps cultures alive. King Arthur realizes this when at the end of *Camelot* (Logan, 1967), he tells the boy, Thomas, to run behind the lines to safety so that he may "tell" later generations that there once was an ideal called Camelot. Thus, allowing students to tell their own stories on standardized writing tests gives voice to the "muthos" found in all students regardless of race, gender, or culture. Closing the reading and writing achievement gap means more than raising standardized test scores. It means realizing there are no gaps between peoples' abilities when tests become literacy windows for viewing each other's rich cultural heritage or human experience.

Cross-Curricular Literacy Celebrations

An optional strategy listed at the end of most plot scaffold lessons involves turning the scaffold into a play and acting it out. With emphases on standardized tests and meeting AYP (adequate yearly progress), classes like art, music, and physical education may fall through the cracks in terms of educational priority. However, the fine arts do improve academic scores (Sweet, 2005) and help meet the needs of diverse learners. Perhaps *optional* is not the appropriate word when discussing teaching the fine arts as a literacy strategy. Within current national standards, performance-based assessment has become a necessity. Students must be able to "show" what they have learned. According to McTighe (1996), "Performance assessments are better suited than traditional tests to measure what really counts: whether students can apply their knowledge, skills, and understanding in important, real-world contexts" (p. 6). Performance-based assessments are part of a final evaluation that needs to use multiple types of assessment because not only does multiple assessment provide more data on student achievement but also it can help "to mitigate a disturbing trend—the tendency to fixate on 'test preparation' as a way of increasing test scores" (McTighe, 2000, p. 5). Therefore, we need to teach in rich, meaningful, engaging ways.

Several teachers who used the plot scaffold lessons reported being very surprised to find one or two students who normally did not participate in writing activities suddenly begin to put forth effort and succeed when they treated the stories as plays. For example, one middle school teacher found that one of her students who was failing her language arts class, and other classes as well, gave the best performance of Cleopatra that she had ever seen. The student did not like to write and would not complete language arts assignments, but the hands-on, creative drama motivated her, and she even performed at the Roman theme banquet. When students acted out the "Tyrant?" plot scaffold, the teacher began to look at this student's literacy in a different way. The student was able to construct a very convincing portrayal of Cleopatra and her intentions and motivations. The teacher stated,

> I think it's drama. She comes to me after class and says, "I think someone should do this." I think she really likes drama; it appeals to her because the drama is the difference between this and simply reading for information. She's good, she's really good.

Several teachers also reported that previously unorganized, unmotivated students, who had not been producing work in class, suddenly started to either perform well as an actor or actress or simply "take over" the class project and start writing the plot scaffold. These teachers were able to broaden their views of literacy as well as recognize the diversity of learning styles that exists in students and encourage, support, and reward their contributions.

There is much support for including the fine arts in writing instruction. Writing is one of several available communication systems (art, music, mathematics, and so forth). However, several sign systems can be used to support emergent literacy—for example, when students use drawing, gesture, or talk to add depth and meaning to their writing. The integration of the fine arts (e.g., drama, drawing) in schools has the potential to enhance and support young students' writing. As a result of expressing in writing ideas such as those generated in drama and drawing, the unique features of drama's immediacy or drawing's visual components may enrich writing. "Features such as these may be particularly relevant to narrative writing, which relies for its success upon creating and manipulating an imaginary world" (Moore & Caldwell, 1993, p. 101).

Using drama as a broad, schoolwide literary strategy has the potential to help all students experience success and honor each student's abilities. Actually, turning the scaffolds into plays can make literacy the focus of cross-curricular theme units. Throughout my teaching career, I have continued not only to use plot scaffolding in my own classroom but also to include other teachers and the community in my efforts to promote a broader meaning of literacy. In an effort to increase the use of plot scaffolding and drama as a literacy strategy, over the past 12 years I have designed and developed an annual thematic dinner theater in which students perform their plays. I not only want my students to write and perform plays, but I also want them to truly inquire, using hands-on methods, into the life and times of writers and historical figures. Students read classic literary works, such as *Hard Times* (Dickens, 1854/1981), *True Grit*

(Portis, 1969), and *Romeo and Juliet* (Shakespeare, 1994e), and then study the costumes, history, art, music, and ideas of that time period. This inquiry culminates in a banquet, at which food, social customs, dress, entertainment, art, and music are presented in a shared atmosphere between students from different schools, their families, administration, and the community. Such themed dinner theaters have included celebrations of Charles Dickens, Leonardo da Vinci, the Middle Ages, the Roman Empire, Sinbad's Middle East, the U.S. Old West, the U.S. Roaring '20s, and even outer space. As a way to diminish barriers between parents, students, and myself, I held these events in my own home until the attendance became too large. Table 3 lists helpful tips for a successful performance task, a thematic dinner theater celebration; Figure 9 presents a letter template that can be used in conjunction with the dinner theater celebrations.

Table 3
Tips for Thematic Dinner Theater Celebrations

1. Plan ahead. During the second week of school, I have students choose a theme based on a time period (e.g., ancient Rome), and we vote on which one we think will work best in terms of resources and student motivation and interest. We also choose a date to hold the event so it does not conflict with sporting events, holidays, or other commitments. Significant student and parent participation is important to making the celebration reach its full potential as a collaborative experience. (Based on my experience, the weekend before Thanksgiving has always been a good time because it is prior to holiday commitments and does not overlap with many sporting events.)

2. Find stories that deal with the theme that may be read, acted out, or illustrated. Write plot scaffolds for your students to use based on the theme. Assign students to research the time period including art, music, costumes, entertainment, and food. Try to choose a time period that requires simple costumes to re-create so everyone may easily participate. As far as food is concerned, I advise my students not to make anything that they would not eat themselves.

3. Do not do this alone. Enlist the help of parents and other teachers and collaborate.

4. Get a head count. Send home a note early and find out who is coming. Figure 9 is an example of a letter that I used; feel free to use this letter as a template for creating your own letter.

5. Either pass out recipes the week before the celebration or review the recipes students have chosen. (I also find it helpful to have dishes brought to the dinner in disposable containers so nothing is lost or broken.)

6. Make simple yet large decorations for the event. For example, for a celebration that focused on The Lord of the Rings triology, we simply gathered large fall leaves, covered them lightly in gold glitter, and hung them in long strands from the ceiling in the cafeteria. Recalling images like those used for heraldry, small groups of students also made large banners with animals and symbols chosen to represent them. The banners were images for their values, ideas, feelings, or personal characteristics. (One student remarked that the cafeteria looked a bit like Hogwarts' main hall from the Harry Potter series.)

7. Set up the dinner, decorations, plates, and so forth the day before the event.

8. Have some sort of entertainment in the form of a play, dance, or games that fits the theme.

9. Call the local media. I have found the local newspapers are supportive about featuring community events. Thematic dinners and performances are a good way to publicize student achievement.

  Strategies contained within plot scaffold minilessons can be used as a basis for either cross-curricular literacy celebrations or to build writing mentor programs. For writing mentor programs, it beneficial to include strategies such as image and dialogue writing. Writing mentor programs have the potential to benefit small groups of students by providing them with more individualized instruction and can serve as practice grounds for teachers so they may hone new skills. Cross-curricular literacy celebrations are collaborative, performance-based assessments; they have the ability to get students, parents, teachers, administrators, and the community involved. Thus, the elaboration, originality, flexibility, and fluency contained within plot scaffolds infuse learning and make literacy an active process of sharing ideas.

CONCLUSION

Plot scaffolding is not just about creating new stories; it is about how the experiences connect to our own lives—and teachers are not immune to the transactional processes that occur when they share stories with their students. In fact, I believe these processes have the potential to make us feel more fulfilled and rewarded as teachers.

Although I have taught for more than 20 years, my most rewarding experience as a classroom teacher came in the second year of teaching. It was a spring afternoon, just after lunch, and I was teaching third grade in an inner-city Catholic school with predominantly African American students. I was reading aloud *Pippi Longstocking* (Lindgren, 1957) to my students. After I had finished, one of my students—a handsome boy, the acknowledged leader of the class—raised his hand. When I called on him, he said with great conviction, "You are Pippi Longstocking." Giving agreement to the leader's statement, the whole class of 30 looked on with a quiet, firm stance. As if they were one unified front, I remember all those eyes filled with a knowing satisfaction.

I recall feeling amused by the boy's statement, thinking his analogy had to do with the color of my hair, but later in the day when my students left, I looked about the classroom and realized what the class meant. Surveying the room with its giant paper daffodils, western civilization timeline, play scenery from a student-written melodrama, and other creative projects, I saw the magic. I really was like Pippi, the strongest girl in the world, and my classroom was evidence of the adventures my students and I were having.

Students empower teachers to reach goals as much as we empower students to realize their potential. The adventures have never stopped. Even many years later, when I was feeling overwhelmed by being a single mother raising two children, working full time as a teacher and graduate student, working part time at Home Depot, and driving home late at night thinking, How can I do all this? I remember the boy's words about being Pippi Longstocking, and I no longer doubt myself. I become the strongest girl in the world.

Teaching is magic, and the spells go both ways. Whether you enable students to act out the characters in a story through plot scaffolds or students bring that character to life in you, the process is still a powerful transaction or "spell" between student, text, and teacher. The history of the Old English word *spell* meant simply to recite a story or tale, but as the Roman alphabet spread throughout Europe, *spell* took on a double meaning: On one hand, it meant to arrange, in the proper order, the written letters that constituted the name of a thing or person, and on the other, it signified a magic formula or charm (Abram, 1997). To assemble the letters in the correct order was to effect a magic, to establish a new kind of influence over something, and to call it forth: "To spell, to correctly arrange the letters to form a name or a phrase, seemed thus at the same time to cast a spell, to exert a new and lasting power over the things spelled" (Abram, 1997, p. 133).

As a teacher, you realize that learning to spell, to use writing, is a way to help students unleash the magic in literacy. With its blend of oral tradition, play, and language arts skills, it is my hope that *Setting the Stage for Creative Writing: Plot Scaffolds for Beginning and Intermediate Writers* will enable you and your students to refine the magic of the written word.

Plot Scaffold Learning Objectives and Rubrics

Plot scaffold learning objectives and rubrics are based on the writer's level of competency, not the student's grade level. Throughout this book, writers have been categorized according to developmental stages. These stages can be found on many current state testing criteria, such as the Georgia Writing Assessment (Georgia Department of Education, 2004a, 2004b), which was the basis for the stages in this book.

The learning objectives have been designed according to national standards for language arts. Learning objectives may be used interchangeably with many of the scaffolds because teachers may have a variety of writing abilities within a specific class. The learning objectives not only cover writing but also listening, speaking, and reading because the scaffolds involve all four components.

Emerging writers typically are in the first grade. Developing writers typically are in second or third grade and have some practice with the writing process. Focusing writers usually are in third and fourth grade because they have enough tools at this point to write stories and pay more attention to surface features such as grammar. Likewise, a fifth- or sixth-grade writer would be experimenting more with style, while a seventh-grade writer may be using that style to engage the reader. Eighth-grade writers should be extending their narrative writing skills, so by high school they are well prepared for persuasive writing, the focus of most high school curriculums as well as the SAT's new essay component.

Learning Objectives for Beginning and Intermediate Writers

	Listening/Speaking	Writing	Reading

Emerging Writer	• Adapts or changes oral language to fit the situation by following the rules of conversation with peers and adults.
	• Listens to a variety of literary forms including plays, stories, songs, movies, videos, and so forth.
	• Follows two- and three-part oral directions.
	• Recalls information presented orally.
	• Interprets the meaning of a question in order to give an appropriate response.
	• Communicates effectively when using descriptive language; relating experiences; and retelling stories read, heard, or viewed.
		• Uses examples from literature to create individual and group stories.
		• Uses correct spelling for frequently used sight vocabulary.
		• Communicates ideas by using the writing process:
		  Prewriting—Generates ideas.
		  Drafting—Focuses on topic; uses prewriting ideas to complete first draft.
		  Revising—Expands use of descriptive words.
		  Editing—Begins each sentence and proper noun with capital letter and uses correct spelling, appropriate punctuation, and complete sentences.
		  Publishing—Shares writing with others.
			• Increases vocabulary to reflect a growing range of interests and knowledge.
			• Uses word order and sentence structure to read.
			• Increases sight vocabulary (instant recognition).
			• Reads with fluency and expression.
			• Recognizes EXPLICIT main ideas, details, sequence of events, and cause–effect relationships in fiction.
			• Recognizes IMPLICIT main ideas, details, sequence of events, and cause–effect relationships in fiction.
			• Identifies main characters.
			• Identifies characters' actions, motives, emotions, traits, and feelings.
			• Draws conclusions and makes predictions and comparisons.
			• Demonstrates comprehension when reading a variety of literary forms including drama.

Developing Writer	• Follows oral directions and works collaboratively with others. • Recalls and interprets information presented orally. • Uses oral language to inform, to persuade, and to entertain. • Uses a variety of language patterns and sentence structures. • Uses increasingly complex sentence structures in oral communication.	• No changes.	• No changes.

(continued)

Adapted from the Georgia English/Language Arts Performance Standards (2004a).
Each stage builds on the previous stage and includes objectives for the previous stages. Only additions to each stage are noted after the Emerging Writer stage.

	Listening/Speaking	Writing	Reading
Focusing Writer	• Actively solicits another person's comments and opinions. • Uses language clues to indicate different levels of certainty or hypothesizing (e.g., What if? questions).	• Applies correct principles of grammar, parts of speech, and usage and mechanics. • Writes complete sentences. • Uses correct capitalization and punctuation. • Uses correct word structure. • Identifies types of sentences according to purpose (declarative, interrogative, imperative, exclamatory). • Identifies the parts of a sentence in various sentence patterns (simple subject and predicate). • Forms singular, plural, and possessive nouns. • Demonstrates knowledge of nouns, pronouns, verbs, and adjectives in writing simple sentences.	• Demonstrates an understanding of semantic relationships by using context clues, word meanings, and prior knowledge in reading.
Experimenting Writer	• No changes.	• Engages the reader by establishing a context, creating a point of view, and otherwise developing reader interest. • Establishes plot, setting, conflict, and/or the significance of events. • Creates an organizing grammatical structure. • Includes sensory detail and concrete language to develop plot and character. • Excludes extraneous details and inconsistencies. • Develops complex characters through actions describing the motivation of characters and character conversation. • Uses a range of appropriate narrative strategies such as dialogue, tension, or suspense. • Provides a sense of closure to the writing.	• Identifies the meaning of common idioms and figurative language. • Identifies playful uses of language (e.g., puns, jokes, palindromes). • Recognizes and uses words with multiple meanings (e.g., *school*, *hard*, *sentence*) and determines which meaning is intended from the context of the sentence.

(continued)

Adapted from the Georgia English/Language Arts Performance Standards (2004a).
Each stage builds on the previous stage and includes objectives for the previous stages. Only additions to each stage are noted after the Emerging Writer stage.

	Listening/Speaking	Writing	Reading
Engaging Writer	• No changes.	• Uses a wider range of appropriate narrative strategies to describe plot and characters such as figurative language, movement, gestures, expressions, and expanded vocabulary. • Lifts the level of language using appropriate strategies including word choice.	• Identifies messages and themes from stories.
Extending Writer	• No changes.	• Engages the reader by establishing a sharpened focus. • Creates an organizing grammatical structure to explain purpose, audience, and context. • Develops a controlling idea that conveys a perspective on the subject.	• No changes.

Adapted from the Georgia English/Language Arts Performance Standards (2004a).
Each stage builds on the previous stage and includes objectives for the previous stages. Only additions to each stage are noted after the Emerging Writer stage.

Beginning Writer Rubric

Name_____

Date_____

Literacy Skills	Standards	Student Evaluation	Teacher Evaluation	Comments
Listening/Speaking	Spoke clearly	1 2 3 4 5	1 2 3 4 5	
	Followed directions	1 2 3 4 5	1 2 3 4 5	
	Remembered information	1 2 3 4 5	1 2 3 4 5	
Reading	Read fluently	1 2 3 4 5	1 2 3 4 5	
	Made predictions by filling in the scaffold	1 2 3 4 5	1 2 3 4 5	
	Read with expression	1 2 3 4 5	1 2 3 4 5	
	Understood the story	1 2 3 4 5	1 2 3 4 5	
	Increased vocabulary	1 2 3 4 5	1 2 3 4 5	
Writing	Filled in the scaffold (prewriting)	1 2 3 4 5	1 2 3 4 5	
	Wrote complete rough draft	1 2 3 4 5	1 2 3 4 5	
	Wrote finished product	1 2 3 4 5	1 2 3 4 5	
	Used descriptive images	1 2 3 4 5	1 2 3 4 5	
	Wrote dialogue correctly	1 2 3 4 5	1 2 3 4 5	
	Grammar:			
	Used complete sentences	1 2 3 4 5	1 2 3 4 5	
	Used appropriate punctuation	1 2 3 4 5	1 2 3 4 5	
	Correct spelling	1 2 3 4 5	1 2 3 4 5	
	Shared ideas with others	1 2 3 4 5	1 2 3 4 5	

Listening/Speaking _____ / 15 points

Reading _____ / 25 points

Writing _____ / 45 points

Total score _____ / 85 points

77–85 = 90%

68–76 = 80%

60–67 = 70%

51–66 = 60%

Literacy Skill	Standard	Student Evaluation	Teacher Evaluation	Comments
Performance	Body movement	1 2 3 4 5	1 2 3 4 5	
	Artwork	1 2 3 4 5	1 2 3 4 5	
	Voice	1 2 3 4 5	1 2 3 4 5	

Performance _____ / 15 points

Directions for Abridging the Beginning Writer Rubric: Making a Checklist

Often in order for younger students to understand how a rubric works, it is easier to start with a checklist. As noted in Davies' (2000) work on assessment, students should have an active role in determining the criteria for a performance assessment. Student involvement in the assessment process makes the learning meaningful to them. For assessment of a plot scaffold, have students brainstorm what they believe is important to writing the story or performing the scaffold. Next, have them sort the suggestions into categories. For example, writing a story may include the following:

- dialogue
- creativity
- images
- plot
- conventions

Based on my experience, teachers should limit the number of categories to four or five and make them worth 20–25 points each. Teachers also can allow students to decide how much weight to place in each category because it makes students critically think about what is most important to a story.

Then, have students define each category or place important criteria under each heading. For example, students might define creativity as "number of changes made to the original scaffold that now make it different" or "addition of more characters." Under the heading of images, students might include, "using sensory details," and for conventions, they might list "using quotation marks correctly," "remembering periods at the end of sentences," or "spelling words correctly."

Finally, the list that has been sorted and categorized becomes a checklist for students to use when they edit their papers. I also allow students to score their own papers based on their checklists. If they can justify their scoring to me, then they are given that grade.

Intermediate Writer Rubric

Name_____

Date_____

Literacy Skills	Standards	Student Evaluation	Teacher Evaluation	Comments
Listening/Speaking	Spoke clearly and with inflection	1 2 3 4 5	1 2 3 4 5	
	Actively solicited another's comments and opinions	1 2 3 4 5	1 2 3 4 5	
	Worked collaboratively	1 2 3 4 5	1 2 3 4 5	
Reading	Read fluently	1 2 3 4 5	1 2 3 4 5	
	Made predictions by filling in the scaffold	1 2 3 4 5	1 2 3 4 5	
	Recognized multiple word meanings	1 2 3 4 5	1 2 3 4 5	
	Identified motives	1 2 3 4 5	1 2 3 4 5	
	Increased vocabulary	1 2 3 4 5	1 2 3 4 5	
Writing	Engaged the reader	1 2 3 4 5	1 2 3 4 5	
	Established a plot	1 2 3 4 5	1 2 3 4 5	
	Created an organized structure	1 2 3 4 5	1 2 3 4 5	
	Used sensory images	1 2 3 4 5	1 2 3 4 5	
	Developed complex characters	1 2 3 4 5	1 2 3 4 5	
	Used a range of strategies	1 2 3 4 5	1 2 3 4 5	
	Created relevant dialogue	1 2 3 4 5	1 2 3 4 5	
	Excluded extraneous information	1 2 3 4 5	1 2 3 4 5	
	Provided a sense of closure	1 2 3 4 5	1 2 3 4 5	
	Grammar:			
	Surface errors did not interfere with meaning	1 2 3 4 5 6 7 8 9 10	1 2 3 4 5 6 7 8 9 10	

Listening/Speaking _____ / 15 points
Reading _____ / 25 points
Writing _____ / 60 points
Total Score _____ / 100 points

Literacy Skill	Standard	Student Evaluation	Teacher Evaluation	Comments
Performance	Body movement	1 2 3 4 5	1 2 3 4 5	
	Artwork	1 2 3 4 5	1 2 3 4 5	
	Voice	1 2 3 4 5	1 2 3 4 5	

Performance _____ / 15 points

Plot Scaffolds

These plot scaffolds have been designed for practical classroom use. They can accommodate any number of children and contain short, easy-to-read dialogue. The scaffolds are meant to be used as an exercise in active reading and critical thinking. To accomplish this, the last line for each character has been left blank, and the students must supply this ending based on their own feelings about the character and the plot. In addition, students need to add images, too.

The first six plot scaffolds incorporate elements of relevant literary genres, such as melodrama or mystery, and can be easily expanded into larger theme units. The next six plot scaffolds are based on historical fact or myth and are open-ended—that is, students may either create new endings to the problems they present or give them the original or historically factual endings.

There's a Bug in My Beans

Characters:

Bug	Bug Spray
Old Lady	Restaurant Owner
Old Man	Cook
Waiter	Harry (the cook's helper)
Businessman	Health Inspector
Businessman's Wife	Lawyer
Artist	Narrator/Writer

Narrator/Writer: We are inside a restaurant, and three to four tables are set for dinner. (Write images that "show" this restaurant. Is it fancy? Expensive? How is the setting like a character in a story?)

_____

_____

It is evening, and there are several people in the Cuccamonga restaurant eating dinner, including an unwanted visitor, a bug. An old couple is eating their dinner when they hear a strange sound.

Bug: Buzz....Buzz....Buzzzzzzzzz...Buzzzzz...humm....Beans! (Bug spies beans and gets into

them. Write an image to describe this situation.)_____

_____

Old Lady: Albert dear, do you hear something odd?

Old Man: No, Martha dear, just a buzzing noise in my ear. There must be something wrong with my hearing aid. (Taps it against the chair or table. Write an image to describe this action.)

_____

_____ Stupid machine.

Old Lady: Albert dear, do you have your glasses? I forgot mine. I can't see too well, but it looks like one of my string beans is taking a walk off the plate.

Old Man: Yes, Martha dear, your beans are most surely taking a little stroll. You would think they would be dead after being cooked.

Bug: Buzzzz...hummmmmmm, gooood beans.....lovvvvve hum.

Old Lady: Glory be! Albert dear, my beans aren't walking. There's an ugly, slimy bug in my beans! Do something! Oh my goodness. I think I'm going to faint.

Old Man: Waiter! Waiter!

Waiter: You rang?

Old Man: My wife just found an awful, dirty bug strolling away with her beans.

Waiter: Sir, this is a gourmet restaurant, but we do not have bugs listed on the menu. Besides bugs do not stroll; they walk or fly.

Old Man: Well I can't tell if it's a fly, but it is bug, and he is strolling in the beans. Tell him to leave. I'm sure he has no reservation here.

(continued)

Narrator/Writer: Everyone in the restaurant hears the noise and comes over to the old couple's table to investigate.

Businessman: What is this I hear about bugs in the beans? If it is true, will the beans cost more to eat? After all, it's extra meat.

Old Man: Look here, sir, right in my wife's beans there's a hungry green bug.

Businessman: Yes, a slithery bug all right. I wonder if bugs like that are good to eat? If so, I am sure I could make a lot of money selling them to restaurants.

Businessman's Wife: What is this I hear about buggy beans? Come, William. We're leaving! Imagine bugs being allowed in a fine restaurant. How disgusting!

Artist: What a new, interesting way to serve beans. Why, bugs are so colorful and nice. I hope there's a bug in my beans.

Old Lady: You can have my bug, young man. I think he's ugly!

Waiter: Ladies and gentlemen, I assure you we do not serve bugs, only snails.

Narrator/Writer: Now the owner of the restaurant comes in to find out what's wrong. (Write an image to describe this situation.)

_____

_____

Restaurant Owner: Waiter, what's the problem?

Waiter: A bug complaint, sir.

Bug: Buzzzz...hummmmmm...love, love, really like these beans.

Owner: Yes, I do hear a buggy little voice. What's the bug's complaint? Call the cook. I'll fire him!

Cook: (Write an image describing the cook entering.) _____

_____

_____ What is the complaint about my cooking? I am a great chef. Do you want my reputation to be ruined! I don't even know how to cook a bug. I certainly would never serve one. Perhaps it is not a bug, just a piece of ground pepper instead. Harry! Get in here! You're fired!

Harry: (Write an image to describe this situation.)

_____

_____

What did I do wrong this time?

Cook: Lazy! You didn't grind the pepper!

Harry: I always grind the pepper too small to be mistaken for a bug. Everyone always blames me for everything.

(continued)

Setting the Stage for Creative Writing: Plot Scaffolds for Beginning and Intermediate Writers by Shannon O'Day.
Copyright © 2006 by the International Reading Association. May be copied for classroom use.

Narrator/Writer: The Health Inspector comes in. (Write an image to describe this situation.)

_____

_____

Health Inspector: I've just had a report that your restaurant is not clean. You serve buggy beans.

Old Lady: Yes, Inspector. Look. He is right here in my beans. Oh, the monster. I still feel faint.

Lawyer: Lady, if you get sick, you can sue the restaurant for one million of your favorite things.

Owner: Please, Lady, don't sue!

Waiter: May I suggest, everyone, that we call in Bug Spray to rescue us from this terrible bean-eating bug?

Old Man: (What would the Old Man say? How would he say it? Write your own line.)

_____

_____

Old Lady: (What would the Old Lady say? How would she say it? Write your own line.)

_____

_____

Bug Spray: (Write an image to describe this situation. What does Bug Spray look like? Is this a superhero?)

_____

_____

Here I am to save the day and the beans! Where's that bug! I'll get him! I'll smash his little head! I'll stomp his little toes!

Artist: Don't hurt the pretty green bug. I'll take him home for a pet.

Health Inspector: Come on Spray! Punch his lights out!

Bug Spray: Don't worry. This bug spray works first time, every time. Squirt! (Write an image to describe this situation.)

_____

_____

Narrator/Writer: (What happens?)

_____

_____

Health Inspector: (What would the Health Inspector say? Write your own line.)

_____

_____

(continued)

Setting the Stage for Creative Writing: Plot Scaffolds for Beginning and Intermediate Writers by Shannon O'Day.
Copyright © 2006 by the International Reading Association. May be copied for classroom use.

There's a Bug in My Beans (continued)

Bug: (What would the Bug say? Write your own line.)

_____

_____

Bug Spray: (What would Bug Spray say? Write your own line.)

_____

_____

Artist: (What would the Artist say? Write your own line.)

_____

_____

Lawyer: (What would the Lawyer say? Write your own line.)

_____

_____

Owner: (What would the Owner say? Write your own line.)

_____

_____

Cook: (What would the Cook say? Write your own line.)

_____

_____

Harry: (What would Harry say? Write your own line.)

_____

_____

Waiter: (What would the Waiter say? Write your own line.)

_____

_____

Businessman: (What would the Businessman say? Write your own line.)

_____

_____

Businessman's Wife: (What would the Businessman's Wife say? Write your own line.)

_____

_____

Narrator/Writer: (What would you say? End the story and resolve the problem.)

_____

_____

The Rent

Characters:

Annabelle	Mr. Snake (Villain)
Mayflower	Mr. Peabody (Villain's helper)
Grandmother	Hero
Grandfather	Spot (the dog)
Sheriff	Narrator/Writer

Narrator/Writer: Annabelle is setting the table for dinner, and Mayflower is combing her hair. Grandmother is knitting while Grandfather is reading the newspaper. Suddenly, there is a knock at the door. (Write your own images. How might you describe the sound of the door knocking? What is the setting of this story? How is the setting like a character in the story?)

_____

_____

Grandmother: Annabelle, would you please answer the door? It must be the paperboy to collect the paper money. Tell him...tell him...to come back...next Tuesday.

Annabelle: Why do I have to answer the door? I always have to answer the door! I always have to do all the work.

Mayflower: That's what younger sisters are for.

Narrator/Writer: Annabelle answers the door. The Villain and his helper enter.

All: Hiss! (Make the sound _Hiss_. This is a speaking/sound part now. Later write it as an image describing the Villain and his helper as they enter.)

_____

_____

Mr. Snake: Good evening. My name is Mr. Snake, and this is my associate, Mr. Peabody. Excuse me for intruding, but I've come to collect the rent.

Mayflower: Let me check my piggy bank. (She goes over to a large piggy bank and shakes out one nickel. Write your own image. What does the piggy bank look like?)

_____

_____

I have a nickel. Is that enough?

Mr. Peabody: I'm sorry, but we don't take nickels.

Mayflower: Grandmother, Grandfather, do you have any money for the rent? Something other than a nickel?

Grandmother: Hummmm...rent money...where did I...put it?

Grandfather: Quiet! Can't you see that I'm trying to read the paper!

(continued)

Setting the Stage for Creative Writing: Plot Scaffolds for Beginning and Intermediate Writers by Shannon O'Day.
Copyright © 2006 by the International Reading Association. May be copied for classroom use.

Mr. Snake: Unless you can pay the rent now, I'll have to throw you out of your dingy little shack into the cold. Excuse me, but you better pay.

All: Boo! (Write an image that describes this situation.)

_____

_____

Mayflower: Mercy! Please don't throw us out of our dingy little shack into the cold.

All: Ah! (Write an image that describes this situation.)

_____

_____

Mr. Snake: Excuse me, but we could make a deal. Marry me, and Mr. Peabody can marry Annabelle. Then I'll let your grandparents stay in this dingy little shack.

All: Hiss! (Write an image that describes this situation.)

_____

_____

Mayflower: Never!

Annabelle: Never! Always never!

Mr. Snake: Excuse me, but you have no choice. You must marry me.

Mr. Peabody: You have no money. If you don't marry us, you'll all be thrown out into the cold.

Grandfather: No! I'm not cold! Can't you see I'm trying to read the paper!

Mr. Snake: Come now and marry us!

Narrator/Writer: Mr. Snake and Peabody begin to chase Annabelle and Mayflower around the room. (Write an image that describes this situation.)

_____

_____

*Optional scene: Mr. Snake and Mr. Peabody tie Annabelle and Mayflower to the train tracks. (This is a stock scene, or scene found in many Victorian melodramas and early films. This is a good opportunity for students who are n___ __served to get involved by playing an inanimate object such as the train. This a___ _____ _pportunity for teaching personification. Write a passage that des___ ___ ___ ___ Or you could choose to have the Villain trap Annabelle and M___fl___ ___ ___v.)

_____

_____

Mayflower: Help!

Annabelle: Help! No one ever helps me!

Narrator/Writer: The Hero enters.

(continued)

Hero: Hi. I'm a hero, so I can help you.

All: Hooray! (Write an image that describes the situation.)

_____

_____

Mr. Snake: They must pay the rent.

Hero: I can pay the rent! I have three coupons and two bus passes.

Mr. Peabody: I'm sorry, but we don't take coupons.

Hero: Then I'll call my dog Spot on you. Come, Spot!

All: Hooray! (Write an image that describes this situation.)

_____

_____

Narrator/Writer: Spot enters and chases the villains into the arms of the Sheriff who is waiting at the door. (Write an image that describes this situation.)

_____

_____

Sheriff: I arrest you in the name of the law for not paying your property taxes for six years.

All: Hooray! (Write an image that describes this situation.)

_____

_____

Mr. Snake: (What would Mr. Snake say? Write your own line.)

_____

Mr. Peabody: (What would Mr. Peabody say? Write your own line.)

_____

Sheriff: (What would Sheriff say? Write your own line.)

_____

Mayflower: (Runs to Spot and hugs him. Write an image that describes this situation.)

_____

_____

I'll marry you!

(continued)

All: Ah! (Write an image that describes this situation.)

_____

_____

Annabelle: You always get to marry the dog. I never get to marry the dog.

Mayflower: (What would Mayflower say? Write your own line.)

_____

_____

Hero: (What would the Hero say? Write your own line.)

_____

_____

Spot: (What would Spot say? Write your own line.)

_____

_____

Grandmother: I just remember what I did with the rent money. I spent it on...Girl Scout cookies.

Annabelle: (What would Annabelle say? Write your own line.)

_____

_____

Grandmother: (What would Grandmother say? Write your own line.)

_____

_____

Grandfather: (What would Grandfather say? Write your own line.)

_____

_____

Narrator/Writer: (What would you say? End the story with a resolution.)

_____

_____

Emergency

Characters:

Orderly 1	Receptionist
Orderly 2	Patient's Mother
Patient	Patient's Father
Doctor Ben	Doctor Ron
Nurse Able	Specialist
	Narrator/Writer

Optional Characters:

Nurses	Doctors

Narrator/Writer: This is the reception area of a hospital, near the emergency room. A patient is wheeled in on a gurney, or table, by two orderlies. Both of his parents are with him. (Write a passage with good images that describes a hospital emergency room. How is the setting like a character in a story?)

_____

_____

Orderly 1:   Boy, this is the third one today. I hope I get overtime!

Orderly 2:   We'll get a new white coat at least. This patient is heavy.

Receptionist: (Looks at the Patient. Write an image that describes this situation.)

_____

_____

Paging Doctor Ben. Paging Doctor Ben. Emergency Room, please.

Patient's Mother: Please hurry. Our son's left big toe hurts.

Receptionist: Did you bring your insurance forms?

Patient's Father: We're covered by Blue Alligator Safety.

Receptionist: Very well. Fill out these papers—all 16 of them. Don't forget the copies, and you have the right to remain silent until questioned. (Hands them forms. Write an image that describes this situation.)

_____

_____

Patient's Mother: Please hurry. I have a hair appointment at 2:00. It's an emergency!

Receptionist: A nurse will admit you soon. Please wait in the waiting room. I hope you brought your lunch.

Narrator/Writer: Doctor Ben enters followed by Nurse Able and Doctor Ron.

Doctor Ben: (Looks at Patient. Write an image that describes this situation.)

_____

_____

Stick out your tongue, and tell me where it hurts.

(continued)

Patient: [cough, cough] It's my toe, doc. [cough, cough] (Write an image that describes this character as he coughs.)

_____

_____

Doctor Ben: It will have to come off, son.

Patient's Mother: Please hurry, Junior, you heard him. Your shoe will have to come off.

Patient: My shoe? Oh no! I haven't washed my feet for two weeks. (Everyone groans. Write an image that describes this situation.)

_____

_____

Nurse Able: Doctor Ron, you are so handsome and all the nurses want to marry you. Why don't you notice me?

Doctor Ron: Not now, Able! Can't you see we're in the middle of a serious operation? He might even have to remove his shoe!

Doctor Ben: You can go out with me anytime, cutie.

Patient: If you think she is cute, [cough, cough] you should meet her sister. She's married to my ex-brother-in-law's brother's cousin. (Write an image that describes this situation. How could this be a twist in the plot?)

_____

_____

Doctor Ron: Really? Is he the one who blackmailed Nurse Johnson for two million dollars?

Patient: [cough, cough] Yes, but she got a TV series. Doctor, what about [cough, cough, gasp] my toe? (Write an image that describes this situation.)

_____

_____

Doctor Ben: We better call in a Specialist.

Narrator/Writer: (The specialist enters and looks at Patient's foot. Write an image that describes this situation.)

_____

_____

Specialist: The shoe will have to be removed. Assistants please. (More nurses and doctors enter. Write an image that describes this situation.)

_____

_____

Patient's Father: How much will this cost me?

(continued)

Receptionist: Don't worry, under Blue Alligator Insurance, only the second visit is covered.

Specialist: I shall remove the shoe. Masks please. (All put on any kind of mask. Write an image that describes this situation.)

_____

_____

Gloves! (Nurse hands him gloves. Write an image that describes this situation.)

_____

_____

Shoehorn! (The nurse hands him a shoehorn, and he removes the shoe. All remove masks. Write images that describe this situation.)

_____

_____

Doctor Ron: It's a success! (Everyone cheers. Write an image that describes this situation.)

_____

_____

Nurse Able: What's that smell?

Doctor Ben: It's the sock. It will have to come off, too.

Patient's Mother: But we're in a hurry.

Specialist: These things take time, madame. (The Specialist starts to remove the sock and stops. Write an image that describes this situation.)

_____

_____

My hands, they're stiff, I can't operate! (Everyone gasps. Write an image that describes this situation.)

_____

_____

Doctor Ron: I, the handsome Doctor Ron, who all the nurses love, will remove it. Stand back! (He removes the sock. Write an image that describes this situation.)

_____

_____

Oh no!

Nurse Able: What is it doctor?

Doctor Ron: I think the patient has a hangus nailius.

(continued)

Patient's Mother: Will it take long?

Patient: Oh, my toe. Do something. (Write an image that describes this situation.)

_____

_____

Doctor Ron: (What would Doctor Ron say? Write your own line.)

_____

_____

Doctor Ben: (What would Doctor Ben say? Write your own line.)

_____

_____

Nurse Able: (What would Nurse Able say? Write your own line.)

_____

_____

Specialist: (What would the Specialist say? Write your own line.)

_____

_____

Patient's Mother: (What would the Patient's Mother say? Write your own line.)

_____

_____

Patient's Father: (What would the Patient's Father say? Write your own line.)

_____

_____

Patient: (What would the Patient say? Write your own line.)

_____

_____

Receptionist: (What would the Receptionist say? Write your own line.)

_____

_____

Orderly 1 and 2: (What would the Orderlies say? End the story with a resolution.)

_____

_____

Shoot Out at the Bottoms Up Saloon

Characters:

Sheriff

Banker

Bad Guy

Doctor

Good Guy

Narrator/Writer

Miss Glitter

Piano Player

Bartender

Deputy

Big Sal

Little Sal

Optional Characters:

Saloon Dancers

Cowboys

Animals

Narrator/Writer: Well folks, it went like this...in the Old West things were wild, especially in the Bottoms Up Saloon. (Write an image to describe this situation. What does an Old West saloon look like? What noises do you hear? What does it smell like?)

_____

_____

Yes, sir, things were wild, really wild, when B.G. came to town.

Bad Guy: (The Bad Guy enters the saloon. Write an image to describe this situation.)

_____

_____

I'm B.G.; that's Bad Guy to my friends. (Goes to bar. Write an image to show how he does this.)

_____

_____

Gimme a cola drink, no straw.

Miss Glitter: (Write an image to describe how she walks over to the Bad Guy.)

_____

_____

Oh Bad Guy, you big hunk of a cowman, buy a pretty lady a soft drink?

Bad Guy: Sure, honey. Drinks on the house. Bottoms up.

(Everyone drinks holding their glasses bottoms up, or in other words upside down. Write an image to describe this action.)

_____

_____

(continued)

Setting the Stage for Creative Writing: Plot Scaffolds for Beginning and Intermediate Writers by Shannon O'Day.
Copyright © 2006 by the International Reading Association. May be copied for classroom use.

Big Sal: (Comes up to Miss Glitter. Write an image to describe this situation.)

_____

_____

Hey Glitter, stay away from my man.

Miss Glitter: Listen, Big Sal! You don't have your name on him!

Little Sal: (Comes over. Write an image to describe this situation.)

_____

_____

Back off, both of you. I wrote my name, Little Sal, on him yesterday.

Bad Guy: Girls, girls. Don't fight over me. I'll buy you all drinks.

Good Guy: (Walks up. Write an image to describe this situation and how he looks.)

_____

_____

I beg your pardon, Mr. B.G., but Miss Glitter has made it known that she has affections only for me. I therefore find it preferable that you mount your horse and exit this town.

Bad Guy: He's got a flat, so what's it to you?! Bug off!

Sheriff: (Write an image showing how he walks up with the deputy.)

_____

_____

Boys! Boys! Play nice.

Deputy: Yeah boys, why don't you go play cards together?

(Bad Guy and Good Guy sit down with the Banker and the Doctor to play cards. Write an image to describe this situation.)

_____

_____

Banker: It's six cents a card and no withdrawals on Sunday.

Bad Guy: Deal me in.

Good Guy: Go fish.

Doctor: Trout or flounder? I can fix them both.

Banker: Heads or tails?

Doctor: You don't eat fish heads or tails.

Bad Guy: Good Guy's mother eats fish heads.

Good Guy: If you insult my mother, I will be forced to violence!

(continued)

Sheriff: Boys! Boys! Play nice.

Piano Player: I play nice. I'll play you "Drinks on the House."

(Everyone drinks from their glasses bottom side up. Write an image to describe this situation.)

_____

_____

Narrator/Writer: Yes, sir. With all that soft drinkin' things got really, really wild that day in the Bottoms Up Saloon.

Bad Guy: (Turns to Good Guy. Describe how he does this.)

_____

_____

All right. I'm sorry. I really meant to say that your horse eats fish heads.

Good Guy: No one insults my horse and lives! Stand and draw! (How does he say this?)

_____

_____

Bad Guy: I don't draw fish heads.

Narrator/Writer: (Write an image to describe this situation.)

_____

_____

Miss Glitter: Good Guy, don't fight. It is true about your horse. He eats the nastiest things when your back is turned.

Doctor: Don't worry about the fight. I brought some bandages in case there was trouble. I have the good kind with little stars on them.

Bartender: I'm out of milk. It's soft drinks only now.

Banker: That's OK. I'm out of money.

All: Just soft drinks! No milk! (A fight starts. Write an image to describe this scene.)

_____

_____

Narrator/Writer: Now things were really, really, really wild. (Write a passage to describe what was happening.)

_____

_____

(continued)

Bad Guy: (What would the Bad Guy say? Write your own line.)

_____

_____

Good Guy: (What would the Good Guy say? Write your own line.)

_____

_____

Miss Glitter: (What would Miss Glitter say? Write your own line.)

_____

_____

Big Sal: (What would Big Sal say? Write your own line.)

_____

_____

Little Sal: (What would Little Sal say? Write your own line.)

_____

_____

Doctor: (What would the Doctor say? Write your own line.)

_____

_____

Banker: (What would the Banker say? Write your own line.)

_____

_____

Piano Player: (What would the Piano Player say? Write your own line.)

_____

_____

Sheriff: (What would the Sheriff say? Write your own line.)

_____

_____

Deputy: (What would the Deputy say? Write your own line.)

_____

_____

Bartender: Quick everyone—a drink on the house! Bottom's up!

(continued)

Cowboys and Dancers: (What would they do or say together?)

_____

_____

Bartender: (What would the Bartender say? Write your own line.)

_____

_____

Narrator/Writer: (What would the Narrator/Writer say to end the story and resolve the plot?)

_____

_____

Just Sleeping

Characters:

Butler (Humphrey)	Gardener
Maid	Cook
Rich Lady (Sarah)	Chauffeur
Rich Man (Monty)	Daughter (Silvia)
Victim	Son (Monty, Jr.)
Police Inspector (Finder)	Mrs. Mush (party guest)
Narrator/Writer	Mr. Mush (party guest)

Narrator/Writer: A party is going on in a rich person's house. (Write an image to describe this setting.)

_____

_____

The Maid and Butler are serving snacks and drinks. People are mingling. Suddenly the lights go off and someone screams!

Victim: Ah! (Screams and falls over and lies on the floor. The lights go back on. Write an image to describe this situation.)

_____

_____

Rich Lady: Monty, what was that? Who screamed? What will people think? Screaming at our party. It just isn't done.

Rich Man: Now, Sarah, don't get upset, honey bunch. Promise you won't get mad, pumpkin, but I think there's a body on the floor. Maybe it was the one who screamed.

Rich Lady: A body! Not in our house. People will think we are messy. Call the Butler to remove it at once.

Rich Man: Humphrey, come here at once and remove this body.

Butler: Sir, we cannot touch it until the police come. It's against the rules in murder mysteries. I'll call the police at once! (Leaves to call the police. Write an image to describe this situation. How does he leave the room? Does he stomp out?)

_____

_____

Daughter: There is a body on the dance floor. Maybe it will add some excitement to just another boring party. Beautiful people like me need entertainment.

Mrs. Mush: How novel, a dead body. Charles, let's have one at our next party.

Mr. Mush: Only if it's not too expensive dear. Ask the body how much he charges.

Son: Maybe the body just had a heart attack?

Daughter: I think he was just bored to death by this party.

Son: Maybe it was the Cook's food again? It makes me ill at times.

(continued)

Narrator/Writer: The Police Inspector enters. (Write a passage or image to describe this situation.)

_____

_____

Police Inspector: I'm Inspector Finder. I always find my man. (Trips over the body and looks down. Write an image to describe this situation.)

_____

_____

See I found the body.

Rich Lady: I don't know whom it belongs to, but find the owner while you're at it. I don't want people to think we keep unclaimed bodies on the carpet.

Son: We haven't touched it. Maybe it's just sleeping?

Police Inspector: Just sleeping? That's what they all say. Ha! Ha! I want no one to leave the room. Bring in the other servant, too. I'll find out who committed this crime.

Narrator/Writer: The Cook, Chauffeur, Maid, Butler, and Gardener enter. (Write an image to describe this situation. What do these characters look like?)

_____

_____

Cook: It wasn't my cooking—not this time. I bet it was those toadstools from the garden. I told Smith the Gardener that those toadstools looked warty.

Gardener: Toads don't have warts. And those mushrooms were not toadstools; they were bamboo shoots. Although who can tell what they were after he cooked them. I'd rather eat cat chow than the cook's chow.

Police Inspector: No more talking unless I say so. It's my job to find the murderer. I'm the policeman. (Use an image to describe how he faces the Maid.)

_____

_____

Where were you when the lights went out?

Maid: In the dark.

Police Inspector: And what did you do in the dark?

Maid: (What would the Maid say? Write your own line.)

_____

_____

Police Inspector: That seems shady to me. (Describe how he faces the Chauffer.)

_____

_____

(continued)

Police Inspector: Where were you when this victim was driven to his death by the murder?

Chauffeur: I didn't drive him anywhere. He took a cab.

Police Inspector: When did he call for a cab? I thought you picked up all the guests.

Chauffeur: (What would the Chauffeur say? Write your own line.)

_____

_____

Police Inspector: (Use an image to describe how the Police Inspector faces the Butler.)

_____

_____

Was there anything unusual about this guest?

Butler: (What would the Butler say? Write your own line.)

_____

_____

Police Inspector: (How would the Police Inspector face the Rich Lady and Rich Man? Write an image to describe this situation.)

_____

_____

What was your relationship to this body?

Rich Lady: (What would the Rich Lady say? Write your own line.)

_____

_____

Rich Man: (What would the Rich Man say? Write your own line.)

_____

_____

Police Inspector: (How would the Police Inspector face the Son and Daughter? Write an image to describe this situation.)

_____

_____

How do you think the body was killed?

Son: (What would the Son say? Write your own line.)

_____

_____

(continued)

Daughter: (What would the Daughter say? Write your own line.)

_____

_____

Police Inspector: (Describe how the Police Inspector faces the Cook.)

_____

_____

Cook: Did you fix the food tonight?

(What would the Cook say? Write your own line.)

_____

_____

Police Inspector: (Describe how the Police Inspector faces the Gardener.)

_____

_____

Gardener: How did you know those mushrooms were not warty toadstools?

(What would the Gardener say? Write your own line.)

_____

_____

Police Inspector: (Describe how the Police Inspector faces Mr. and Mrs. Mush.)

_____

_____

Mrs. Mush: Did you hear anything unusual tonight?

(What would Mrs. Mush say? Write your own line.)

_____

_____

Mr. Mush: (What would Mr. Mush say? Write your own line.)

_____

_____

*Optional scene: The Police Inspector also can question any other additional guests or characters at this time.

Police Inspector: Well, all the evidence seems to point to...(Complete the line. Write your own conclusion.)

_____

_____

(continued)

Victim: (Starts to snore loudly on the floor. Everyone looks at the Victim. Write an image to describe this situation.)

_____

_____

Daughter: He was just put to sleep by this boring party. The party is guilty. I'll give him a kiss and he will wake up.

Son: He might turn into a frog if you kiss him.

Gardener: He also might get warts.

Police Inspector: Well, I've solved another unsolvable case. Call me anytime.

Narrator/Writer: (Write the conclusion to the story.)

_____

_____

The Book Fine

Characters:

Judge Justice
Defense Lawyer
Prosecution Lawyer
Miss Copy (court recorder)
Miss Shhh (librarian)
Ralph Ransom
Bailiff
Witness
Narrator/Writer

Jury members:
Jury Leader
Old Lady
Plumber
Housewife
Dog Catcher
Doctor
Teacher
Actress
Waitress
House Painter
Sleepy Person
Journalist

Narrator/Writer: This is the Kangaroo Court with Judge Justice presiding. The jury is sitting in the jury box in a courtroom and a trial is about to begin. (Write an image to describe this situation. Describe the setting like you would describe a character in the story.)

_____

_____

Bailiff: Court in the order! I mean order in the ort! No, order in the port! Oh, I mean, everyone get up. Here comes the Judge. (Everyone stands as the Judge enters. They sit down when he sits down. Write an image to describe this situation.)

_____

_____

Judge: OK. Bring in the next victim. (Hits his gavel on his desk. Write an image to describe this situation.)

_____

_____

(Lawyers and their clients enter the court and sit at tables in front of the Judge. Write an image to describe this situation.)

_____

_____

Bailiff: Your majesty, the next case is the Never-Lend Library versus Ralph Ransom. The charge is ook ept. I mean book leap. No, it's look theft. Oh, I mean the creep lost his library book.

Judge: I'm "your honor" not "your majesty." And please don't call people names. It's against the law. Besides, my mother says it's not nice.

Bailiff: Sorry, sire.

(continued)

Judge: (Use an image to describe how the Judge turns to the Defense Lawyer.)

_____

_____

How does your client plead—guilty, not guilty, or in between?

Defense Lawyer: My client pleads not guilty to the crime of book stealing. I will prove that my poor, innocent, nice, wonderful, trusting client is not at fault. He better pay me a lot of money for doing this, too.

Prosecution Lawyer: I object, sir! My client, the forever hardworking librarian, Miss Shhh, and I, the most famous lawyer on television, can prove that Ralph Ransom is a book thief and a terrible person.

Defense Lawyer: You're wrong! He's innocent. Rich people are always proven innocent.

Prosecution Lawyer: He's guilty!

Defense Lawyer: Innocent!

Prosecution Lawyer: Guilty! Guilty! Guilty! You dodo bird!

Defense Lawyer: Innocent! Innocent! Innocent! You bubble brain!

Judge: Order in this court! (Write an image describing how the Judge bangs his or her gavel.)

_____

_____

No name-calling or I'll call my mother. Miss Copy, strike those last words from the court record.

Miss Copy: Done, sire. (Describe how she hits her computer keyboard.)

_____

_____

Oh, no! I broke a nail!

Actress: You poor thing. Will you ever be able to type again?

Bailiff: I hope so. She never could before.

Miss Copy: Who types anymore? It's all voice activated nowadays, and I own a patent to the latest software. I invent things in my spare time.

Judge: (Use an image to describe how he turns to Defense Lawyer.)

_____

_____

Let's hear your side and hurry. It's almost my snack time.

Bailiff: Your highness, will you be having crackers and milk?

(continued)

Judge: It's "your honor," not "your highness"!

Bailiff: Of course it's my honor. It's my honor to serve you ackers and ilk.

Judge: Enough of the crackers. Hurry up.

Defense Lawyer: I call Ralph Ransom to the stand. (Write an image describing how Ralph goes to the witness box.)

_____

_____

Bailiff: Raise your right hand and sear to tell the old trith.

Ralph: You mean the whole truth? I do. (Write an image describing this situation.)

_____

_____

Defense Lawyer: Did you check out a book and lose it?

Ralph: I did. I was going to return it, but my little brother ate it.

Housewife: (Write an image describing this situation. Where is this character sitting? How does she speak and look?)

_____

_____

Poor man. I have the same problem. My son eats books all the time. He likes them with his crackers and milk.

Doctor: I wonder if his little brother got sick. I don't believe that story. Only goats eat paper. (Where is this character? Write an image describing the setting.)

_____

_____

Waitress: I've seen kids eat paper napkins at my restaurant. They seem to like them, especially with ketchup.

Prosecution Lawyer: That's not a good excuse! It's the old "my brother ate it" explanation.

Teacher: Yes, I've heard that one before from my students. Little brothers eat homework, too.

Prosecution Lawyer: So do computers.

Defense Lawyer: I have a witness to prove my client is telling the truth. I call Witness to the stand. (The Witness comes to the stand. Describe how the Witness walks up to the stand.)

_____

_____

Witness: I swear to tell the whole truth because I am paid to tell the truth.

Jury Leader: How much are you paid?

Witness: All the crackers and milk I can eat.

(continued)

House Painter: That's more than they pay me. I'm calling my painter's union.

Defense Lawyer: Did you see Ralph's little brother eat the library book?

Witness: I did see it. He ate the book and then threw up. The book didn't look very good after that.

Plumber: I bet it looked like something that's been down the drain, like a garbage clog.

Sleepy Person: (Snoring loudly. Write an image describing this situation.)

_____

_____

Journalist: Wake up! You're missing the best part!

Actress: Did you say part? Will I get a part in this trial? I can play the beautiful girl helping the poor innocent Ralph.

Prosecution Lawyer: I call Miss Shhh to the stand. (Miss Shhh goes to the stand and swears in. Write an image describing this situation.)

_____

_____

Miss Shhh: I swear to tell the real truth. I am a good librarian. I always guard my books.

Dog Catcher: Yes, she looks like a good guard. She looks like a dog, too.

Old Lady: I used to have a guard dog. I think you caught him.

Prosecution Lawyer: Miss Shhh, did the defendant sign a library card saying that he would be responsible for his book?

Miss Shhh: Yes, he did.

Prosecution Lawyer: I rest my case. Ladies and gentlemen of the jury, Ralph Ransom signed a library card. He is guilty because...(Complete the line.)

_____

_____

Defense Lawyer: Ladies and gentlemen of the jury, Ralph is not guilty. It is not his fault because...(Complete the line.)

_____

_____

Judge: Ladies and gentlemen of the jury, you must now go into another room and decide if Ralph Ransom is guilty or innocent of the crime of book theft. (Bailiff leads the jury to another corner of the stage. Write an image describing this situation.)

_____

_____

(continued)

Judge: Ladies and gentlemen of the jury, how do you vote?

Jury Leader: Plumber, how do you vote and why?

Plumber: (Write the last lines. Decide if Ralph is guilty or innocent.)

_____

_____

Jury Leader: Sleepy Person, wake up! How do you vote and why?

Sleepy Person: (Write the last lines. Decide if Ralph is guilty or innocent.)

_____

_____

Jury Leader: Actress, how do you vote and why?

Actress: (Write the last lines. Decide if Ralph is guilty or innocent.)

_____

_____

Jury Leader: Doctor, how do you vote and why?

Doctor: (Write the last lines. Decide if Ralph is guilty or innocent.)

_____

_____

Jury Leader: Teacher, how do you vote and why?

Teacher: (Write the last lines. Decide if Ralph is guilty or innocent.)

_____

_____

Jury Leader: Dog Catcher, how do you vote and why?

Dog Catcher: (Write the last lines. Decide if Ralph is guilty or innocent.)

_____

_____

Jury Leader: Housewife, how do you vote and why?

Housewife: (Write the last lines. Decide if Ralph is guilty or innocent.)

_____

_____

Jury Leader: Old Lady, how do you vote and why?

Old Lady: (Write the last lines. Decide if Ralph is guilty or innocent.)

_____

_____

(continued)

Jury Leader: Waitress, how do you vote and why?

Waitress: (Write the last lines. Decide if Ralph is guilty or innocent.)

_____

_____

Jury Leader: Journalist, how do you vote and why?

Journalist: (Write the last lines. Decide if Ralph is guilty or innocent.)

_____

_____

Jury Leader: House Painter, how do you vote and why?

House Painter: (Write the last lines. Decide if Ralph is guilty or innocent.)

_____

_____

Jury Leader: (Write the last lines. Add your own vote to decide if Ralph is guilty or innocent.)

_____

_____

Judge: The jury had voted Ralph Ransom _____ (guilty or innocent) of the charges. (Write the last lines. What would the Judge say?)

_____

_____

Bailiff: (Write the last lines? What would the Bailiff say?)

_____

_____

Witness: (What would you say? Make up your own line.)

_____

_____

Ralph: (What would Ralph say? Write his last lines.)

_____

_____

Narrator/Writer: (End the story. Provide a resolution to the problem.)

_____

_____

Guess Who Moved in Next Door?

Characters:

Beowulf	14 warriors (Geats)
Grendel	Door of Hall Heorot
Grendel's Mother (SHE)	Servant 1
King Hrothgar	Servant 2
Unferth	People in Hall Heorot
Queen Wealhtheow	Narrator/Writer

Narrator/Writer: In the fen, Grendel and his mother are having breakfast. (Write an image that describes this situation.)

_____

_____

Grendel: Mom, what was all that noise next door last night? I couldn't get my beauty sleep.

Grendel's Mother: I know, my little bone cruncher. It must be the new neighbors with that gaudy house. After dark, they should be more respectful of our quiet little swamp. Honey, take your elbows off the table when you are gorging.

Grendel: Mom, can I go visit them tonight? I promise to make them be quiet.

Grendel's Mother: Yes, mommy's baby. You go along and be a good monster tonight. Oh...and bring me home a snack dear.

Grendel: Yes, mom. (Grendel goes toward Heorot. Write an image that describes this situation.)

_____

_____

Narrator/Writer: King Hrothgar and his men are feasting. Grendel knocks at the door. (Write an image that describes this situation.)

_____

_____

Door of Hall Heorot: (How might the door react? Think of the door as a character in the story. Would you fall or faint when Grendel knocks on you?)

_____

_____

Grendel: Hey, guys. My, my, if you all don't look good enough to eat! Excuse me if I help myself.

**People in
Hall Heorot:** (What would they say? Write your own line.)

_____

_____

Grendel: It was nice visiting you. I have to go home to my mom now. (Grendel leaves. Write an image that describes this situation.)

_____

_____

(continued)

Setting the Stage for Creative Writing: Plot Scaffolds for Beginning and Intermediate Writers by Shannon O'Day.
Copyright © 2006 by the International Reading Association. May be copied for classroom use.

Narrator/Writer: (Describe the scene of Hall Heorot the next day.)

_____

_____

Two servants are discussing the noise in the hall last night.

Servant 1: Let me tell you, it must have been some party at Heorot last night. I swear the hall was rockin'.

Servant 2: Probably because King Hrothgar built it next to the fen, a swamp. Who in their right mind builds a golden hall next to a swamp? I hope he at least got the land cheap.

(Both servants see the hall. Write an image that describes this situation.)

_____

_____

Servant 1: (What would the character say? Write your own line.)

_____

_____

Servant 2: (What would the character say? Write your own line.)

_____

_____

Narrator/Writer: A month later, Beowulf and 14 of his friends have come to help King Hrothgar. (Write an image that describes this situation.)

_____

_____

Beowulf: I hear you have problems with the neighbors eating your guests.

King Hrothgar: Yes, every time I try to throw a party, this really ugly party crasher breaks in the door and wrecks the place.

Queen Wealhtheow: It is getting so _nobody_ will come to our gorgeous new vacation spot.

Beowulf: Vacation spot in a swamp?

King Hrothgar: It was my dream.

Unferth: And it was a deal. Talk about cheap.

Queen Wealhtheow: Would you be our bouncer?

Beowulf: Don't worry. I've got a good grip on the situation.

Narrator/Writer: Later that night, all the Geats are pretending to sleep in Heorot, waiting for Grendel to appear. (Write an image that describes this situation.)

_____

_____

(continued)

Grendel: (knocking at the door) Hi, guys! It's your party animal again! (Knocks down the door and enters the hall. Write an image that describes this situation.)

_____

_____

Door of Hall Heorot: (What would the door do? How would it react? Write an image that describes this situation.)

_____

_____

Beowulf: Not without an invitation! Mind if I check your wrist? (He grabs Grendel by the arm.)

_____

_____

Grendel: Now look here. I've been here loads of times. (He tries to get his arm free. Write an image that describes this situation.)

_____

_____

Beowulf: Please don't mess up my fur. By the way, the arm is attached, you know.

(What would the character say? Write your own line.)

_____

_____

Grendel: (What would the character say? Write your own line.)

_____

_____

Narrator/Writer: Back at the swamp, Grendel has dragged himself home. (Write an image that describes this situation.)

_____

_____

Grendel's Mother: Grendel! What happened? You look terrible!

Grendel: (What would Grendel say? Write your own line.)

_____

_____

Grendel's Mother: That's it! Nobody messes with my baby and gets away with it! I'm going right now to have a word with that Beowulf. (She leaves for Hall Heorot. Write an image that describes this situation.)

_____

_____

(continued)

Guess Who Moved in Next Door? (continued)

Narrator/Writer: Everyone is celebrating Beowulf's success. (Write an image that describes this situation.)

_____

_____

King Hrothgar: I have to hand it to you, Beowulf. You really pulled it off!

Queen Wealhtheow: My hero. Here is a gold ring, a golden collar, and many other tokens of our thanks.

Beowulf: Your praise is reward enough, really. The treasure I will give to my king, Hygelac.

Warriors: (What would they say? Write your own line.)

_____

_____

Narrator/Writer: Everyone gets tired and goes to sleep. Grendel's Mother knocks quietly at the door and enters. (Write an image that describes this situation.)

_____

_____

Door of Hall Heorot: (What would the door say or do? Write your own line.)

_____

_____

Grendel's Mother: Everyone is asleep. Well, I will grab a quick snack and come back later. (She leaves and takes a warrior with her. The people in Hall Heorot wake up and find Aschere missing. Write an image that describes this situation.)

_____

_____

King Hrothgar: It looks like another monster has been here. It took away my best friend. Not again!

Unferth: Looks like it was SHE. I know because I have admired her work for years. What a monster! (Everyone gasps. Write an image that describes this situation.)

_____

_____

Queen Wealhtheow: Not SHE! SHE is so evil people don't even give her a name. SHE is Grendel's Mother.

Beowulf: No problem. I'll get rid of this one, too.

Narrator/Writer: Beowulf and his men follow Grendel's Mother's trail back to the fen and reach a pool. (Write an image to describe the pool. How can the pool be a character in this story?)

_____

_____

Warriors: Boss, it looks like she went into this pool.

(continued)

Beowulf: So? I can swim. (He dives into the pool. Describe how the pool feels. Make it a character.)

_____

_____

(Beowulf reaches Grendel's Mother's den. Write an image that describes this setting.)

_____

_____

I am Beowulf, son of Ecgtheow.

Grendel's Mother: Am I supposed to be impressed? I'm the *most* evil monster in the fen.

Beowulf: (What would Beowulf say? Write your own line.)

_____

_____

Grendel's Mother: (What would Grendel's Mother say? Write your own line.)

_____

_____

Narrator/Writer: (Resolve the problem and end the story.)

_____

_____

That Apple

Characters:

Paris
Aphrodite
Athena
Helen
King Menelaus
Cupid
Discord

Thetis
Zeus
Hera
Gods and Goddesses of Olympus
Peleus
Narrator/Writer

Narrator/Writer: Many gods and goddesses are on Mount Olympus to celebrate the wedding of Peleus, a mortal, to Thetis, a sea goddess. (Describe the scene of a wedding on Mount Olympus in Greece.)

_____

_____

Hera: Zeus, aren't you glad you married Thetis off to Peleus?

Zeus: Yes, dear. Besides making you jealous, Thetis would have a child greater than me. Being married to a mortal like Peleus makes my position as King of Olympus safer.

Hera: I heard Thetis wasn't too happy about your choice of bridegrooms, but she certainly can't complain about you giving her a wedding on Olympus.

Athena: And it was so smart of you to invite everybody who is somebody.

Discord: (Enters very angry. Write an image that describes this situation.)

_____

_____

Well, I, Discord, did not get an invitation...but I still brought a little "present." (She throws a golden apple on the table. Write an image that describes this situation.)

_____

_____

It is "For the Fairest."

Aphrodite: How pretty! What does it say on the tag? I don't read very well...I mean I forgot my reading glasses. Would some big, strong, handsome god read it for me?

Discord: (What would Discord say? Write your own line and an image that describes this situation.)

_____

_____

Thetis: I'm the bride. The apple is my wedding present.

Peleus: You are right. The bride is always the fairest.

Aphrodite: I'm the prettiest here. So of course the apple is mine.

Athena: Brains before beauty. It's mine you airhead.

(continued)

That Apple (continued)

Hera: Hold it, both of you! Who's the Queen of Heaven here?

Thetis: (What would Thetis say? Write your own line.)

_____

_____

Peleus: (What would Peleus say? Write your own line.)

_____

_____

*Optional scene: Other goddesses and gods may be added here to argue over the apple. (Write an image that describes this situation.)

_____

_____

Narrator/Writer: Weeks go by and everyone on Mount Olympus is still arguing over who deserves the apple. (Describe the situation on Mount Olympus.)

_____

_____

Hera: Zeus, that apple belongs to me! I'm your wife and I better get it!

Aphrodite: But I'm the cutest! Especially when I'm straight from the sea.

Athena: You are such a stereotypical female. Women are more than just good looks!

Zeus: Ladies, please! This racket is enough to make me hurl a thunderbolt.

Hera: No, you can't go and play with your toys until you make a decision right now about who gets the apple. You better pick me, too!

Athena: That's not fair. He can't judge. He's your husband.

Aphrodite: And he's your father.

Zeus: You are right, Athena. We need an impartial judge who doesn't know any of you. I choose Paris, a mortal who has never seen any of you three.

Athena: Paris has never been to school, but it seems fair, Daddy.

Hera: Paris also is a poor shepherd—but he really is the abandoned son of King Priam, who tried to get rid of the bad luck Paris was predicted to bring to Troy by disposing of him. Paris doesn't know about his royal birth and the bad luck...however, I agree to him if we keep peace in the family.

Aphrodite: I understand he has seen nothing but sheep and is married to some plain wood nymph...sounds like a good judge to me. I agree.

Zeus: (What would Zeus say? Write your own line.)

_____

_____

(continued)

Narrator/Writer: The three goddesses appear to Paris, and he has to pick who will get the apple. (Write an image that describes this situation and new setting.)

_____

_____

Paris: (Holds the apple and looks at it.) Um...apples and females.... Doesn't this cause a problem in another story?

Hera: (Approaches Paris and whispers in his ear. Write an image that describes this situation.)

_____

_____

Pick me, you lowly shepherd, and I will make you king of the world.

Athena: (Approaches Paris and whispers in his ear. Write an image that describes this situation.)

_____

_____

Be smart. Show what little brains you have. Choose me, and I will make you the wisest man in the world.

Aphrodite: (Approaches Paris and whispers in his ear. Write an image that describes this situation.)

_____

_____

You are a very handsome man and obviously know the fairest when you see her. Choose me and I will give you the most beautiful woman in the world as your wife.

Paris: (What would Paris say? Write your own line.)

_____

_____

Hera: (What would Hera say? Write your own line.)

_____

_____

Athena: (What would Athena say? Write your own line.)

_____

_____

Aphrodite: (What would Aphrodite say? Write your own line.)

_____

_____

(continued)

Narrator/Writer: Although King Priam and his Queen Hecuba have heard the prophecy about their son, Paris, causing the destruction of Troy, Aphrodite has made them forget this unpleasant prophecy and accept him. They make Paris a prince and send him to visit the court of King Menelaus, a Greek king who is married to the most beautiful woman in the world, Helen. (Describe this situation and the new setting in King Menelaus's court.)

_____

_____

King Menelaus: Welcome to my palace, Prince Paris. You are my guest.

Paris: Thank you, great king. Being a prince is new to me...so I am not sure of all the rules yet.

King Menelaus: I like you, my boy. As my guest, I will share what I have with you.

(Helen enters. Everyone acts overwhelmed by her beauty. Write an image that describes this situation.)

_____

_____

Helen: Hi, everyone. I'm Helen, and I'm the fairest and I know it. I've got a face that could launch 1,000 ships.

King Menelaus: This is _my_ lovely queen, Helen.

Aphrodite: (Enters invisible to all but Paris. She whispers in his ear. Write an image that describes this situation.)

_____

_____

Helen is the most beautiful woman in the world and she is all yours!

Paris: But she is married.

Aphrodite: No problem. Cupid!

Cupid: Yes, mother.

Aphrodite: Shoot Helen with one of your love arrows.

Cupid: (What would Cupid say? Write your own line.)

_____

_____

Helen: (What would Helen say? Write your own line.)

_____

_____

Paris: (What would Paris say? Write your own line.)

_____

_____

(continued)

King Menelaus: (What would King Menelaus say? Write your own line.)

_____

_____

Narrator/Writer: (Resolve the problem and end the story.)

_____

_____

Beware of Gifts

Characters:

King Priam	Odysseus
Hecuba	Laocoon
Cassandra (a prophet)	Trojan Soldier 1
King Agamemnon	Trojan Soldier 2
King Menelaus	Narrator/Writer
Greek Soldier 1	
Greek Soldier 2	

Optional Characters:

Two Snakes
Laocoon's Children
Additional Greek Soldiers and Trojan Soldiers

Agamemnon: OK, people. We have been outside the walls of Troy now for 10 years, trying to get in and conquer the place so we can all go home rich and famous.

Narrator/Writer: (Describe the setting.)

_____

_____

Menelaus: I thought we were just trying to get my wife, Helen, back.

Agamemnon: I know she is the most beautiful woman in the world, but hey, get real, she isn't that beautiful...but she made a beautiful excuse to attack Troy. Still, it has been 10 years, and my armies are starting to complain about the time factor. Anybody have any good ideas?

Odysseus: Being the tricky one among you, I say we use the old gift trick and hope they don't look it in the mouth, if you get my drift.

Menelaus: Gift? Is that what I have to give my wife to get her back?

Agamemnon: Trust me—that's a never-ending tactic.

Odysseus: Look, we tell the Trojans they've won and give them a prize to prove it...a huge wooden.... What is it they like?

Greek Soldiers: Bunnies?

Odysseus: No, horses! That's it. Poseidon will like it, too. Anyway we make it a real big horse—so big they might even have to tear down a wall or two to take it into the city. Even if they don't take it into the city, we can make the horse hollow and hide men inside so they can sneak out at night and open the gates for us. We can pretend to leave but sneak back just as the doors open....and surprise! We get them.

Greek Soldiers: Won't they be expecting us?

Odysseus: Hardly. They will probably be tired from all the victory celebrations.

(continued)

Agamemnon: Sounds like a plan. Let's go for it.

Narrator/Writer: Odysseus and the Greek soldiers build the horse, leave it in front of Troy's walls, and pretend to sail away. (Write an image describing the situation.)

_____

_____

Trojan Soldier 1: (Write an image describing the situation.)

_____

_____

Look! The Greeks have left!

King Priam: We must have won!

Hecuba: Look! They left us a present! A big present!

Cassandra: Beware of Greeks bearing gifts.

King Priam: What is that supposed to mean?

Hecuba: Now don't fuss at her, dear; you know she's crazy. No one believes a thing she says.

Cassandra: (What would this character say? Write your own line.)

_____

_____

Trojan Soldier 2: I say we take the present into the city! (Everyone cheers. Then, they begin to drag the horse into the city. Write an image describing the situation.)

_____

_____

Laocoon: Wait! I am a priest and I say you should burn that horse as an offering to the god Poseidon.

King Priam: He might have a point there. Poseidon did help us.

Greek Solider 1: (inside of horse) Great! We are in trouble now! (Write an image describing the situation.)

_____

_____

Greek Soldier 2: (inside of horse) Quick, everyone pray hard to Poseidon—he owes us one.

Odysseus: How do you figure that?

Greek Soldier 2: We made this thing a horse didn't we?

Narrator/Writer: Two snakes enter and attack Laocoon. (Write an image describing the situation.)

_____

_____

(continued)

Laocoon: Help! Two big serpents! (His children run to help and everyone gets dragged out to sea. Write an image describing the situation.)

_____

_____

King Priam: Guess Laocoon was wrong. We should take the horse into the city.

Laocoon: (What would he say? Write your own line.)

_____

_____

Narrator/Writer: Later that night after the Trojans have had a big party.... (Write an image describing the situation.)

_____

_____

Greek Soldier 1: It sure is stuffy in the horse. Do you think we can go out now?

Greek Soldier 2: I think it is quiet outside.

Odysseus: Let's go, men. (They get out of the horse. Write an image describing the situation. How do they get out? What happens?)

_____

_____

Trojan Soldier 1: (What would the soldier say? Write your own line.)

_____

_____

Trojan Soldier 2: (What would the soldier say? Write your own line.)

_____

_____

Greek Soldier 1: (What would the soldier say? Write your own line.)

_____

_____

Greek Soldier 2: (What would the soldier say? Write your own line.)

_____

_____

King Priam: (What would King Priam say? Write your own line.)

_____

_____

(continued)

Hecuba: (What would Hecuba say? Write your own line.)

_____

_____

Odysseus: (What would Odysseus say? Write your own line.)

_____

_____

Agamemnon: (What would Agamemnon say? Write your own line.)

_____

_____

Menelaus: (What would Menelaus say? Write your own line.)

_____

_____

Narrator/Writer: (End the story and resolve the problem.)

_____

_____

Are We Home Yet?

Characters:
Ulysses (also known as Odysseus)
Hermes
Cyclops (Polyphemus)
Circe
Crewman 1, 2, 3, 4, 5 (you may later wish to give them names rather than numbers)
Aeolus
Lotus Lander
Calypso
Other Cyclops
Narrator/Writer

Narrator/Writer: (Describe the scene on Ulysses' ship. What does the ship look like? How long have they been sailing from Troy? Write an image that describes this situation.)

_____

_____

Crewman 1:   Are we home yet?

Crewman 2:   I'm hungry.

Crewman 3:   I want a drink of water. Can we stop at that island for lunch?

Ulysses: All right, but remember the last time when we stopped at Ciconia?

Crewman 4:   But, boss, the place looks like easy pickings. And we need the loot because the treasure from Troy was dumped overboard when Poseidon sent that storm that almost sank us. We can't go home without surprises and treats for our families.

Narrator/Writer: (Describe what happens when they land on Ciconia.)

_____

_____

The crew then sails on to another island.

Crewman 1:   Are we home?

Crewman 2:   Not yet.

Crewman 1:   We need to land here, but what about our time on Ciconia?

Ulysses: Yes, it seemed like a plan, but what did we all learn, boys?

Crewman 3:   Looks are deceiving. They attacked us and we lost two ships. Now we are down to only one.

Ulysses: Good answer. So we land—but no looting!

(continued)

Narrator/Writer: They land on Lotus land. (Write an image describing the setting here.)

_____

_____

Lotus Lander: Hi, welcome to the island of your dreams! Care to eat some flowers?

Crewman 2: I'm starved. Why not? It's not looting; it's a gift. (He eats the flowers). Wow, great stuff! Makes you feel very relaxed. Hey guys, try the flowers.

Narrator/Writer: The crew begins to eat the flowers. (Write an image describing the situation.)

_____

_____

Crewman 1: This is great! (He looks around then falls asleep.) What a nice dream. I feel like I'm home. (Write an image describing the situation.)

_____

_____

Crewman 3: I can sleep here forever and just dream. (Falls asleep, snoring.)

Ulysses: What is this? Everyone is asleep!

Lotus Lander: Want some flowers? They will make all your troubles fade away. Just take a bite; it's great stuff.

Ulysses: No way! I'm not giving control of my life over to some flower. I'm going home to my wife and kids. (To his men.) Get up all of you. (They don't move. Write an image describing the situation.)

_____

_____

Very well, I'll carry you all back to the ship. (He takes them back to ship. Write an image describing the situation.)

_____

_____

You guys weigh a ton and I always have to bail you out of trouble—but then I'm the smartest one, so it is part of the job.

Lotus Lander: (What would the Lotus Lander say? Write your own line.)

_____

Narrator/Writer: Ulysses and his men sail on. (Write an image describing the situation.)

_____

_____

(continued)

Are We Home Yet? (continued)

Crewman 2: I'm hungry.

Crewman 1: Are we home yet?

Crewman 3: I'm thirsty. Can we stop at that island for lunch?

Ulysses: All right, but what did we learn last time, boys?

Crewman 2: Don't take flowers from strangers.

Crewman 5: But they made you feel good!

Crewman 3: Yes, but I'm thirsty...and we need to go home.

Crewman 4: I know the answer! No looting!

Ulysses: Yes, boys. Now behave yourselves.

Narrator/Writer: They land and find a large cave. (Write an image describing the situation.)

_____

_____

Crewman 4: Let's go in. There's no one home.

Crewman 5: Maybe we can "borrow" some food and stuff.

Crewman 2: But we haven't been invited.

Crewman 4: Look, food! (Dives in and starts eating. Write an image describing the situation.)

_____

_____

Cyclops: (Enters the cave and looks around.) I'm Polyphemus. Who has been eating my food and laying on my bed?

Ulysses: Uh...Nobody.

Cyclops: Well, Nobody, looks like that's my cheese and bread you are eating. Who invited you in into my cave?

Ulysses: Well...where I come from, there are rules for hospitality, including taking care of strangers. I know you feel the same way here. We will pay you for the food.

Cyclops: Mind if I close the door? (Closes door of the cave.) I'll start with a tasty human. (He grabs a person and eats him. Write an image describing the situation.)

_____

_____

A bit stringy.

Narrator/Writer: Ulysses' men get scared, but he stays calm. (Write an image describing the situation.)

_____

_____

(continued)

Ulysses: I have just the thing to help with that. Wine?

Cyclops: Nobody, I've never had any, but anything to get the stringy taste out of my mouth. (Drinks the wine.) Tasty! I think I will drink all of it! More! (The men give him all their wine and he falls asleep. Write an image describing the situation.)

_____

_____

Ulysses: Well, it's the smart guy to the rescue again, boys. Where would you be without me? Go sharpen that pole and heat it up. We'll stab his eye and escape. (They sharpen the pole, heat it up, and then get ready to stab the Cyclops's eye while he is sleeping. Write an image describing the situation.)

_____

_____

Hope you get the point of this lesson on manners! (Stabs him in the eye. Write an image describing this event.)

_____

_____

Cyclops: My eye! (He blindly gropes around, looking for the men. Then he goes to the door, opens it, and yells for help. Write an image describing the situation.)

_____

_____

Help! Nobody blinded me! Nobody hurt me!

Other Cyclops: (grumbling) It's Poseidon's son again. If Nobody has hurt you, why are you yelling? The guy is a flake.

Narrator/Writer: Ulysses and his men escape past the blind Cyclops, get on their ship, and sail away.

Cyclops: (What would the Cyclops say? Write your own line.)

_____

_____

Narrator/Writer: Many days later. (Describe the long trip.)

_____

_____

Crewman 1: Are we home yet?

Crewman 2: I'm hungry!

Crewman 3: I see another island!

Ulysses: OK, guys, but what have we learned?

Crewman 5: (What would the crewman say? Write your own line.)

_____

_____

(continued)

Narrator/Writer: They land on the island of the winds. There Aeolus feeds them, and Ulysses tells him of their adventures. (Write an image describing these scenes.)

_____

_____

Ulysses: (What would he say? Recount his adventures in Troy and on his way home.)

_____

_____

Aeolus: Great story! As a reward, I will help you get home. Here is a bag. In it are the north, south, and east winds. You must keep them prisoner in here. I'll send the west wind to blow you home. Whatever you do, _don't open the bag_ or who knows where you'll get blown.

Ulysses: Thanks, Aeolus. I promise to stay awake the whole time and guard the bag.

Aeolus: (What would Aeolus say? Write your own line.)

_____

_____

Narrator/Writer: The men get back on the ship and after nine days, they are almost home. (Write an image describing the situation.)

_____

_____

Ulysses: Well, boys, I can almost see Ithaca. I'm beat and going to take a little nap. Don't open the bag! (He goes to sleep. Write an image describing the situation.)

_____

_____

Crewman 1: I wonder what is in that bag?

Crewman 2: I bet it is gold. He better share with us!

Crewman 3: Let's take a peek. (He opens the bag and they are blown off course. They land on an island far from Ithaca. Write an image describing the situation.)

_____

_____

Ulysses: What did you do?

Crewman 3: (What would the crewman say? Write your own line.)

_____

_____

Crewman 1: I guess we are not home yet.

Crewman 2: I'm hungry.

(continued)

Crewman 3: I'm thirsty.

Ulysses: Well, this time you are on your own! I am staying right here on this beach.

Crewman 1: Well, that is no kind of attitude! We are going inland and finding something to eat. (They all leave Ulysses. Write an image describing the situation.)

_____

_____

Narrator/Writer: A few hours later....

Crewman 1: (Comes running in) Ulysses, you've got to help! The men—they have been turned into pigs!

Ulysses: Really? Somehow I don't see the change.

Crewman 1: You don't understand. _Real swine_. There is a sorceress on the island named Circe. She invited us in for lunch and then when everyone started eating, whatever she gave them turned them into pigs! Of course, I didn't eat anything. I was waiting outside on guard in case anything went wrong.

Ulysses: Umm. Well I guess it is smart, handsome old me to the rescue _again_. I'll go have a talk with Miss Circe.

Narrator/Writer: Ulysses goes to get his men back from Circe. Of course, being a clever man, he gets some help from the god Hermes who gives him a special herb. As long as he carried it, Ulysses was not affected by Circe's magical food.

Circe: Ah, the famous Ulysses. My, aren't you cute! Care for lunch?

Ulysses: Sure, no problem. (He eats lunch and doesn't change into a pig. Write an image describing the situation.)

_____

_____

Circe: How are you feeling? Piggish?

Ulysses: No, your magic won't work on me, and you will turn my men back now or I'll get rough.

Circe: Moi? Look, I'll offer you a deal. Stay with me for a day and I'll turn back your men, although to be honest, they really acted like pigs.

Ulysses: You have a deal.... I know they are hard to manage, but they are my responsibility.

Circe: Here piggy, piggy, piggy. (She changes them back into men. Write an image describing the situation.)

_____

_____

Crewman 2: (What would the character say? Write your own line.)

_____

_____

(continued)

Narrator/Writer: Ulysses stays the night with Circe, which turns out to be longer than he thinks. (Write an image describing the situation.)

_____

_____

Crewman 4: Ulysses, I've just come back from checking the ship like you told me and it is buried in sand and looks years older!

Ulysses: That can't be right. We've only been here a day and night. Circe, what magic have you done now, you little sneak?

Circe: No magic...it has been only a day and night. Oh, did I forget to mention the time change on the island? One night in your world is seven years here. It keeps me from aging.

Ulysses: Oh, just great. I was in Troy for 10 years and now it's been another 7 years. My wife Penelope is going to kill me for coming home late.

Circe: Why not stay with me, handsome? You won't age here.

Ulysses: Nice offer...but I love my wife, so I'll be going.

Circe: Have it your way, but it won't be fun. You still have to pass many dangers: The Sirens, The Land of the Dead, Scylla and Charybdis...oh, and whatever you do, don't eat the Sun God's cattle.

Crewman 1: Are we going home yet?

Ulysses: Yes, and there's no time like the present. Off we go, men.

*Optional scenes: This plot can be expanded by adding other adventures, people, and places, such as those mentioned by Circe.

Crewman 1: Are we home yet?

Crewman 2: I'm thirsty.

Crewman 3: I'm hungry and that looks like the Island of the Sun God. Look at those cows! I could use a steak!

Ulysses: All right, we land—but no eating steaks!

Narrator/Writer: The men land on the Island of the Sun but can't find much to eat. (Write an image describing the situation.)

_____

_____

Ulysses: OK men, I'm taking a nap. Please be good and don't eat the cattle.

Crewman 1: I am getting very tired of eating shellfish.

Crewman 2: Yeah, and the winds won't blow, so we can't leave this island. I think it means we have to eat steak.

Crewman 4: What gave you that idea?

(continued)

Crewman 2:   I'm a genius, I know.

Narrator/Writer: The crew kills one of the Sun God's cattle and are in the midst of eating it when Ulysses wakes up. (Write an image describing the situation.)

_____

_____

Ulysses: What is that wonderful smell?

Crewman 1:   Uh...chicken.

Ulysses: (Takes a bite) Funny, it doesn't taste like chicken.

Crewman 4:   The winds have changed! We can leave now!

Ulysses: Good. And I am proud of you boys for obeying orders and not eating any of the Sun God's cattle.

Narrator/Writer: As they leave the island, a terrible storm begins and the ship is wrecked. All of Ulysses' men drown. (Write an image describing the situation.)

_____

_____

Ulysses: I knew it! They ate those cattle! Now I am the only one left.

Narrator/Writer: Ulysses lands upon Calypso's island. Calypso, a Titan, keeps Ulysses on her island. Three years pass. (Write a scene describing the new setting and situation.)

_____

_____

Calypso: Ulysses, you are so cute. Aren't you glad I rescued you?

Ulysses: You are beautiful...but I miss my wife and want to go home.

Calypso: What kind of gratitude is that?

Hermes: (flies in) Look, Calypso, the gods have decided it is time for Ulysses to go home, so you have to let your plaything go.

Calypso: That is not fair.

Hermes: Who said the gods were fair?

Ulysses: You have a point there.

Calypso: (What does Calypso say? Write your own line.)

_____

_____

Hermes: (What does Hermes say? Write your own line.)

_____

_____

(continued)

Ulysses: (What would Ulysses say? Write your own line.)

_____

_____

Narrator/Writer: (What happens when Ulysses gets home? Resolve the problem and end the story.)

_____

_____

Wolf Kids

Characters:

Romulus

Remus

She-Wolf

Grey Wolf

Faustulus (a shepherd)

Acca Larentia (Faustulus's wife)

Guard 1

Guard 2

King Numitor

Rhea Silvia

King Amulis

Narrator/Writer

Narrator/Writer: In the kingdom of Alba Longa, King Amulis is sitting on the throne talking to his guards. (Describe the setting and this situation. Don't forget to include images.)

_____

_____

King Amulis: You say that Princess Rhea, my dear departed elder brother's daughter, just had twin baby boys. Well, I helped him "depart" by throwing him out of the country so I could get the throne for myself. It seems I am going to have to help the little twins depart, too. One's throne can never be safe with unwanted relatives about the place. Guards, go murder those brats!

Guard 2: Sure, sir.

Guard 1: We will do the old basket-in-the-river number.

King Amulis: Good choice—no blood, no mess, and no bodies. By the way, make sure the basket leaks.

Guard 1: Nice touch.

Guard 2: No problem.

Narrator/Writer: The guards take the twin boys away from their mother. (Write an image that describes this situation.)

_____

_____

Rhea Silvia: What do you want with my children?

Guard 1: They are going to take some swimming lessons.

Guard 2: You can never start them too young.

Guard 1: Come, little fishes, into the basket.

Guard 2: They are not fish. We are supposed to drown them, not fish with them.

Rhea Silvia: You can't drown my children. They are princes!

Guard 2: Sorry lady, we have our orders.

Rhea Silvia: (What would Rhea Silvia say? Write your own line.)

_____

_____

(continued)

Narrator/Writer: The guards take the boys, put them in the basket, and throw them in the Tiber River. They float down the river, and just when they are about to sink, they are rescued by a She-Wolf. (Write some images to make this more interesting to the reader.)

_____

_____

Grey Wolf: Hey, what did you fish out of the river? Boy, are they ugly.

She-Wolf: Well, they are a little strange looking, but I think I had a cousin once in the jungle with a cub like this. She called him...something that started with _m_ I think.

Narrator/Writer: Romulus cries and begins to shove Remus. (Write an image that describes this situation.)

_____

_____

Remus: (He cries and starts shoving him back. Write an image that describes this situation.)

_____

_____

Grey Wolf: I think I'd call these two trouble. Look, fighting already.

She-Wolf: It is only sibling rivalry. I'll feed them, and they will be fine.

Narrator/Writer: And so Romulus and Remus are cared for by the She-Wolf until they are discovered one day by a shepherd named Faustulus and his wife, Acca Larentia.

Faustulus: Darling, look what I found out in our flock today. They were growling and pulling on one of our sheep. A wolf came up to me and actually led me to them.

(The boys start growling and pushing each other. Write an image that describes this situation.)

_____

_____

Acca Larentia: They would probably be cute if they were cleaned up. Are you sure they are tame?

Faustulus: Don't worry. It's just sibling rivalry. They appear to be twins after all.

Acca Larentia: You know, they look a lot like Rhea Silvia. They have her eyes.

Faustulus: (What would Faustulus say? Write your own line.)

_____

_____

Narrator/Writer: Acca Larentia raises the boys until they reach manhood and then she takes them to see King Numitor. (Add some backfill to explain this to the reader.)

_____

_____

(continued)

Setting the Stage for Creative Writing: Plot Scaffolds for Beginning and Intermediate Writers by Shannon O'Day.
Copyright © 2006 by the International Reading Association. May be copied for classroom use.

Wolf Kids (continued)

Acca Larentia: Now boys, behave yourselves. We are going to see the old king, Numitor.

Romulus: I get to see him first!

Remus: You always get to be first! It's my turn.

Romulus: It is not!

Remus: Is so, you toad!

Romulus: Dog face!

Acca Larentia: Boys! You are acting like wild wolves. Your highness, you'll have to excuse them. They have experienced a great childhood trauma.

King Numitor: You know, they have my daughter's eyes.

Acca Larentia: I thought so, too. I think they are your long lost grandchildren.

King Numitor: I think you are right. Boys, if you are my grandchildren, you must win back the throne from my wicked younger brother, Amulis.

Romulus: Remus, I told you younger brothers were a pain!

Remus: How do you know I'm younger? We're twins. Maybe you're younger! You're a pain!

Acca Larentia: (What would Acca Larentia say? Write your own line.)

_____

_____

Narrator/Writer: Romulus and Remus travel to Alba Longa and depose King Amulis. (Write a description of this happening in the story.)

_____

_____

Romulus: Amulis, you will have to leave. You tried to kill us!

Remus: But we are back, so get off the throne!

King Amulis: (What would King Amulis say? Write your own line.)

_____

_____

Guard 1: (What would Guard 1 say? Write your own line.)

_____

_____

Guard 2: (What would Guard 2 say? Write your own line.)

_____

_____

(continued)

Wolf Kids (continued)

King Numitor: Now I have my old throne back. Thanks boys. How about you two go build a city of your own?

Remus: Great idea! How about a spot on the other side of the Tiber, one of those seven hills?

Romulus: Let's build it on the Palatine Hill.

Remus: No way. I like the Capitoline Hill to the left of the Palatine Hill.

Romulus: Not *that* spot. This spot. And I'm building a wall, so there!

Narrator/Writer: Romulus builds the wall and to show its inadequacy, Remus leaps over it. (Describe this situation.)

_____

_____

Remus: (What would Remus say? Write your own line.)

_____

_____

Romulus: (What would Romulus say? Write your own line.)

_____

_____

King Numitor: (What would King Numitor say? Write your own line.)

_____

_____

Grey Wolf: (What would the Grey Wolf say? Write your own line.)

_____

_____

She-Wolf: (What would She-Wolf say? Write your own line.)

_____

_____

Narrator/Writer: (Write the last lines and resolve the plot.)

_____

_____

Tyrant?

Characters:

Julius Caesar

Mark Anthony

Casca

Lepidus

Soothsayer (a person believed to be able
  to read the future)

Titinus

Cleopatra

Brutus

Metellus

Cinna

Flavius

Portia

Cicero

Octavius

Calpurnia

Cassius

Servant

Murellus

Narrator/Writer

Optional Characters:

Senators

Servants

Narrator/Writer: The scene is ancient Rome, 44 B.C. Queen Cleopatra is talking with her servant. (Describe the setting and this situation. Don't forget to include images.)

_____

_____

Cleopatra: Well, what is the latest gossip? I know I set everyone's tongues wagging when I, the Queen of Egypt, came to visit Caesar in Rome and brought our child.

Servant: What would you expect? He does have a wife here.

Cleopatra: Some wife. She can't even have children. He married me in Egypt. That's what counts. Together we will rule the entire Roman Empire from Gaul to Egypt, and I will be his beautiful queen. Our son will inherit the empire. (Describe how she might walk around the room.)

_____

_____

Servant: Sounds wonderful, but the Roman people may have something to say about Caesar becoming a king. They have a republic here, not a monarchy. Also, Caesar's current heir is his grandnephew, Octavius.

Cleopatra: Well, Caesar was just made Dictator for Life by the senate in gratitude for all he has done. He goes around carrying a scepter and wearing the robe and crown of a triumphant general and uses the title *Imperator*. It's only a matter of time before they make him supreme ruler of Rome, and I'll be right there at his side. As for an heir, what's a grandnephew compared to a direct son?

Servant: There are some ugly rumors to the effect that certain important people may not

(continued)

tolerate Caesar too much longer. If I were you, I'd have a back-up plan. (Describe the servant's actions as he or she talks.)

_____

_____

Narrator/Writer: The setting is Caesar's home in the early morning. (Describe the setting and this situation. Don't forget to include images.)

_____

_____

Narrator/Writer: (A Soothsayer appears outside the window of Caesar's home. Describe the setting and this situation. Don't forget to include images. What does the Soothsayer look like?)

_____

_____

Soothsayer: Caesar, beware the Ides of March! (How would the Soothsayer say this?)

_____

_____

Calpurnia: Dearest, do you have to go to the senate today? That Soothsayer is outside again shouting warnings.

Caesar: Not again. Even after I reformed the current calendar and gave Rome a rational means of recording time, they still mark bad and good days on them. I don't even remember seeing the Ides marked as bad, do you? Besides, it is all superstitious nonsense. (Describe the setting and this situation. Don't forget to include images.)

_____

_____

Portia: My husband, Brutus, says that superstitions often have real bases.

Caesar: As Marcus Junius Brutus is one of my best friends, I won't dispute that with you. However, I still plan to go to the Senate today, and I will probably come home with some big news. I expect we will be moving to the palace soon. Ah, here is my great friend, Mark Anthony, to escort me to the Senate. (Describe the setting and this situation. Don't forget to include images.)

_____

_____

Mark Anthony: Hail Caesar. There's a rumor that you are to be made Emperor of Rome today. No one deserves the title more, and the people love you. You have certainly helped to straighten out the political mess in our republic. You eliminated the highly corrupt tax system, reconstituted the courts, and increased the number of senators. The government of our large empire needs a strong leader. (Does he admire Caesar? What might he be doing while he says this?)

_____

_____

(continued)

Caesar: It is only my duty as a citizen. I live to serve Rome.

Portia: Here is my beloved husband, Brutus. (This is said in an aside, without the other characters hearing. How might a character say an aside? Don't forget to include images.)

_____

_____

Why do you look so worried?

Brutus: (This also is said in an aside, without the other characters hearing. How might a character say an aside? Don't forget to include images.)

_____

_____

It's this rex thing with Caesar. I love and admire Caesar, but we have a republic, and kings are tyrants and enemies to our Roman republic.

Portia: You have been talking to Cassius again. He is bad news, that one. He has a lean, hungry look. He's just jealous of Caesar. Many people are.

Brutus: You are probably right, still.... (to Caesar, how would he say this?)

_____

_____

Hail Caesar, I've come to escort you to the Senate today. Mark Anthony, Metellus said he needs your help with one of the speeches he is writing and would like you to come to his house right now.

Mark Anthony: The price of being a good orator. I'll meet you at the Senate, Caesar. (He leaves. Describe this image.)

_____

_____

Calpurnia: I really wish you wouldn't go today.

Caesar: Don't be ridiculous. We need to go. (Brutus and Caesar leave. Describe how they would leave by using an image.)

_____

_____

Portia: If it had been Cleopatra asking, he would have stayed.

Calpurnia: He doesn't listen to _that woman_.

Narrator/Writer: Meanwhile at the Senate, all the senators are talking. (Describe the setting and this situation. Don't forget to include images.)

_____

_____

(continued)

Cassius: Fellow Romans, Caesar is a tyrant. We must destroy him before he destroys us by taking away our freedom.

Metellus: Yes, our great ancestors will haunt us forever if we allow Caesar to be king!

Lepidus: But the people love him. Why, he has cut the welfare dole by half!

Titinus: The army loves him, too. He has sponsored colonies of veterans and extended Roman citizenship. Why, he conquered Gaul, and the Roman Empire is twice as big as when he first became a general! I think you are also forgetting that he is still in total command of the armies. (How might Titinus say this? Don't forget to include images.)

_____

_____

Cinna: I told you he was a tyrant—nothing but a military dictator. It is only a matter of time before he takes away our basic voting rights.

Octavius: I am not going to sit here while you badmouth my uncle! Why, the government was a mess before he came in and got things running smoothly. Think of all he has done for us and his plans for a new harbor.

Cassius: What do you know? You are too young to even be a senator. Go home and leave this business to men who care about what is really important to the republic—freedom.

Octavius: You are just jealous. (He leaves. Describe this in an image.)

_____

_____

Flavius: What can we do? Caesar may be ambitious, but he is a good man.

Casca: But Cassius is right. We, as older and wiser men, have a duty to protect the republic from kings.

Cicero: Caesar is not a king.

Cassius: But Caesar is ambitious. He is now Pontifex Maximus, and the Senate will make him Rex if we don't persuade them that he is just using them to gain power over us all. It is obvious that Caesar only created more senatorial positions so he could get more people on his side.

Metellus: They will never believe us. The people love Caesar.

Casca: The people are too easily fooled. Remember how Caesar became so popular. He gave the most lavish gladiatorial games. The people have elected us to lead them to protect their rights, to do what is in their best interest.

Flavius: But is it in their best interest to destroy Caesar? How else can we stop him?

Cassius: Caesar comes to the senate today. He has already been made dictator for life, a title *formally* given only for six months in a state of national emergency. Do you see any emergencies? Must he also be given the crown?

Murellus: We don't have a crown. We are a republic.

Setting the Stage for Creative Writing: Plot Scaffolds for Beginning and Intermediate Writers by Shannon O'Day.
Copyright © 2006 by the International Reading Association. May be copied for classroom use.

Casca: Well, Caesar has a crown on his mind and so do the people. Better to stop him here before it is too late.

Cicero: How do we stop him? What do we do?

Murellus: (What would Murellus say? Write your own line.)

_____

_____

Cicero: (What would Cicero say? Write your own line.)

_____

_____

Lepidus: (What would Lepidus say? Write your own line.)

_____

_____

Cassius: (What would Cassius say? Write your own line.)

_____

_____

Flavius: (What would Flavius say? Write your own line.)

_____

_____

Narrator/Writer: Caesar and Brutus enter the senate. (Describe the setting and this situation. Don't forget to include images.)

_____

_____

Caesar: My fellow Romans, greetings. I know you are pleased to see me today, and I am so happy to be with you.

Casca: (What would Casca say? Write your own line.)

_____

_____

Brutus: (What would Brutus say? Write your own line.)

_____

_____

Caesar: (What would Caesar say? Write your own line.)

_____

_____

Cinna: (What would Cinna say? Write your own line.)

_____

_____

Metellus: (What would Metellus say? Write your own line.)

_____

_____

Narrator/Writer: Back at Caesar's home.

Portia: (Rushes in. Describe in an image what she might be about to say.)

_____

_____

My lady, have you heard the news about Caesar?

Calpurnia: No, tell me.

Portia: (What would Portia say? Write your own line.)

_____

_____

Calpurnia: (What would Calpurnia say? Write your own line.)

_____

_____

Narrator/Writer: At Cleopatra's villa.

Servant: (Rushes in. Describe this in an image.)

_____

_____

My lady, have your heard that...? (What would the servant say? Write your own lines.)

_____

_____

Cleopatra: (What would Cleopatra say? Write your own line.)

_____

_____

Soothsayer: (What would the Soothsayer say? Write your own line and end the story.)

_____

_____

The Guinea Pig Paper Model

Guinea Pig Paper

Research Question
Why did the Inca Indians keep guinea pigs?

Review of Literature
Archeologists have found many drawings of guinea pigs on temple walls in the jungles of Peru, and there are many theories as to why the Incas kept guinea pigs. Guinea pigs can still be found in Peru and have been there for thousands of years. Today we keep guinea pigs as pets or use them for lab experiments. The Incas may have had other uses for them.

One theory by Whitworth (1968) states that the Incas kept guinea pigs as a type of watchdog. He points out that most of the temple drawings show guinea pigs in small cages hanging outside of what are obviously shops and houses. Guinea pigs would squeak when an intruder approached and warn their masters. "Other societies such as the Chinese use a similar type of alarm system when they hang cages of crickets outside their shops and homes" (Whitworth, 1968, p. 186). When the crickets stop chirping, an intruder must be present. Guinea pigs are practical and eat less than dogs. There is no evidence that the Incas kept large dogs. Guinea pigs were one of the first alarm systems.

Another theory by Sims (1998) states that guinea pigs were kept as a food source. Evidence for this are the mounds of literally millions of guinea pig bones found outside most Inca ruins. Like rabbits, guinea pigs breed rapidly and would prove an excellent food source. "Guinea pigs taste like chicken" (Sims, 1998, p. 333). Sims has also noted that the pictures on temple walls show very large guinea pigs, some as big as ten pounds. This huge South American guinea pig may have become extinct due to disease as guinea pigs are notorious for getting viruses easily, and that is why they are used in labs today (Sims, 1977). Guinea pigs could have been a food source for the Incas.

Yet another possibility is that guinea pigs may have been raised for their fur and skins (Myers, 1944). Guinea pigs have very warm, soft fur, which comes in a great variety of colors. Their skins could be used for leather products such as belts or shoes.

Myers also found a necklace made of hundreds of tiny guinea pig feet, but as this is the only one ever found, "...guinea pig feet as a form of jewelry may be not a wide spread use of the animal" (Myers, 1935, p. 99).

Analysis
There are four theories for guinea pig use, and they do not seem to have much in common with each other. They could have been used as watchdogs, a food source, for clothing, and for jewelry. It is true that some societies keep small animals as watchdogs. These animals, like the Mexican Hairless [dog], are very small and bark at intruders to scare them away. As a food source, guinea pigs might be edible, but it would take many of them to make a meal. Their fur is soft and long and might have been used like we use rabbit skins today. Decorating oneself with guinea pig feet may have been a fad just as today we have fads like wearing owl-dropping jewelry. All four theories do not seem to have much in common.

Methodology (Depending on one's project, this section is optional.)
In order to test the theories on guinea pig use this researcher will raise guinea pigs for ten months in order to find out how fast they breed. The researcher will also then eat guinea pig and serve it to other people to determine if it is edible. The researcher will also attempt to make clothing and jewelry from the remaining skins and feet.

(continued)

Guinea Pig Paper (continued)

Conclusion

The most likely explanation seems to be that guinea pigs were kept as a food source. As watchdogs, guinea pigs would not scare someone away because they cannot attack. Besides, they only squeak when they want food so the intruder would have to be bringing them their dinner. Guinea pigs could not be used for clothing because it would take over 200 skins to make a small coat (Whitworth, 1968). This is not practical when making clothing, and their skins are too thin to make good soles for shoes. The guinea pig necklace mentioned by Myers seems to be an isolated incident or perhaps just a one-time use. The most practical use of guinea pigs appears to be as a food source for the Incas. The evidence which might prove this are the mounds of guinea pig bones found outside temples, and the fact that guinea pigs do taste good. This researcher has raised and eaten guinea pigs herself and finds that, indeed, they taste like chicken. The Incas used guinea pigs for food.

Sources (APA)

Borman, W.C., Hanson, M.A., Oppler, S.H., and White, L.A. (1993) Role of early Incan people in food production. *Journal of Applied Foodstuff*, 78, 433–449. Retrieved October 23, 2000, from Psycarticles database.

Hammond, T, (2000, July 14). New resources for the giant guinea pig [Msg 311]. Message posted to http://groups.yahoo.com/group/visualcognition/message/31 (Message posted to online forum or discussion group)

Myers, M. (1935, October 29). Jewelry in the ancient world. *Journal of Anthropology*, 2, 67–99. (magazine article)

Myers, M. (1944). New Coats. In *The new encyclopedia Britannica* (Vol. 26, pp. 501–588). Chicago: Encyclopedia Britannica. (entry in an encyclopedia)

Sims, N.L. (1998). *It tastes like chicken*. Washington, DC: American Psychological association. (one-author book)

Whitworth, S. (Ed.). (1968). *The new Grove dictionary of animals* (6th ed., Vols. 1–20). London: Macmillan. (encyclopedia or dictionary)

Learning Objectives for Research Writing

Students produce a piece of writing that

1. Uses research and technology to support writing.

2. Cites references and gives credit for both quoted and paraphrased information.

3. Uses various reference materials.

4. Includes appropriate, relevant information and arguments.

5. Supports arguments with detailed evidence, citing sources of information as appropriate.

6. Defines a thesis.

7. Poses relevant and tightly drawn questions about the topic.

8. Excludes information and arguments that are irrelevant.

9. Provides details, reasons, and examples, arranging them effectively by anticipating and answering reader concerns and counterarguments.

Research Paper Rubric

Research Skills	Standards	Student Evaluation	Teacher Evaluation	Comments
Purpose	Clear thesis	1 2 3 4 5	1 2 3 4 5	
Evidence	Literature review had three or more various sources	1 2 3 4 5	1 2 3 4 5	
	Summarized ideas	1 2 3 4 5	1 2 3 4 5	
Analysis	Analyses drawn from literature	1 2 3 4 5	1 2 3 4 5	
Experiment	Methodology	1 2 3 4 5	1 2 3 4 5	
Conclusion	Conclusion is valid	1 2 3 4 5	1 2 3 4 5	
Grammar	Surface errors and grammar do not interfere with meaning	1 2 3 4 5 6 7 8 9 10	1 2 3 4 5 6 7 8 9 10	
References	Cited all reference sources	1 2 3 4 5	1 2 3 4 5	
Organization	Organized format	1 2 3 4 5	1 2 3 4 5	

Total score _____ / 50

Teacher Handouts for Writing Mentor Program

Meeting One: Graphic Organizers for Narrative, Persuasive, and Expository Writing

Meeting One is designed to help students realize how they will be evaluated and how to use a simple scaffold, such as a graphic organizer, to help focus and direct their writing. Most standardized tests are timed, so organization is a key factor in helping emerging, developing, and focusing writers stay on task and have a clear plan for writing.

Procedures

1. Review the specific rubric for the standardized test to be administered. Both students and teachers need to know how test evaluation will occur. Compare the rubric to a sample essay students have written before this meeting.

2. Explain the three common choices for standardized writing tests: narrative, persuasive, and expository. Often in K–8 testing, narrative text receives higher scores, so encourage students to write narratives or stories. Scoring usually is higher because this type of writing lends itself to student individuality and creativity.

3. Explain the components of a story and introduce the types of graphic organizers to use in conjunction with narrative, persuasive, and expository formats. Emphasize to students the importance of using a graphic organizer *before* they begin a writing project. A graphic organizer can be used to store notes and to scaffold students' writing. As a prewriting strategy, graphic organizers provide a means for writers to organize information and stay on the topic. Encourage students to check off the notes in their graphic organizer *during* the writing process. The following are some examples for graphic organizers. Write them on the board or place them on an overhead projector to explain narrative, persuasive, and expository writing.

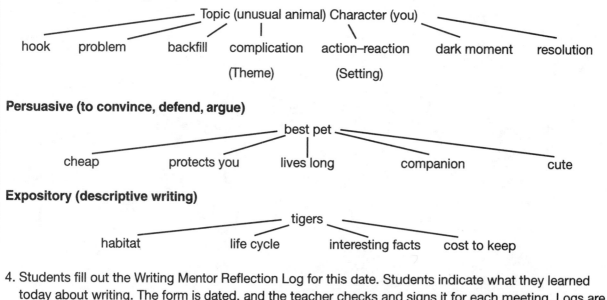

Narrative (story writing)

Topic (unusual animal) Character (you)

hook   problem   backfill   complication   action–reaction   dark moment   resolution

(Theme)   (Setting)

Persuasive (to convince, defend, argue)

best pet

cheap   protects you   lives long   companion   cute

Expository (descriptive writing)

tigers

habitat   life cycle   interesting facts   cost to keep

4. Students fill out the Writing Mentor Reflection Log for this date. Students indicate what they learned today about writing. The form is dated, and the teacher checks and signs it for each meeting. Logs are collected at the end of the program, and the data are used to help determine any changes to next year's program. Whoever is in charge of the writing mentor program should maintain these logs.

Meeting Two: Image Strategy

Meeting Two is designed to make students aware of the importance of using images in their writing to give the reader a clear picture of the writer's feelings and ideas. Writing images in standardized tests is often regarded as a higher level skill, but beginning writers can achieve this engaging- or extending-writer status by learning to include images, too.

Procedure

Opening: Show students an interesting picture; for example, a picture of an optical illusion of a cow. Ask, "What is it?" After students have made guesses or offered suggestions, explain that the picture is a cow. Once students know what the picture is, explain how having prior knowledge or describing something allows people to "see" the image. A picture that can be interpreted in various ways is useful also for understanding point of view. Also explain that a good literary image shows not tells; for example, taste and smell can evoke past experiences and make for very powerful images. The following two lessons can aid students in writing good images.

1. Hand out one jellybean to each student. Ask students to describe the taste of their jellybeans. Students' descriptions should include how they feel about the taste and of what it reminds them. Like the interpretive picture, the taste of one flavor may be very different for each person. For example, following are two descriptions of jellybeans:

   Chocolate pudding jellybean: The jellybean reminds me of curling up late on a rainy night and drinking cocoa while watching an old movie on television.

   Yellow and white jellybean: The jellybean reminds me of a comfortable movie theatre, and it tastes like the warm popcorn my family and I eat when we see movies at the movie theatre.

   Review students' images by reading them aloud. Then, correct grammar and meaning.

2. Have students write a description of a smell. Bring in a scented candle, perfume (sprayed on paper), or some other object with an interesting odor. Then, have students brainstorm topics for the writing test and think of ways they could use images (incorporating smell or taste) that describe their feelings toward the topic. The following is an example of an image describing the topic "My best day at school."

   Like warm apple pie, my best day at school was when I met my best friend, Sammy. She just knew how to talk to me and make school a cozy place to be.

3. Finally, students fill out the Writing Mentor Reflection Log for this date by explaining what they learned. The teacher checks the log to gain feedback and signs it.

Meeting Three: Interesting Sentences and Dialogue

Meeting Three is designed to emphasize the importance of varying types of sentences and creating interesting dialogue. Have students focus on using the strategy of "flipping" sentences to avoid the overuse of articles or pronouns at the beginning of sentences. Have students focus on adding interesting dialogue through "dressing" their characters—that is, describing characters by showing readers what characters are wearing, which relates to the story setting and plot.

Procedure

1. Review students' original stories and count how many times they use *the* or a pronoun at the beginning of sentences. Students can complete this task using a highlighter; have them highlight the words and then count them. This calls students' attention to how many times their sentences may begin with repetitive, dull words that do not grab the reader's interest.

2. Introduce the flip-sentence strategy. Have students focus on starting sentences with clauses or phrases, although teachers will need to warn students to avoid dangling modifiers. Following is an example that illustrates this strategy:

   The red dog ran over the hill.
   Over the hill ran the red dog.

3. Have students flip some of their own sentences in their stories.

4. Emphasize the importance of using interesting words, and have students choose three higher level vocabulary words to include in their essays. For example, use the series Word Within the Word (Fireworks Press) as a source for vocabulary words. Have students note these words in their graphic organizers and check them off as they use them.

5. Emphasize the importance of dialogue. Advise students to avoid overuse of the word *said*. The reader needs to "see" the character as he or she talks. Use the Fred and Mary dialogue strategy:

   • Write the lines. (Remember to space dialogue or go to the next line and indent when you change characters.)

   • Add some movement. (What are the characters doing?)

   • Add some scenery (images).

   • Put your characters in costume. (What are the characters wearing or what do they look like?)

I tell students to think of writing dialogue in a story as writing lines in a play or movie. We use the following lines as a starting point:

Fred: There is a dog.

Mary: It is a big dog.

Fred: It bit me.

Students recognize that the dialogue sounds pretty flat. Reading lines from a script can be dull because the reader cannot see the actors or the action. To help readers visualize what is going on, I have students add stage directions or add movement to the script. I also have students give the characters some expression with more exact dialogue.

(continued)

Fred: (calls out to Mary) There is a huge bulldog coming this way!

Mary: (turns to Fred) It is a gigantic bulldog with fangs and a blue tail. I think it is glaring at us. Do you have a gun?

Fred: (looking down in disbelief) Too late. I think the creature just took my hand off. Ouch!

The dialogue is improving, but the scenery is missing. I have students add some images so readers know where the characters are and then put the dialogue into story form. Finally, I remind students to dress the characters in costumes that match the setting. The final version of the dialogue read as follows:

While exploring the dense jungle on planet Xenon, Fred, flipping back his space helmet visor, calls out to Mary, "There is a huge bulldog coming this way."

Turning both of her heads in his direction, Mary quickly responds in a high squeaky voice, "It is a gigantic bull dog with sharp fangs and a blue tail. I think it is glaring at us. Do you have a gun?"

Jumping forward at light speed, the rabid creature leaps at Fred and then quickly retreats into the tall purple vegetation surrounding them. "Too late," Fred sighs, "I think the creature just took my hand off. Ouch!" Fred shrugs his shoulders, "Guess I will just have to grow another hand."

Once students realize that creating dialogue in this way is not intimidating, they become eager to participate and to continually revise and rewrite the story's ending until they are satisfied that the plot says what they want it to say.

6. Students fill out the Writing Mentor Reflection Log for this date by explaining what they learned. The teacher checks the log to gain feedback and signs it.

Meeting Four: Overall Appearance and Varying Sentence Length

Meeting Four, the last meeting before the standardized test, is designed to focus on the appearance of students' writing, which should appear neat, legible, and balanced. Students' writing should look appealing because presentation is a large part of any exhibition.

Procedure

1. Have students count the word length of their original essays. For rhythm, beat, and interest, sentences should have a variety of lengths. If all sentences roughly had the same amount of words and syllables, the story would have a four-four-four beat, which can become monotonous. If all sentences had the same number of words and those numbers were placed as points on graph paper, the line connecting the numbers would be straight. My students and I refer to this as a "flat line" or "dead" story because it has no up and down rhythm. Teachers also can choose to count the words in each sentence and draw an analogy to lines of music or poetry. For example, William Shakespeare's sonnets, which are written in iambic pentameter, have the same rhythm as a beating human heart. As well as being heard, Shakespeare's language also is "felt" because it matches the rhythm of our hearts.

2. Review the use of hook. Ask students how they would grab readers' interest in the first sentence. Ask how to avoid using pronouns and articles at the beginning of sentences.

3. Have students focus on the overall appearance or presentation of their writing. Emphasize the importance of handwriting. Just as a good oral storyteller must use clear enunciation and body language, the writer must ensure that his or her written story appears fluent and easy to decode. Handwriting is a life skill. For example, explain to students that the post office hires people simply to read hand-addressed envelopes because millions of letters are lost each year due to illegibility.

   Use the following handwriting strategy with students as a class warm-up activity in the morning while the teacher takes roll or collects homework or while waiting for the rest of the class to arrive. This daily exercise improves students' handwriting, sets the tone for productivity for the day, and results in a more quiet environment first thing in the morning. Later, make the activity more exciting by incorporating special pens or fancy paper. Students ultimately learn that handwriting does matter despite the current emphasis and reliance on computers.

4. Students fill in Writing Mentor Reflection Log for this date by explaining what they learned. The teacher checks the log to gain feedback and then signs it.

Handwriting Strategy

1. At the beginning of the week, give students one handwriting sheet that will be used to practice writing on the lines and writing larger. Purchase reproducible handwriting practice books or make photocopies from the school district's handwriting book. To save paper, teachers can place on overhead transparencies whatever handwriting books or forms the school district has mandated. Teachers also can create their own sheets. Each sheet can focus on a specific letter or letter combination and should have space to practice writing words and a complete sentence including that specific letter-writing exercise.

2. For the next four days, have students complete the activity on the handwriting sheet, writing each section three times on lined paper. Award students one point each day if they are able to complete the task before the bell for first period rings and if their writing is neat and complete, and sentences end with periods. These points can be used to raise assignment grades five points, so students' papers are stapled onto those assignments.

3. Ask students to submit their handwriting at the end of each day. Write appropriate comments on students' papers or display them.

Meeting Five: Celebration

Meeting Five is designed for discussing the results of the writing test with students. Teachers review individual scores with each mentee and share information regarding the meaning and significance of the scores. Students provide the teacher with feedback about what students thought was helpful or what needs improvement in the mentor program. Students explain what strategies worked best for them during the test as well as what difficulties they experienced. At this last meeting, teachers make sure that the Writing Mentor Reflection Log is completed and this information is given to whoever is in charge of the writing mentor program. This last mentor meeting also is a celebration of writing achievement, so some teachers may choose to bring treats or snacks to share with their students while they are discussing the test results.

Writing Mentor Reflection Log

Meeting One:

Date of meeting_____ time_____

What did you learn from this session? What concerns about writing do you have?

Mentee signature _____   Mentor signature _____

Meeting Two:

Date of meeting_____ time_____

What did you learn from this session? What concerns about writing do you have?

Mentee signature _____   Mentor signature _____

Meeting Three:

Date of meeting_____ time_____

What did you learn from this session? What concerns about writing do you have?

Mentee signature _____   Mentor signature _____

Meeting Four:

Date of meeting_____ time_____

What did you learn from this session? What concerns about writing do you have?

Mentee signature _____   Mentor signature _____

Meeting Five:

Date of meeting_____ time_____

What did you learn from this session? What concerns about writing do you have?

Mentee signature _____   Mentor signature _____

GLOSSARY

Action–reaction: An element of plot; the first serious attempt by the main character to solve the problem, but the problem gets worse. Action–reaction may occur more than one time in a story as the main character or characters continue to try, unsuccessfully, to solve the problem. Thus, the characters' actions cause a "reaction" rather than a solution.

Anticipation–reaction guide: A prereading strategy that helps activate students' ideas about a topic by asking students to react to a series of guided statements related to that topic.

Backfill: An element of plot; the background information in the story.

Collaboration: In literacy scaffolding, refers to the teacher's role being that of facilitator rather than evaluator so that students feel comfortable exploring different solutions rather than giving a recitation and display of previous learning.

Complication: An element of plot; a twist to the plot in which the character attempts to solve a problem, but the problem gets worse. A complication is a condition that challenges the hero.

Constructed response: A written task based on short, open-ended questions that measure application-level cognitive skills as well as content knowledge. Written descriptions of complex problem solutions can also provide insight into reasoning proficiency. Constructed or free-response assessment models require students to develop their own responses, which include structured interviews and essays—for example, an essay that taps understanding of relationships among elements of knowledge.

Constructivism: An educational theory based on the idea that learners construct knowledge for themselves and do so individually and socially as they learn. Constructing meaning is learning. The focus is on the learner and the experience constructed by the learner or community of learners.

Creative drama: A process that enhances problem solving in an active organic sense as solutions grow into more possibilities. An original play text provides learners with an initial dilemma or situation, but it is soon supplemented by the texts that arise among students and teacher as they interact. The product, a final performance or solution, is highly linked to literacy because learners must communicate their ideas to other participants, which may include the instructor, fellow students, and an audience.

Creativity: The ability to produce work that is novel and appropriate, useful, and adaptive despite task constraints (Sternberg, 1997).

Cross-curricular units: Thematic instruction based on macro themes. Thematic instruction integrates content areas such as reading, math, and science with the exploration of a broad subject, such as communities, the hero, Middle Ages, or the Renaissance. Cross-curricular units are created based on the idea that people acquire knowledge best when learning in the context of a coherent "whole" and when they can connect what they are learning to the real world. McTighe (2000) argues that learning is meaningful and more likely to grab the learner's attention when it contains broad questions that relate to their world. Essential questions need to identify big ideas to create enduring understandings, which by their nature would cross disciplines. Big ideas are important, enduring, and transferable beyond the scope of just one particular content area. For example, an essential question such as Do the arts reflect society or shape it? would cross many content areas including music, art, social studies, and language arts.

Dark moment: An element of plot; the climax of the story, or the "moment of one candle." This image is helpful to writers because it clarifies for them the concept of dark moment. At the dark moment, the hero only has one light or one opportunity to take action, or the situation will become dark or disastrous.

Developing writer: A writer who is able to begin developing the topic. The student's response to writing has the start of an organizational plan, but it is not complete. This writer has a limited awareness of audience and uses simple word choice and sentence patterns. Errors in surface features interrupt the fluency of communication.

Elaboration: A component of creativity that enables one item of information to lead to another as a kind of extension or completion, with a variety of implications. These new changes are the transformations—that is, the revisions, redefinitions, or modifications—by which any product of information in one state is altered to another state.

Emerging writer: A writer who needs to work on topic development, organization, and detail because he or she has little awareness of audience or the writing task. This type of writer has a message but needs structure to make the message known. The writer makes errors in grammar that prevent the reader from understanding the message.

Empathy: A literacy process that is important for creating connections between writer and reader such that the reader is able to understand the writer's message. It is the deeper understanding that comes about through shared emotional experiences.

Engaging writer: A writer who uses well-developed story topics with a clear, focused beginning, middle, and end. This type of writer engages the reader's interest with an effective use of varied language and sentence patterns. Surface features do not interfere with meaning.

ESL: A program that deals specifically with students who are studying English as a second language. Students within the program are often referred to as ESL students.

Evaluative questions: These types of questions ask students to decide whether or not they agree with an issue that is being explored in text and assess how it fits in with their experiences.

Experimenting writer: A writer who includes a clear topic but whose development may be uneven, making the beginning and ending of the story awkward. The writer is aware of the audience and is experimenting with language and sentence patterns. Word combinations and choice may be unique, but errors in surface features may interrupt fluency.

Explicit questions: These types of questions ask the reader to recall particular details or events from a story. They may be answered using factual information found in the text. Normally, there is only one correct answer.

Extending writer: A writer who has a good grasp of how to create images and novel language. Surface structure does not interfere with meaning.

Facilitation: A teaching style that creates a positive climate that makes it easier for students to achieve their potential. The teacher gives a clear, visible priority to students' prior knowledge and shows a willingness to diverge from or modify the planned curriculum to meet students' needs. There is a high degree of tolerance and skill in managing and allowing students' choices about the form and content of their work, which occurs in an atmosphere where all participants feel safe in taking risks.

Flexibility: A component of creativity; the ability to produce a number of changes to material—changes that are neither immediate nor obvious, but appropriate to a general requirement that needs to be fulfilled (Alpaugh & Birren, 1977). Flexibility is sometimes spontaneous and allows for solutions or interpretations to a problem from more than one perspective.

Fluency: A component of creativity; the rate of generation of a quantity of ideas that are possible solutions to a problem. For example, students might attempt to name as many possible solutions or scenarios as they can think of for a plot in which "boy meets girl," "boy loses girl," and "boy wins girl."

Focusing writer: A writer who includes a clear topic even though development is not complete. Although this type of writer has a sense of audience, the writer's plan is loosely organized, and he or she uses a minimal variety of vocabulary and sentence patterns. Errors in surface features interrupt the fluency of communication.

Formal assessment: A form of evaluation that usually focuses on selected responses. For example, multiple-choice, true-or-false, and matching formats often are given at the end of a unit of study to determine the degree of a student's mastery of the subject. Formal assessments also include criterion references tests and standardized tests. A constructed or performance-based assessment also can be used if set criteria are established and assessment occurs to determine subject mastery.

Graphic organizer: A visual aid that defines hierarchical relationships among concepts and that lends itself to the organization of ideas. Like mapping, it can be used as a blueprint or guide for writing papers.

Guinea Pig Paper Model: A term affectionately given to a scaffold used to write a research paper. (See Appendix C for The Guinea Pig Paper.)

Hook: An element of plot; the event usually found at the beginning of a story that grabs the reader's attention.

Image: A writer's description that shows the reader what something looks, smells, tastes, feels, or sounds like using figurative language, such as metaphor or simile.

Imaging: A mental visualization process that helps readers to store information in their memory, organize schemata, recall information such as the climax of a story, and elaborate.

Implicit questions: These types of questions have more than one answer that can be supported through evidence found in the text. They ask the reader to think carefully about what happens in the story and to consider the meaning of the story.

Impressionistic literacy: An impression of current thought, usually captured in writing, as writers express meanings dependent on and developed by prediction, empathy, voice, imagination, and reflection. In a sense, these verbal or nonverbal impressions are the reflections based on different interpretations of the same event.

Informal assessment: A short, frequent evaluation of students' progress that can be as simple as stopping during instruction to observe or to discuss with them how learning is progressing. This is especially useful when students have difficulty putting their thoughts on paper.

Internalization: This criterion for literacy scaffolding allows for students to take ownership and control of their newly acquired skills and strategies.

Learned focus: A teaching style that focuses on teachers asking questions based on core concepts, principles, theories, and processes that serve as the focal point of curricula, instruction, and assessment.

Literacy: The ability to communicate; to explain the obscure, to inquire (Levison, 1983). Literacy as communication is such an active mental process that when a transaction between the reader and text occurs, the reader is, in fact, in a state of empathy with the writer's message due to the writer's skill in eliciting an emotional or mental response from the reader.

Metacognition: The active, mental process of constructing meaning related to text while reading.

Multiple sign systems: The concept that literacy as communication may include such modes as art, music, mathematics, and dance (Harste, 1999; Harste, Woodward, & Burke, 1984).

Multiple intelligences: Gardner's (1990) view of intelligence as the capacity to solve problems or to fashion products that are valued in one or more cultural settings. The seven signs of intelligence include linguistic, logical-mathematical, musical, bodily-kinesthetic, spatial, interpersonal, and intrapersonal. Students perform best when using their personal, strongest intelligence.

National standards: In 2000, the U.S. Department of Education set forth the following objective: "All states and schools will have challenging and clear standards of achievement and accountability for all children, and effective strategies for reaching those standards" (n.p.). Since then, national education organizations and state departments of education also have implemented sets of standards or guidelines. These standards are the baseline that all students must achieve.

No Child Left Behind Act of 2001: The No Child Left Behind Act (NCLB; 2002) is a reauthorization of the Elementary and Secondary Education Act (ESEA), a law first passed in 1965, which reflects a commitment to ensuring that all students, regardless of their background, receive a quality education. To reach this goal, NCLB refocuses federal education programs on the principles of stronger accountability for results, more choices for parents and students, greater flexibility for states and school districts, and the use of research-based instructional methods.

Originality: A component of creativity; the production of a unique, fresh response. This response may be far-fetched, remote, or have never existed. Originality involves the ability to produce new ideas by changing their original contexts and redefining them.

Ownership: A criterion of instructional scaffolding that allows for students to make their own contributions to ongoing tasks so students' products reflect their personal thoughts and opinions.

Performance-based tasks: Assessments that evaluate higher level thinking skills and other skills and abilities that students will use in their lives using authentic, real-world tasks.

Play: A learning strategy that contains dimensions of cognitive, social, and physical spontaneity; manifest joy; and a sense of humor.

Plot scaffold: A temporary linguistic scaffold that teachers may use to assist learners in moving to more complex levels of performance that they would be unable to obtain at that time without the scaffolding. *Linguistic* refers to the structures language takes in order to convey meaning. The short, simple framework includes a hook, problem, complication, action-reaction, backfill, and possible dark moment, but no resolution. Learners complete the plot using originality, elaboration, flexibility, and fluency.

Prediction: A literacy process that involves the critical thinking skill of attempting possible solutions to a problem by applying prior knowledge to the current situation. Prediction allows a reader to think ahead, reflect on, and to hypothesize about character actions based on the story plot.

Prior knowledge: Ideas and concepts learners possess and bring to a learning situation before they experience the lesson being taught.

Problem: An element of plot; the dilemma or issue in a story that has to be solved, usually by the main character.

Reflection: A literacy process that occurs when students digest or ponder different solutions to a problem.

Resolution: An element of plot; the closure, or the resolution, of the problem in a story.

Rubric: A set of rules that communicates standards; shows levels of quality and students' expectations for assessment tasks; and includes dimensions (criteria), indicators, and a rating scale that can be used to assess depth of student understanding. Rubrics are used to assess quality of work while checklists assess quantity of completed work.

Selected response: Teacher-driven assessments whereby students choose from given responses. Selected responses methods include true or false, multiple choice, matching, keyed surveys, and, to a certain extent, fill in the blank.

Sociocognitive interactive model: A meaning-construction process that contains three major components: reader, teacher, and text (all within classroom context). During the reading process, these three components are in a state of dynamic change and interchange as meaning negotiation and meaning construction take place (Ruddell & Unrau, 1994). New ideas are created as text, reader, and teacher interact because each of these components brings its own original stance to the task. The completed task reflects a blending of all three major components.

Standards-based performance: A system in which the classroom curriculum is designed to help students attain defined learning goals or proscribed standards. A performance task uses a student's knowledge to effectively act or bring to fruition a complex product that reveals the student's knowledge and expertise.

Support: A criterion of instructional scaffolding that ensures that students' natural sequence of thought and language exists, providing effective routines for them to internalize.

Triangulation: The collecting of data for assessment in which at least three pieces of data are used to evaluate and determine accomplishment of a task.

Voice: A learner's personal input into a learning task.

Whole language: The concept that reading is a dynamic, constructive process involving the whole psycholinguistic process of constructing meaning (Goodman, 1996).

REFERENCES

Abram, D. (1997). *The spell of the sensuous: Perception and language in a more-than-human world*. New York: Vintage Books.

Alpaugh, P.K., & Birren, J.E. (1977). Variables affecting creative contributions across the adult life span. *Human Development, 20*, 240–248.

Annarella, L.A. (1992). *Creative drama in the classroom*. Unpublished manuscript. (ERIC Document Reproduction Service No. ED391206)

Applebee, N.A. (1991). Environments for language teaching and learning: Contemporary issues and future directions. In J. Flood, J.M. Jensen, D. Lapp, & J.R. Squire (Eds.), *Handbook of research on teaching the English language arts* (pp. 549–558). New York: Macmillan.

Barnett, L.A. (1998). The adaptive powers of being playful: Diversions and divergences in fields of play. In M.C. Duncan, G. Chick, & A. Aycock (Eds.), *Play and culture studies* (Vol. 1, pp. 97–119). Westport, CT: Ablex.

Bean, T.W. (2002). Making reading relevant for adolescents. *Educational Leadership, 60*(3), 1–6.

Buege, C. (1993). The effect of mainstreaming on attitude and self-concept using creative drama and social skills training. *Theory Into Practice, 24*, 151–156.

Bolton, G. (1985). Changes in thinking about drama in education. *Theory Into Practice, 24*, 151–157.

Booth, D. (1985). Imaginary gardens with real toads: Reading and drama in education. *Theory Into Practice, 24*, 193–198.

Bruner, J. (1996). *The culture of education*. Cambridge, MA: Harvard University Press.

Bryson, B. (1990). *Mother tongue: English and how it got that way*. New York: William Morrow.

Campbell, J. (1989). *The power of myth*. New York: Doubleday.

Celce-Murcia, M., Brinton, D., & Goodwin, M. (1996). *Teaching pronunciation: A reference for teachers of English to speakers of other languages*. Cambridge, England: Cambridge University Press.

College Entrance Examination Board. (2003). *The new SAT and your school: For teachers, counselors, and administrators* [Brochure]. New York: Author.

Courtney, R. (1989). Culture and the creative drama teacher. *Youth Theatre Journal, 3*(4), 18–23.

Davies, A. (2000). *Making classroom assessment work*. Courtenay, BC: Connections Publishing.

Dreher, M.J. (2003). Motivating struggling readers by tapping the potential of informational books. *Reading & Writing Quarterly, 19*(1), 25–39.

DuPont, S. (1992). The effectiveness of creative drama as an instructional strategy to enhance the reading comprehension skills of fifth-grade remedial readers. *Reading Research and Instruction, 31*(3), 41–52.

Dwyer, E.M. (1990). *Enhancing reading comprehension through creative dramatics*. (ERIC Document Reproduction Service No. ED316849)

Eastman, R.M. (1970). *Style: Writing as the discovery of outlook*. New York: Oxford University Press.

Eichenberger, C.J., & King, J.R. (1995). Two teacher roles in language experience: Scaffold-builder and gatekeeper. *Reading Research and Instruction, 35*(1), 64–84.

Fillmer, H.T., & Parkway, F.W. (1990, May). *Imagery: A neglected correlate of reading instruction*. Paper presented at the Annual Convention of the International Reading Association, Atlanta, GA. (ERIC Document Reproduction Service No. ED319039)

Fisher, D., & Frey, N. (2003). Writing instruction for struggling adolescent readers: A gradual release model. *Journal of Adolescent & Adult Literacy, 46*, 396–405.

Fitzgerald, J., & Noblit, G. (1999). About hopes, aspirations, and uncertainty: First-grade English-language learners' emergent reading. *Journal of Literacy Research, 31*(2), 133–182.

Gardner, H. (1990). Multiple intelligences: Implications for art and creativity. In W.J. Moody (Ed.), *Artistic intelligences: Implications for education* (pp. 11–27). New York: Teachers College Press.

Gardner, H. (2000). *Intelligence reframed: Multiple intelligences for the 21st century*. New York: Basic.

Georgia Department of Education. (2004a). *English/language arts performance standards*. Retrieved February 6, 2006, from http://georgiastandards.org/english.aspx

Georgia Department of Education. (2004b). *Writing assessments*. Retrieved December 30, 2005, from http://www.doe.k12.ga.us/curriculum/testing/writing.asp

Goodman, K. (1996). *Ken Goodman on reading: A common-sense look at the nature of language and the science of reading.* Portsmouth, NH: Heinemann.

Gourney, A.P., Bosseau, J., & Delgado, J. (1985). The impact of an improvisational dramatic program on student attitudes and achievement. *Children's Theatre Review, 34,* 9–14.

Handford, S.A., & Herber, M. (1966). *Landenscheidt's pocket Latin dictionary.* Maspeth, NY: Langenscheidt Publishers.

Harste, J.C. (1999). *Curriculum, multiple literacies, and democracy: What if English/language arts teachers really cared?* Presidential address from the National Council of Teachers of English. Retrieved December 29, 2005, from http://www.indiana.edu/~langed/faculty/harste/speech.html

Harste, J.C., Woodward, V.A., & Burke, C.L. (1984). *Language stories and literacy lessons.* Portsmouth, NH: Heinemann.

Haycock, K. (2001). New frontiers for a new century: A national overview. *Thinking K–16, 5*(2), 1–23.

Heathcote, D., & Herbert, P.A. (1985). A drama of learning: Mantle of the expert. *Theory Into Practice, 24,* 173–180.

Hiebert, E. (1991). *Literacy for a diverse society.* New York: Teachers College Press.

Ignoffo, M. (1993). Theatre of the mind: Nonconventional strategies for helping remedial readers gain control over their reading experience. *Journal of Reading, 37,* 310–321.

Knight, N., Dixon, D., Golden, C., Graham, M., Strickland, B., & Weis, M. (2004). Writer's free-for-all. Panel discussion conducted at Dragoncon convention, Atlanta, GA.

Levison, M.E. (1983). The basics—The etymology of reading, writing, and arithmetic. *NASSP Bulletin, 67,* 49–53.

McTighe, J. (1996). Teaching for authentic student performance. *Educational Leadership, 54*(4), 6–12.

McTighe, J. (2000). Meaningful learning for all students. *Asilomar, 24,* 1–8.

Meade, M. (Speaker). (2002). *The great dance: Finding one's way in troubled times* [CD recording]. Seattle, WA: Mosaic Voices of the Community.

Moore, B., & Caldwell, H. (1993). Drama and drawing for narrative writing in primary grades. *Journal of Educational Research, 87*(2), 100–110.

Morain, G. (1990). Kinesics and cross-cultural understanding. In J.M. Valdes (Eds.), *Culture bound: Bridging the cultural gap in language teaching* (pp. 64–77). New York: Cambridge University Press.

National Assessment of Educational Progress (NAEP). (2003). *Research in adolescent literacy.* Retrieved December 30, 2005, from http://grants.nih.gov/grants/guide/rfa-files/RFA-HD-03-012.html

Neelands, J. (1998). *Beginning drama, 11–14.* London: David Fulton.

No Child Left Behind Act of 2001 (NCLB), Pub. L. No. 107-110, 115 Stat. 1425 (2002).

O'Day, S. (2000). *Creative drama as a literacy strategy: Teachers' use of a scaffold.* Unpublished doctoral dissertation, Georgia State University, Atlanta.

O'Neill, C. (1995). *Drama worlds: A framework for process drama.* Portsmouth, NH: Heinemann.

Pelligrini, A.D. (1997). Dramatic play, context, and children's communication behavior. In J. Flood, S.B. Heath, & D. Lapp (Eds.), *A national policy perspective on research intersections between literacy and the visual/communicative arts* (pp. 486–491). New York: Macmillan.

Readence, J.E., Bean, T.W., & Baldwin, R.S. (1981). *Content area reading: An integrated approach.* Dubuque, IA: Kendall/Hunt.

Robbins, P., & Alvy, H.B. (2003). *The principal's companion* (2nd ed.). Thousand Oaks, CA: Corwin Press.

Rosenblatt, L. (1985). The transactional theory of the literary work: Implications for research. In C.R. Cooper (Ed.), *Researching response to literature and the teaching of literature* (pp. 33–53). Norwood, NJ: Ablex.

Ruddell, R.B., & Unrau, N.J. (1994). Reading as a meaning-construction process: The reader, the text, and the teacher. In R.B. Ruddell, M.R. Ruddell, & H. Singer (Eds.), *Theoretical models and processes of reading* (4th ed., pp. 996–1056). Newark, DE: International Reading Association.

Sadoski, M., & Paivio, A. (1994). A dual coding view of imagery and verbal processes in reading comprehension. In R.B. Ruddell, M.R. Ruddell, & H. Singer (Eds.), *Theoretical models and processes of reading* (4th ed., pp. 582–601). Newark, DE: International Reading Association.

Scarborough, E., McCaffery, T., McCullugh, K., Crispin, A., & Weis, M. (2003, September). *How to write plots.* Writers' panel conducted at Dragoncon, Atlanta, GA.

Schonmann, S. (1996). Jewish-Arab encounters in the drama/theatre class battlefields. *Research in Drama Education, 1,* 175–188.

Smith, F. (1978). *Understanding reading: A psycholinguistic analysis of reading and learning to read.* New York: Holt, Rinehart and Winston.

Sternberg, R.J. (1997). *Successful intelligence: How practical and creative intelligence determine success in life.* New York: Plume.

Stewart, R.A., Paradis, E.E., & Ross, B.D. (1996). Student voices: What works in literature-based developmental readings. *Journal of Adolescent & Adult Literacy, 39*(6), 468–478.

Sweet, A.P. (2005). A national policy perspective on research intersections between literacy and the visual/communicative arts. In J. Flood, S.B. Heath, & D. Lapp (Eds.), *Handbook of research on teaching literacy through the communicative and visual arts* (pp. 264–285). Mahwah, NJ: Erlbaum.

Thompson, M. (1998). *The word within the word.* New York: Royal Fireworks Press.

U.S. Department of Education. (2000). *Overview: Mission.* Retrieved January 23, 2006, from http://www.ed.gov/about/overview/mission/archived-priorities.html#4

Valdes, J.M. (1990). *Culture bound.* New York: Cambridge University Press.

Van Doorn, M. (2004, June). *Double helix.* Session presented at Mythic Journeys Conference, Atlanta, GA.

Verriour, P. (1985). Face to face, negotiating meaning through drama. *Theory Into Practice, 24,* 181–186.

Wagner, B.J. (1998). *Educational drama and language arts: What the research shows.* Portsmouth, NH: Heinemann.

Wolf, S., Edmiston, B., & Enisco, P. (2005). Drama worlds: Places of the heart, head, voice, and hand in dramatic interpretation. In J. Flood, S.B. Heath, & D. Lapp (Eds.), *Handbook of research on teaching literacy through the communicative and visual arts* (pp. 492–505). Mahwah, NJ: Erlbaum.

Wright, L. (1985). Preparing teachers to put drama in the classroom. *Theory Into Practice, 24,* 205–210. (ERIC Document Reproduction Service No. EJ324615)

Zukav, G. (1979). *The dancing wu li masters: An overview of the new physics.* New York: Morrow.

Literature Cited

Applebaum, S. (Ed.). (1993). *Euripides, Medea.* New York: Dover Publications.

Carroll, L. (2002). *Alice in Wonderland.* New York: Scholastic. (Original work published 1865)

Conan Doyle, A. (2003). *The adventures of Sherlock Holmes.* New York: Scholastic.

Cushman, K. (1995). *Catherine, called Birdy.* New York: HarperCollins.

Dickens, C. (1981). *Hard times.* New York: Bantam Books. (Original work published 1854)

Dickens, C. (1986). *A Christmas carol.* New York: Bantam Classics. (Original work published 1843)

Heaney, S. (2000). *Beowulf.* New York: Farrar, Straus and Giroux.

Johnston, J. (1979). *King Arthur: His knights and their ladies.* New York: Scholastic.

King, S. (1983). *Pet sematary.* New York: Signet.

Lewis, B.R. (1980). *Timeless myths.* Cambridge, England: Brimax Books.

Lindgren, A. (1957). *Pippi Longstocking.* New York: Viking Press.

Nickl, P., & Schroeder, B. (1976). *Crocodile, crocodile.* New York: Tundra Books.

Nye, R. (1968). *Beowulf: A new telling.* New York: Bantam Doubleday Dell Books for Young Readers.

Osborne, W., & Osborne, M.P. (1988). *Jason and the Argonauts.* New York: Scholastic.

Portis, C. (1969). *True grit.* New York: Simon & Schuster.

Rieu, E.V., & Rieu, D.C.H. (1991). *Homer: The Odyssey.* London: Penguin.

Rowling, J.K. (1998–2005). Harry Potter series. New York: Scholastic.

Schaefer, J. (1975). *Shane.* New York: Bantam. (Original work published 1949)

Shah, I. (1979). *World tales: The extraordinary experience of stories told in all times, in all places.* New York: Harcourt Brace Jovanovich.

Shakespeare, W. (1994a). A midsummer's night dream. In P. Alexander (Ed.), *Complete works of William Shakespeare: The Alexander text* (pp. 218–242). Glasgow, England: HarperCollins.

Shakespeare, W. (1994b). As you like it. In P. Alexander (Ed.), *Complete works of William Shakespeare: The Alexander text* (pp. 277–307). Glasgow, England: HarperCollins.

Shakespeare, W. (1994c). Julius Caesar. In P. Alexander (Ed.), *Complete works of William Shakespeare: The Alexander text* (pp. 1019–1048). Glasgow, England: HarperCollins.

Shakespeare, W. (1994d). Macbeth. In P. Alexander (Ed.), *Complete works of William Shakespeare: The Alexander text* (pp. 1051–1078). Glasgow, England: HarperCollins.

Shakespeare, W. (1994e). Romeo and Juliet. In P. Alexander (Ed.), *Complete works of William Shakespeare: The Alexander text* (pp. 950–985). Glasgow, England: HarperCollins.

Tolkien, J.R.R. (1956). *The fellowship of the ring.* New York: Ballantine Books.

Tolkien, J.R.R. (1966). *The hobbit.* New York: Houghton Mifflin.

Van Allsburg, C. (1985). *The polar express.* New York: Houghton Mifflin.

White, A.T. (1964). *The golden treasury of myths and legends*. New York: Golden Press.
Williams, S. (1992). *Working cotton*. New York: Voyager.

Motion Pictures Cited

Brown, D., Zanuck, D. (Producers), & Spielberg, S. (Director). (1975). *Jaws* [Motion picture]. United States: Universal Pictures.

Coen, E. (Producer), & Coen, J. (Director). (2000). *O brother, where art thou?* [Motion picture]. United States: Touchstone Pictures.

Donner, R. (Director). (1978). *Superman* [Motion picture]. United States: Warner Bros.

Fleming, V. (Director). (1939). *The wizard of Oz* [Motion picture]. United States: Metro-Goldwyn-Mayer.

Logan, J. (Director). (1967). *Camelot* [Motion picture]. United States: Warner Brothers.

Lucas, G. (Director). (1977). *Star wars* [Motion picture]. United States: Lucasfilm.

INDEX

Note. Page numbers followed by *f* or *t* indicate figures or tables, respectively.

for, 28–29, 39*t*, 105–106; "Shoot Out at the Bottoms Up Saloon" scaffold for, 48–52; "There's a Bug in My Beans" scaffold for, 31, 32*f*, 34–38; types of, 29–30; voice of, 32–33. *See also* students

BEOWULF: A NEW TELLING (NYE), 13, 63–67

BEOWULF (HEANEY), 12, 13, 14

"BEWARE OF GIFTS" SCAFFOLD, 70–76, 147–150

BIRREN, J.E., 185

BODY LANGUAGE, 10

BOLTON, G., 33

"THE BOOK FINE" SCAFFOLD, 54–57, 131–136

BOOTH, D., 4, 6, 30, 33

BOSSEAU, J., 5, 33

BRINTON, D., 8, 9

BROWN, D., 12

BRUNER, J., vi, 2

BRYSON, B., 82

BUEGE, C., 33

BURKE, C.L., 26, 186

BURNOUT, TEACHER, 90

C

CALDWELL, H., 95

CAMPBELL, J., 62

CARROLL, L., 43, 73

CATHERINE, CALLED BIRDY (CUSHMAN), 97*f*

CELCE-MURCIA, M., 8, 9

CHARACTER FLAWS. *See* flaws, character

CHARACTERS: in "Are We Home Yet?" scaffold, 77; and beginning writers' images, 33; in "Beware of Gifts" scaffold, 71–72; in "The Book Fine" scaffold, 56; importance of, 17–18; in "Just Sleeping" scaffold, 53; in scaffold creation, 58; in "Shoot Out at the Bottoms Up Saloon" scaffold, 48–52; in "That Apple" scaffold, 69

CHEERING SIGN, 40, 41

A CHRISTMAS CAROL (DICKENS), 43

CLICHÉS, 16–17

CLIMAX. *See* dark moment

CLOSING ARGUMENTS, 55

COEN, E., 78

COEN, J., 78

COLLABORATION: and beginning writers' images, 33; as scaffolding criteria, 2; for "Shoot Out at the Bottoms Up Saloon" scaffold, 51

COLLEGE ENTRANCE EXAMINATION BOARD, 93

COMMAS, 57

COMPARATIVE LITERATURE, 66

COMPLEX-COMPOUND SENTENCES, 2

COMPLICATION, 14

COMPREHENSION: achievement in, 89; and constructivist theory, viii

CONAN DOYLE, A., 43

CONFLICT, 12–13

CONSTRUCTIVE ASSESSMENT, 20

CONSTRUCTIVE CRITICISM, 65

CONSTRUCTIVIST THEORY, viii, 33

COSTUMES: for "Are We Home Yet?" scaffold, 77; and dialogue, 19; in lesson format, 22; for "Tyrant?" scaffold, 84; for "Wolf Kids" scaffold, 80–81

COURTNEY, R., viii, 29

COURTROOM PROCEEDINGS, 55–56

CREATIVE DRAMA. *See* drama

CREATIVITY: versus grammar, 22; and mentor programs, 90; suppression of, vi–vii

CRISPIN, A., v, 13, 33, 49, 62, 80

CRITICISM, 65

CROCODILE, CROCODILE (NICKL & SCHROEDER), 85–86

CULTURE, 62–63

CURRICULUM: literacy celebrations across, 94–97; writing across, 84

CUSHMAN, K., 97*f*

D

DANGLING MODIFIERS, 73

DARK MOMENT: overview of, 14; in scaffold creation, 58; in "There's a Bug in My Beans" scaffold, 37

DAVIES, A., 19, 21, 106

DELGADO, J., 5, 33

DEVELOPING WRITERS: grade level of, 101; objectives of, 101, 102; overview of, 30

DIALOGUE: in "Are We Home Yet?" scaffold, 77; in "The Book Fine" scaffold, 56; in "Emergency" scaffold, 45; in "Guess

WILLIAMS, S., 86
THE WIZARD OF OZ (FLEMING), 61
"WOLF KIDS" SCAFFOLD, 78–82, 160–163
WOLF, S., viii, 4, 29
WOODWARD, V.A., 26, 186
WORD BANKS, 16, 38
WORKING COTTON (WILLIAMS), 86
WORLD TALES (SHAH), 64
WRIGHT, L., 6, 31, 32
WRITING: across the curriculum, 84; acting before, 12; as art, 10; and benefits of plot scaffolds, viii–ix, 11; criteria for, 11; development of, 29–30; focus of instruction in, 89; inquiry approach to, 11–12; integration of fine arts in, 95; and lesson format, 21–26; of plot scaffolds, 85–86; shortcomings of students', 10; and theater-of-the-mind technique, 5–6. *See also specific aspects of writing*

Z

ZANUCK, D., 12
ZUKAV, G., viii